Teaching English Language Learners

Teaching English Language Learners

A Differentiated Approach

Carol Rothenberg
City Heights Educational Collaborative

Douglas Fisher
San Diego State University

Upper Saddle River, New Jersey
Columbus, Ohio

Library of Congress Cataloging-in-Publication Data

Rothenberg, Carol.
 Teaching English language learners: a differentiated approach/Carol Rothenberg,
Douglas Fisher.
     p. cm.
 Includes index.
 ISBN 0-13-170439-7
 1. English language—Study and teaching—Foreign speakers.   I. Fisher, Douglas
II. Title.
PE1128.A2R68 2007
  428.2¢4—dc22   2006021973

Vice President and Executive Publisher: Jeffery W. Johnston
Executive Editor: Debra A. Stollenwerk
Production Editor: Alexandrina Benedicto Wolf
Production Coordination: Carlisle Publishers Services
Design Coordinator: Diane C. Lorenzo
Cover Designer: Candace Rowley
Cover Image: Super Stock
Production Manager: Susan W. Hannahs
Director of Marketing: David Gesell
Senior Marketing Manager: Darcy Betts Prybella
Marketing Coordinator: Brian Mounts

This book was set in Galliard by Carlisle Publishers Services. It was printed and bound by R.R. Donnelley & Sons
Company. The cover was printed by R.R. Donnelley & Sons Company.

Pearson Education Ltd.   Pearson Education Australia Pty. Limited
Pearson Education Singapore Pte. Ltd.   Pearson Education North Asia Ltd.
Pearson Education Canada, Ltd.   Pearson Educación de Mexico, S.A. de C.V.
Pearson Education—Japan   Pearson Education Malaysia Pte. Ltd.

10 9 8 7 6 5 4
ISBN 0-13-170439-7

Preface

Teaching English Language Learners: A Differentiated Approach is a methods book for preservice and inservice teachers on facilitating the literacy and academic development of K–12 learners who speak a language other than English. Designed to move teachers through theory into practice, it begins by providing background knowledge and a solid grounding in language acquisition and learning theory. It then asks readers to apply that understanding to the teaching cycle of planning, teaching, assessing, reflecting, and revising. The text offers a Differentiated Approach that allows teachers to focus on specific needs of English language learners (ELLs) with respect to language, literacy development, and academic achievement.

Across the nation, schools are engaged in innovation and reform efforts to improve the achievement of all students. Specific interventions have been targeted toward "closing the achievement gap." This book is grounded in our belief that, just as we can improve achievement for all our students, we can increase the rate at which ELL students achieve English proficiency by engaging families, providing quality instruction across the curriculum and throughout the grade levels, using students' funds of knowledge, and linking our assessments with instruction.

This book is a guide to accomplish exactly that, to help teachers and administrators examine their own practice and design purposeful, differentiated instruction that accelerates the achievement of students who are learning English.

A DIFFERENTIATED APPROACH

"Specially Designed Academic Instruction in English (SDAIE) strategies are just good teaching strategies. Sheltered instruction is just good teaching." These are common refrains heard as teachers learn about effective instruction for ELLs. In the Differentiated Approach, we propose a model of instruction that takes those "good teaching strategies" and differentiates their use to match the students' needs. English language learners come to our classrooms with differing levels of English proficiency, different funds of background knowledge, and different styles of learning. A "one-size-fits-all" approach—no matter how well intentioned, no matter how closely matched to the standards, no matter how engaging—is simply not sufficient to help ELLs reach high levels of English proficiency and meet grade-level standards for achievement. This book shows teachers how to design lessons that consider the individual needs of students learning a new language and learning *in* a new language.

Research suggests that it takes from five to seven years to gain proficiency in a second language (Cummins, 1979). There are many factors that influence English language acquisition, including program configuration, parental involvement, socioeconomic status, and motivation (Brock, Boyd, & Moore, 2003). (For information on common program models for teaching ELLs, see the Spotlight on Instruction in Chapter 1.)

There are also many factors that influence the rate at which students learn to read—cognitive, linguistic, psychological, social, emotional, physical, or educational—any of which can affect ELLs as much as native English speakers (Li & Zhang, 2004). This book focuses on the factors over which teachers exert the most control, the educational factors that contribute to low achievement for ELLs. Materials that are not accessible to students learning a new language, pacing that does not allow adequate time for students to process new language and new concepts, assessments that ask students to use an unfamiliar language to demonstrate their understanding of content, instructional methods that do not differentiate for students at different levels of language proficiency, and schools where teachers do not know who their ELLs are, or their English proficiency levels, all equate to students not learning English and not achieving academically (Allington & Walmsley, 1995; Garcia, 2003; Gunning, 2002).

HOW THIS BOOK IS ORGANIZED

This book models effective strategies for teaching English language learners: building on background knowledge, focusing on key concepts, differentiating curriculum and instruction, and providing opportunities for self-reflection, interaction, and application. It will be most effective if used as part of a class or study group where readers can discuss the ideas with colleagues, reflect on their practices, and construct meaning based on individual situations. Lesson plans and a case study provide opportunities to apply key principles in each chapter. Each chapter provides an in-depth look at one of the eight aspects of teaching English language learners:

Chapter 1: A Differentiated Approach: Core Principles of Learning

Chapter 2: Language Acquisition: Dimensions of Proficiency

Chapter 3: Purposeful Planning: Equal Access for All

Chapter 4: Assessment: Guide to Purposeful Planning

Chapter 5: Oral Language: The Foundation of Literacy

Chapter 6: Academic Language: Building Proficiency

Chapter 7: Grade-Level Content: Integrating Language and Learning

Chapter 8: Differentiated Instruction: High Expectations for All

Epilogue: Mary's Top Ten: A Guide for Teaching English Language Learners

Special features

Strong research base. Each chapter contains a summary of current thinking on the topic at hand. We synthesize and translate this research into units that teachers can use. In addition, boxed features highlight specific research topics and provide readers with practical ideas for moving from research to practice.

Focus questions. Using focus questions at the start of each chapter allows readers to organize their thinking and ideas into useable categories, and guides them through the chapter's content.

Accessing Prior Knowledge tasks. These build on readers' background and are organized differently in each chapter. We ask readers to engage in tasks designed to access prior knowledge—visualizing, brainstorming, completing anticipatory guides, previewing, reflecting, observing their own use of strategies, and thinking about their own learning styles.

We include these tasks for a number of reasons. First, we want to ensure that we have activated readers' prior and background knowledge so that they get the most out of the chapter. Second, we hope that readers will use these building background activities in their own classrooms. And finally, we know that anticipatory activities create a purpose for reading that is critical to comprehension.

Margin notes. Throughout the text, margin notes ask readers to make connections between the content being presented and other parts of the text or their own lives, offer additional information, direct readers to Web sites, and provide opportunity for reflection.

Spotlight on Instruction. In each chapter, we spotlight effective teachers of ELLs and allow readers to "visit" the classrooms and observe what the teacher is doing. These embedded vignettes provide an authentic context for the information being presented and demonstrate classroom application.

Application to Practice. At the end of each chapter, we provide a number of reflection questions, the opportunity to engage in a case study focused on a specific English language learner, and develop a unit of study that meets the needs of ELL students. Each chapter builds on the previous chapter, and the Application to Practice section allows readers to continually apply what they have learned to their own classrooms.

Teacher Tools. A collection of resources for use in the classroom—from planning tools to self-reflection tools—is found at the end of the book. Before reading this book, we suggest that readers complete the self-assessment found in the Teacher Tools section and keep these key elements of instruction for English language learners in mind as they read the book. After reading the book, readers may complete the self-assessment again, reflecting on how their thinking or instruction has changed (or will change). Also included in the Teacher Tools section are two different versions of a guide for self-reflection. Readers can use these to reflect on their own instruction or to identify concrete examples of the principles of instruction for ELLs as they observe another teacher's classroom. Any of the Teacher Tools may be reproduced for classroom or personal use.

Teaching English Language Learners: A Differentiated Approach provides readers with the tools they need to effectively engage all students in content and language learning.

References

Allington, R. L., & Walmsley, S. A. (Eds.). (1995). *No quick fix: Rethinking literacy programs in America's elementary schools.* Newark, DE: International Reading Association.

Brock, C. H., Boyd, F. B., & Moore, J. A. (2003). Variation in language and the use of language across contexts: Implications for literacy learning. In J. Flood, D. Lapp, J. R. Squire, & J. M. Jensen (Eds.), *Handbook of research on teaching the English language arts* (2nd ed.) (pp. 446–458). Mahwah, NJ: Lawrence Erlbaum.

Cummins, J. (1979). Cognitive/academic language proficiency, linguistic interdependence, the optimum age question and some other matters. *Working Papers on Bilingualism, 19,* 121–129.

Garcia, G. G. (Ed.). (2003). *English learners: Reaching the highest level of English literacy.* Newark, DE: International Reading Association.

Gunning, T. G. (2002). *Assessing and correcting reading and writing difficulties.* Boston: Allyn & Bacon.

Li, X., & Zhang, M. (2004). Why Mei still cannot read and what can be done. *Journal of Adolescent & Adult Literacy, 48,* 92–101.

ACKNOWLEDGMENTS

My thanks go first of all to Doug. He was my motivating force for this book and without his support, encouragement, and belief in me, I would not have embarked on this journey.—*CR*

Carol has challenged my thinking, engaged me in wonderful conversations, and become a trusted colleague and friend.—*DF*

Together we want to thank the teachers who so graciously opened their classrooms to us, shared their successes and their challenges—Aida Allen, Nancy Frey, Dani Cole, Hilda Martinez, Dave Hanula, Chris Johnson, Angie Kania, Sheryl Segal, Rita ElWardi, Maria Grant, and Carol Shirley. Special thanks, of course, to all the students with whom we have had the honor and pleasure of working over the years. They have opened our eyes to the possibilities and helped to clarify and define our thinking.

Many researchers have influenced our work over the years, but we are particularly indebted to Pauline Gibbons, whose influence is woven throughout this book.

We'd like to thank Debbie Stollenwork, our Merrill/Prentice Hall editor, who helped shape this book and bring our ideas into focus, and the reviewers who shared their time and expertise to make this a better book: Rafael Lara-Alecio,

Texas A&M, College Station; Henri Sue Bynum, Indian River Community College; Paul A. Flores, Azusa Pacific University; Emiliano Gonzalez, University of St. Thomas; Daniel Holm, Indiana University, South Bend; Linda Holley Mohr, Blinn College; Solange A. Lopes-Murphy, James Madison University; A. Y. "Fred" Ramirez, California State University, Fullerton; W. Robert Walker, Northern Arizona University, Yuma; Laurie R. Weaver, University of Houston, Clear Lake; and David A. Whitenack, San Jose State University.

Finally we'd like to thank our families for their constant encouragement and love.

Teacher Preparation Classroom

See a demo at
www.prenhall.com/teacherprep/demo

Your Class. Their Careers. Our Future. Will your students be prepared?

We invite you to explore our new, innovative and engaging website and all that it has to offer you, your course, and tomorrow's educators! Organized around the major courses pre-service teachers take, the Teacher Preparation site provides media, student/teacher artifacts, strategies, research articles, and other resources to equip your students with the quality tools needed to excel in their courses and prepare them for their first classroom.

This ultimate on-line education resource is available at no cost, when packaged with a Merrill text, and will provide you and your students access to:

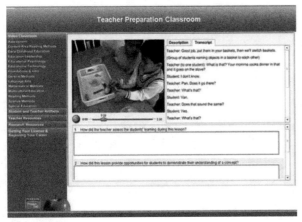

Online Video Library. More than 150 video clips—each tied to a course topic and framed by learning goals and Praxis-type questions—capture real teachers and students working in real classrooms, as well as in-depth interviews with both students and educators.

Student and Teacher Artifacts. More than 200 student and teacher classroom artifacts— each tied to a course topic and framed by learning goals and application questions—provide a wealth of materials and experiences to help make your study to become a professional teacher more concrete and hands-on.

Research Articles. Over 500 articles from ASCD's renowned journal *Educational Leadership*. The site also includes Research Navigator, a searchable database of additional educational journals.

Teaching Strategies. Over 500 strategies and lesson plans for you to use when you become a practicing professional.

Licensure and Career Tools. Resources devoted to helping you pass your licensure exam; learn standards, law, and public policies; plan a teaching portfolio; and succeed in your first year of teaching.

How to ORDER Teacher Prep for you and your students:

For students to receive a *Teacher Prep* Access Code with this text, instructors must provide a special value pack ISBN number on their textbook order form. To receive this special ISBN, please email **Merrill.marketing@pearsoned.com** and provide the following information:
- Name and Affiliation
- Author/Title/Edition of Merrill text

Upon ordering Teacher Prep for their students, instructors will be given a lifetime Teacher Prep Access Code.

Brief Contents

Contents

CHAPTER 4   Assessment: Guide to Purposeful Planning   76

CHAPTER 5   Oral Language: The Foundation of Literacy   106

CHAPTER 6   Academic Language: Building Proficiency   136

CHAPTER 7   Grade-Level Content: Integrating Language and Learning   186

CHAPTER 8   Differentiated Instruction: High Expectations for All   224

Epilogue: Mary's Top Ten: A Guide for Teaching English Language Learners   251

Teacher Tools   255

Index   267

About the Authors

Carol Rothenberg is the coordinator of English learner support for the City Heights Educational Collaborative. She provides coaching, professional development, and guidance in policy development for teachers and administrators in the area of literacy and English language learners. She has worked with secondary and elementary schools throughout the San Diego Unified School District, training teachers and administrators on effective programs and instruction for English language learners. She has taught English, Spanish, and bilingual special education. She currently teaches classes for new teachers on effective instruction of English language learners.

Douglas Fisher is Professor of Literacy and Language Education in the College of Education at San Diego State University. A former teacher and language development specialist, Doug currently works with veteran teachers, guide teachers, new teachers, and student teachers in a variety of classroom settings. He is also the Co-Director for the Center for the Advancement of Reading for the California State University, Office of the Chancellor. Dr. Fisher's work focuses on ensuring that all students have access to content knowledge through quality instruction.

I saw the angel in the marble and I carved until I set him free.

Michelangelo

1

A Differentiated Approach: Core Principles of Learning

Barbara Schwartz/Merrill

Dear Teacher,

I'd like to introduce you to my son, Wind-Wolf. He is probably what you would consider a typical Indian kid. He was born and raised on the reservation. He has black hair, dark brown eyes, and an olive complexion. Like so many Indian children his age, he is shy and quiet in the classroom. He is 5 years old, in kindergarten, and I cannot understand why you have already labeled him a slow learner. At the age of 5 he has already been through quite an education compared to his peers in Western society. . . . His aunts and grandmothers taught him to count and know his numbers while they sorted out complex materials used to make abstract designs in the native baskets. He listened to his mother count each and every bead and sort out numerically according to color while she painstakingly made complex beaded belts and necklaces. He learned his basic numbers by helping his father count and sort the rocks to be used in a sweat lodge – seven rocks for medicine sweat, say, or thirteen for summer solstice ceremony. . . .

He is not culturally disadvantaged, but he is culturally different. If you ask him how many months are in a year, he will probably tell you thirteen. He will respond this way not because he doesn't know how to count properly, but because he has been taught by our traditional people that there are thirteen full moons in a year, according to the native tribal calendar, and that there are really thirteen planets in our solar system, and thirteen tail feathers on a perfectly balanced eagle, the most powerful kind of bird to use in ceremony and healing. . . . My son Wind-Wolf is not an empty glass coming into your classroom to be filled. He is a full basket coming into a different environment and society with something special to share. Please let him share his knowledge, heritage, and culture with you and with his peers.

(Lake, 1990, pp. 48–49)

Focus Questions

1. Who are our English language learners?
2. How can students' "funds of knowledge" be used to design instruction?
3. What are the most common program models of instruction for English language learners?
4. How is the Zone of Proximal Development a foundation of planning for differentiated instruction?
5. What are the conditions of learning, and what evidence of these conditions would you look for in a classroom for English language learners?

ACCESSING PRIOR KNOWLEDGE: LEARNING IN ANOTHER LANGUAGE

Imagine that your school has received a grant to study science instruction in Japan. Although you are not a science teacher, as a member of your school's School Reform Committee, you have been selected as part of a team of teachers to attend a weeklong seminar in Japan. When you were in high school, you took three years of Japanese. Now you teach English, or math, or social studies and love it, but you've never paid much attention to science. Now imagine that the seminar is designed for Japanese teachers, not specifically for those from other countries, so your team may be the only ones there who do not speak Japanese. Close your eyes for a moment and put yourself there.

Visualize: What are you feeling? Observe yourself closely as you enter the classroom, watch yourself move through the weeklong workshop. How do you feel as you walk into the room? How do you feel when the instructor begins to talk to the class in Japanese?

What do you do to support your own learning? What do you wish for to support your learning?

Visualize the hustle and bustle of Tokyo, the silent serenity of the temples, the majesty of the mountains. . . . Visualize yourself in this seminar. . . .

If you are like the teachers in our classes on teaching English language learners (ELLs), you probably experienced some of these feelings: nervous, overwhelmed, inadequate, intimidated, alone, unengaged, frustrated, excited, stupid, angry.

And these are some of the things you did, or wanted, in order to help you:

- An outline of each day's agenda
- Teacher and students who make me feel welcome
- An English-speaking partner
- Teacher using gestures
- A mini–science course and an explanation of the Japanese school system before I go
- An English science text for reference
- An English-Japanese dictionary
- Extra think time
- Hands-on experiences—field trips to the schools
- Pictures, graphics, demonstrations
- Charts with key vocabulary
- A teacher who knows my needs

These are some of the key strategies that comprise quality instruction for English language learners (ELLs). These are the kinds of supports we need to offer our students who are *learning* English and *learning in* English. A significant difference between our ELLs and you in the scenario you just visualized is that you are a confident, capable adult with a wealth of background knowledge and experience upon which you can draw. Our students also bring a wealth of background knowledge and experiences that can support learning new content in a new language, but they may need guidance in making those connections and drawing upon their prior knowledge. Regardless of their previous experiences and their educational level, they may have difficulty connecting new ideas to what they already know if their teacher does not build upon that knowledge and help students make the link to new learning.

You might now be asking yourself, "If I was able to brainstorm all these supports for my English language learners in just a few minutes, why do I need to read an entire book about how to teach them?" Good question. Let's take a look at the need for an in-depth discussion and reflection about our teaching practice before we talk about the practice itself.

WHAT IS THE NEED?

The population of students learning English has increased dramatically in the last 15 to 20 years. Between 1991 and 2004 the number of English language learners in grades K–12 more than doubled, from 2.4 million to 5 million

(National Clearinghouse for English Language Acquisition [NCELA], 2004), while the total K–12 enrollment growth during the same period was just over 7%. And while ELL growth declined by 1% between 2002/03 and 2003/04, overall enrollment declined by 2%. (NCELA, 2005). Our ELLs hail from all over the world. The majority (more than 75%), however, now come from Central and South America and Asia (Van Hook & Fix, 2000). The most commonly spoken languages among our immigrant students are Spanish, Vietnamese, Hmong, Haitian Creole, Korean, Arabic, Chinese, Russian, Tagalog, Portuguese, Urdu, Serbo-Croatian, Lao, and Japanese. California, Texas, Arizona, Florida, New York, and Illinois have the largest numbers of students who are not proficient in English, though many states, Oregon, Nevada, Idaho, Nebraska, Kansas, Arkansas, Tennessee, and Kentucky, to name a few, experienced more than 200% growth in their English language learner population during the 1990s and the first part of this decade (NCELA, 2005). In some parts of the country, the ELL students at a given school may comprise as much as 90% of the student population.

For updated statistics, see www.ncela.gwu.edu/stats.

In this age of accountability, there is a growing concern regarding the progress, or lack thereof, of our English language learners. Although there is little disaggregate data that tracks the dropout rates of English language learners, the U.S. Census does provide dropout rates for immigrant children.

You can look up local census information at www.census.gov.

If we assume that a high percentage of these immigrant children would be classified as English language learners, we can extrapolate an estimate of their dropout rate. From 1970 to 1995, the census data show dropout rates that are significantly higher for first-generation immigrant children than for native-born children. For those born in Mexico, by far the largest segment of our English language learner population, the dropout rate is two to three times higher (Van Hook & Fix, 2000). An analysis of the 2000 U.S. Census data by the Pew Hispanic Center found that Hispanic students ages 16 through 19 who believed they were not proficient in English were four times more likely to drop out than their proficient peers (Fry, 2003). There are many factors that contribute to students' dropping out, but we raise the issue here to provoke a critical examination of the school-related factors, in particular the instructional factors. For many English language learners, the impact of accountability testing has resulted in increased numbers of dropouts. This is especially true for English language learners who enter the U.S. school system during adolescence, as many believe that there is no way for them to pass the tests required under the No Child Left Behind Act.

Research your school's ELL population. How many have been enrolled in U.S. schools 5 or more years and remain classified as ELLs? Have any been reclassified as Fluent English Proficient in less than 5 years? What can you find out about the differences between the two groups?

Certainly, the majority of our ELL students do not drop out. However, even those we consider to be the success stories may lack the skills required for success in university-level courses. Robin Scarcella, a professor at the University of California at Irvine (UCI), received the letter in Figure 1.1 from Van, a student who had been accepted at UCI. Based upon the results of the English Placement Test, this student was required to take an English as a Second Language (ESL) writing class. Since she had received straight A's in her high school English courses, she did not believe she needed this class. Using her

Figure 1.1   Letter Requesting a Waiver from a College English Class

Note the errors you see that you would *not* be likely to see in a letter written by a native English speaker, even though the native speaker may be a struggling reader/writer.

Dear Mrs. Robbin

I really not need humanity 20 writing class because since time I come to United State all my friend speak English. Until now everyone understand me and I dont' need study english. I don't know Vietnam language. I speak only English. I have no communication problem with my friend in dorm. My english teacher in high school key person to teach me. My teacher explain to me that how important the book was for the student and persuaded me read many book. I get A in English through out high school and I never take ESL. I gree that some student need class but you has not made a correct decision put me in english class. Please do not makes me lose the face. I have confident in english.

(Scarcella, 2000, p. 223)

knowledge of how the educational system works, she wrote a letter to request an exemption.

Van is a student who has lived in the United States and attended school since the age of 5. Her experience is typical of many students in our public schools today. Each year, approximately 300 freshmen enter the University of California at Irvine and are required to take ESL. The average length of time these students have lived in the United States is 8 years. Most graduated from California high schools in the top 12% of their class. Over half had been in honors or AP classes. Most had received A's and B's in their English courses (Scarcella, 2000). Yet, even with high scores on the Scholastic Aptitude Test (SAT), their level of performance in writing would prevent them from meeting the standards required in freshman writing courses.

PROFICIENCY DESCRIPTORS

As you read these descriptors, think of your students and which level most closely matches their performance. What patterns do you notice?

English language learners are often identified by their proficiency levels. In general, there are three proficiency levels: Beginning, Intermediate, and Advanced. In some districts and states, English language learners are further classified and may be referred to as Beginning, Early Intermediate, Intermediate, Early Advanced, and Advanced. Others categorize their students as Level 1, 2, 3, 4, or 5. Still others classify them in terms of the stages of language acquisition—Preproduction, Early Production, Speech Emergence, or Intermediate Fluency. Newer guidelines from the Center for Applied Linguistics describe proficiency levels as Entering, Beginning, Developing, Expanding, and Bridging. Tables 1.1 through 1.9 describe the common language characteristics for students at the beginning, intermediate, and advanced levels.

English language development proficiency descriptors

Table 1.1

Listening and Speaking: Comprehension		
Beginning	**Intermediate**	**Advanced**
• Answer simple questions with one- to two-word responses. • Respond to simple directions and questions by using physical actions and other means of nonverbal communication (e.g., matching objects, pointing to an answer, drawing pictures). • Begin to speak with a few words or sentences by using a few standard English grammatical forms and sounds (e.g., single words or phrases). • Use common social greetings and simple repetitive phrases independently (e.g., "Thank you," "You're welcome"). • Ask and answer questions by using phrases or simple sentences. • Retell stories by using appropriate gestures, expressions, and illustrative objects.	• Ask and answer instructional questions by using simple sentences. • Listen attentively to stories and information and identify important details and concepts by using both verbal and nonverbal responses. • Ask and answer instructional questions with some supporting elements (e.g., "Which part of the story was the most important?").	• Demonstrate understanding of academic classroom discussions by participating appropriately. • Demonstrate understanding of most idiomatic expressions (e.g., "Give me a hand") by responding to such expressions and using them appropriately. • Ask for clarification as needed. • Respond to humor.

Table 1.2

Listening and Speaking: Organization and Delivery		
Beginning	**Intermediate**	**Advanced**
• Begin to be understood when speaking, but usage of standard English grammatical forms and sounds (e.g., plurals, simple past tense, pronouns [he or she]) may be inconsistent. • Orally communicate basic personal needs and desires (e.g., "May I go to the bathroom?").	• Participate in social conversations with peers and adults on familiar topics by asking and answering questions and soliciting information. • Make oneself understood when speaking by using consistent standard English grammatical forms and sounds; however, some rules are not followed (e.g., third-person singular, male and female pronouns).	• Negotiate and initiate social and academic conversations by questioning, restating, soliciting information, and paraphrasing the communication of others. • Expresses thoughts in clear sequence or organization.

Table 1.3

Reading: Phonemic Awareness, Decoding and Word Recognition, Concepts about Print		
Beginning	**Intermediate**	**Advanced**
• Recognize and produce the English phonemes that are like the phonemes students hear and produce in their primary language. • Recognize and produce English phonemes that are unlike the phonemes students hear and produce in their primary language. • Produce most English phonemes while beginning to read aloud.	• Produce English phonemes while reading aloud. • Recognize sound/symbol relationships and basic word-formation rules in written text (e.g., basic syllabication rules and phonics). • Apply knowledge of English phonemes in oral and silent reading to derive meaning from literature and texts in content areas.	• Apply knowledge of sound/symbol relationships and basic word-formation rules to derive meaning from written text (e.g., basic syllabication rules, regular and irregular plurals, and basic phonics).

Table 1.4

Reading: Vocabulary and Concept Development		
Beginning	**Intermediate**	**Advanced**
• Produce simple vocabulary (e.g., single words or very short phrases) to communicate basic needs in social and academic settings (e.g., locations, greetings, classroom objects). • Demonstrate comprehension of simple vocabulary with an appropriate action. • Retell stories by using simple words, phrases, and sentences. • Recognize simple affixes (e.g., educate, education, dislike, preheat), synonyms (e.g., big, large), and antonyms (e.g., hot, cold). • Begin to use knowledge of simple affixes, synonyms, and antonyms to interpret the meaning of unknown words. • Recognize the difference between the use of the first- and third-person points of view in phrases or simple sentences.	• Use more complex vocabulary and sentences to communicate needs and express ideas in a wider variety of social and academic settings. • Recognize simple antonyms and synonyms (e.g., good, bad, blend, mix) in written text. Expand recognition of them and begin to use them appropriately. • Apply knowledge of vocabulary to discussions related to reading tasks. • Read simple vocabulary, phrases, and sentences independently. • Read narrative and expository texts aloud with the correct pacing, intonation, and expression. • Use expanded vocabulary and descriptive words in oral and written responses to written texts. • Recognize and understand simple idioms, analogies, and figures of speech in written text. • Recognize that some words have multiple meanings and apply this knowledge to written text. • Recognize the function of connectors in written text (e.g., first, then, after that, finally).	• Apply knowledge of academic and social vocabulary while reading independently. • Be able to use a standard dictionary to find the meanings of unfamiliar words. • Interpret the meaning of unknown words by using knowledge gained from previously read text. • Understand idioms, analogies, and metaphors in conversation and written text.

Table 1.5

Reading: Comprehension and Analysis of Grade-Level-Appropriate Text		
Beginning	**Intermediate**	**Advanced**
• Respond orally to stories read aloud and use physical actions and other means of nonverbal communication (e.g., matching objects, pointing to an answer, drawing pictures). • Respond orally to stories read aloud, giving one- to two-word responses to answer factual comprehension questions (who, what, when, where, and how). • Understand and follow simple one-step directions for classroom-related activities.	• Understand and follow simple written directions for classroom-related activities. • Read text, orally identify the main ideas, and draw inferences about the text by using detailed sentences. • Read and identify basic text features, such as the title, table of contents, and chapter headings. • Respond to comprehension questions about text by using detailed sentences (e.g., "The brown bear lives with his family in the forest").	• Read and orally respond to familiar stories and other texts by answering factual comprehension questions about cause-and-effect relationships. • Read and orally respond to stories and texts from content areas by restating facts and details to clarify ideas. • Explain how understanding of text is affected by patterns of organization, repetition of main ideas, syntax, and word choice. • Write a brief summary (two or three paragraphs) of a story.

Table 1.6

Reading: Structural Features of Informational Materials		
Beginning	**Intermediate**	**Advanced**
• Identify the basic sequence of events in stories read aloud, using important words or visual representations, such as pictures and story frames. • Respond orally to stories read aloud, using phrases or simple sentences to answer factual comprehension questions.	• Identify, using key words or phrases, the sequence of events in texts read. • Identify common text structures such as problem/solution or cause/effect.	• Read for information, using text structures and features, in grade-level texts. • Identify common text structures such as problem/solution or cause/effect.

Table 1.7

Writing: Penmanship		
Beginning	**Intermediate**	**Advanced**
• Copy the alphabet legibly. • Copy words posted and commonly used in the classroom (e.g., labels, number names, days of the week).	• Write legible, simple sentences that respond to topics in language arts and other content areas (e.g., math, science, history, social science).	• Compose original pieces of text in multiple genres.

Table 1.8

Writing: Organization and Focus		
Beginning	**Intermediate**	**Advanced**
• Write simple sentences by using key words commonly used in the classroom (e.g., labels, number names, days of the week, months). • Write phrases and simple sentences that follow English syntactical order.	• Write simple sentences about an event or a character from a written text. • Follow a model given by the teacher to independently write a short paragraph of at least four sentences. • Create cohesive paragraphs that develop a central idea and consistently use standard English grammatical forms, even though some rules may not be followed. • Produce independent writing that is understood when read but may include inconsistent use of standard grammatical forms.	• Develop a clear thesis and support it by using analogies, quotations, and facts appropriately. • Write a multi-paragraph essay with consistent use of standard grammatical forms.

Table 1.9

Writing Conventions: Capitalization, Punctuation, and Spelling
Beginning, Intermediate, and Advanced
• Use capitalization when writing one's own name.
• Use capitalization at the beginning of a sentence and for proper nouns.
• Use a period at the end of a sentence and a question mark at the end of a question.
• Produce independent writing that includes partial consistency in the use of capitalization and periods and correct spelling. (Beginning/Intermediate)
• Produce independent writing with consistent use of capitalization, punctuation, and correct spelling. (Advanced)

TEACHER EXPECTATIONS

After reading Van's request, we cannot help but think about the role that expectations play in student achievement. There are two very real but different perspectives on this situation. Van believes, because of her grades and success in school, that she should not have to take remedial classes. In effect, she has been lied to—receiving excellent grades, but unable to write. Alternatively, the university has data showing that Van is not performing at the levels expected of a college student.

Teacher expectations play a profound role in the education of English language learners (e.g., de la Luz Reyes & Halcón, 2001; Gutiérrez, 2002; Slavin & Calderón, 2001). Far too often, teachers hold their English language learners to lower standards, accept inferior work, and make excuses for students' proficiency levels and achievement.

These lower expectations often are manifested in subtle ways. Even the teachers themselves believe that their expectations for their English language learners are just as high as for their other students. Their intentions are admirable—they don't want to embarrass the students by asking questions that require expression of a complete thought, or frustrate them by giving them a difficult assignment, or inhibit them by correcting errors. The outcome, however, is often that ELLs are not held accountable for the same level of performance as native English speakers. In chapter 5 we will see how a simple interchange between teacher and student can either hold students to high standards, or allow them to sit in silence and become passive learners while the teacher turns to another student for the answer. Teacher expectations extend to beliefs about the families as well as the students. As educators we often underestimate the capacity of ELL parents to help their children succeed

> We will discuss ways to address teacher expectations in chapter 8.

High expectations require meaningful activities
Doug Fisher

in school. In fact, parents of language-minority students express both the willingness and the ability to do exactly that (August & Shanahan, 2006). Teachers who know their students well can involve parents in their children's learning. The National Council of Teachers of English suggests that we must develop two types of relationships with our students—the teacher-learner relationship and the adult-child relationship (NCTE, 2006). Knowing our ELL students as learners, of course, means that we know their proficiency levels in English and their literacy skills, and that we are aware of what background knowledge they bring to the specific content we are teaching. The adult-child relationship is a personal one that involves knowing about our students' lives, their families, and their own backgrounds. This knowledge allows us to help bridge the gap between school and the world in which our students live, a world that often is very different from the world of school. Knowing our students as children or as adolescents allows us to draw upon their funds of knowledge, integrating what they already know and understand with our grade-level content.

Luis Moll and his colleagues (e.g., 1992, 2005) believe that educators must focus on high-level, high-quality, high-expectation instruction coupled with the use of students' funds of knowledge (for more information about funds of knowledge, see the *Research in Focus: Funds of Knowledge* on page 14). In doing so, teachers ensure that they build on what students already know, clearly express their high expectations for achievement, and motivate students to learn.

What can you do to develop the adult-child relationship with your students? How can you use this relationship in your instruction?

Research in Focus:
Funds of Knowledge

Luis Moll, an educator, and his colleagues in anthropology, Carlos Velez-Ibanez and James Greenberg, have studied Mexican-American families who have survived successfully in spite of debilitating circumstances such as poverty and discrimination. Particular constellations of cultural patterns—strategies, if you will—that value learning and the transmission of knowledge to children distinguish these families. Moll et al. argue that schools can draw on the social and cognitive contributions that parents can make to their children's academic learning.

Moll and his colleagues discovered that Mexican-American households are clustered according to kinship ties and exchange relationships. These clusters of households develop rich **funds of knowledge** that provide information about practices and resources useful in ensuring the well-being of the households. Each household in the cluster is a place where expertise in a particular domain can be accessed and used; examples of domains include repair of vehicles and appliances, plumbing, knowledge of education, herbal medicine, and first aid. Together, the households form a cluster for the exchange of information and resources. Often, everyone seems to congregate at one core household.

Families create settings in which children carry out the tasks and chores in the multiple domains of clustered households. The children's activities have important intellectual consequences. They observe, question, and assist adults as various tasks are done. For example, the son may indicate interest in fixing a car by asking questions. The father takes his cue from the child and then decides whether or not the child is capable of doing a task; if not, he may suggest a task that the child can accomplish. Even though the son's help may be minimal, such as helping to put in screws or checking the oil, his participation in the whole task is encouraged as an essential part of learning. He is allowed to attempt tasks and to experiment without fear of punishment if he fails. In such families, learning and questioning are in the hands of the child.

With time children develop expertise as well. They have many opportunities in the cluster of households to apply what they have learned to tasks of their own design. For example, the son may have a workplace where there are many "junk" engines that he can manipulate and with which he can experiment. He may use what he has learned in observing and assisting his father to rebuild a small engine for a go-cart he is constructing.

Moll and his colleagues are exploring ways of using the community to enrich children's academic development. To accomplish this, teachers have developed an after-school laboratory. One teacher created a module on constructing houses, which is a theme of great interest to the students in this teacher's classroom and also one of the most prominent funds of knowledge found in the students' households. The students started by locating information on building or construction in the library. As a result of their research, they built a model house or other structure as homework and wrote reports describing their research and explaining their construction. To extend this activity, the teacher invited parents and other community members who were experts to share information on specific aspects of construction. For example, one parent described his use of construction tools and how he measured the area and perimeter of his work site. Thus, the teacher was mobilizing the funds of knowledge in the community to achieve the instructional goals that she and her students had negotiated together.

The students then took the module one step further. They wanted to consider how they could combine these individual structures to form a community. This task required both application of their earlier learnings and considerable research. Students went out to do research, wrote summaries of their findings, and shared the results orally with others in the class. Thus, students fulfilled their own interests and designed the learning task, while the teacher facilitated and mediated the learning process and fulfilled her curricular goal of teaching language arts.

Source: Luis Moll—Funds of Knowledge, Learning Point Associates/NCREL. Excerpted from *What Is the Collaborative Classroom?* (http://www.ncrel.org/sdrs/areas/issues/students/learning/lr1luis.htm). Used with permission.

Spotlight on Instruction

Program Models for Teaching English Language Learners

There are four major instructional methods for serving English language learners, characterized by the degree to which they incorporate a student's native language and the approach they take to delivering academic content. In addition, several specific program models have been developed using these instructional methods as a guide (Linquanti, 1999).

We have not attempted to evaluate or compare these methods and models, or to draw conclusions as to the best design for a particular district, school, or classroom. In their report, *Program Alternatives for Linguistically Diverse Students* (Genesee, 1999), researchers from the Center for Research on Education, Diversity, & Excellence (CREDE) observed: "No single approach or program model works best in every situation. Many different approaches can be successful when implemented well. Local conditions, choices, and innovation are critical ingredients of success" (p. 4).

1. **Instructional methods using the native language:** These programs use the ELL's primary language to provide lessons in core academic subjects and/or to teach reading and language arts. Classes are usually taught by a teacher who is fluent in the ELL's primary language.

    Transitional Bilingual programs (also known as Early-Exit Bilingual): The primary goal of this model is to mainstream students to all-English classrooms. Teachers use the native language to help students keep up with academic content, but the focus is on phasing students into English-only instruction as quickly as possible. After students have been mainstreamed, no emphasis is put on the retention and development of their native language skills.

Developmental Bilingual programs (also known as Late-Exit Bilingual):
Developmental programs differ from transitional programs "primarily in the amount and duration that English is used for instruction" (Ramirez, Yuen, & Ramey, 1991, paragraph 3, as cited in Rennie, 1993) and in the length of time students are in the program. Developmental programs typically last throughout elementary school and students may continue to receive up to 40% of their instruction in their native language even after they have been reclassified as English-proficient.

Two-Way Immersion programs (also known as Dual-Language or Bilingual Immersion): The goal of these programs is to develop proficiency in the student's first or native language (L1) and in a second language (L2). Usually about half the students are native English speakers and half are English language learners from the same language group and similar cultural backgrounds. Instruction can be 90/10: that is, starting at 90% in non-English and 10% in English, gradually increasing to 50/50. Or instruction can be 50/50 from the beginning. These programs require significant school, family, and community commitment, significant peer interaction, and bilingual teachers who are trained to teach in both languages.

Newcomer programs: These programs are designed to meet the needs of incoming ELL students with low-level English literacy skills and often limited formal schooling in their native countries. Students enrolled in newcomer programs are usually recent arrivals to the United States. The goal of these programs is to help students acquire beginning English skills and core academic skills, and to acculturate to the U.S. school system. Some programs may have the additional role of promoting students' native language skills. These programs can vary widely in their organization.

2. **Instructional methods using the native language as support:** These instructional methods can exist within nearly every program model. Some programs use bilingual paraprofessionals within the mainstream classroom to provide native language support. Other programs may use teachers trained in a variety of sheltering strategies. In its most general sense, these are methods in which teachers or paraprofessionals use the ELL's primary language to translate unfamiliar vocabulary or clarify lessons taught in English.

3. **Instructional methods using English as a Second Language:** These include various approaches to teaching English to non-native speakers. The three common subdivisions of ESL emphasis are:

Grammar-based ESL: Instruction in English that teaches about the language, including its structure, functions, and vocabulary.

Communication-based ESL: Instruction in English that emphasizes using the language skillfully in meaningful contexts.

Content-based ESL: Instruction in English that attempts to develop language skills while preparing students to study grade-level material in English. Although using content as a means, these programs are still focused primarily on the learning of English, which distinguishes them from sheltered instructional methods. (Adapted from Linquanti, 1999.)

4. **Content-Based Instruction/Sheltered Instruction Method:** This method of instruction is also known as Structured Immersion. In California it is known as

Specially Designed Academic Instruction in English (SDAIE). This involves the teaching of grade-level subject matter in English in ways that are comprehensible and engage students academically, while also promoting English language development. Sheltered instructional strategies are part of almost every other method and model, but can also be organized into a unified program model in their own right. This method of instruction requires significant teaching skills in both English language development and subject-specific instruction; clearly defined language and content objectives; modified curriculum, supplementary materials, and alternative assessments (Echevarria, Vogt, & Short, 2000).

Sheltered Instruction Observation Protocol (SIOP): A program model for teaching grade-level content in a way that is understandable for ELL students while at the same time promoting their English language development. SIOP was developed by researchers at the Center for Research on Education, Diversity & Excellence in response to the variability, both in design and delivery, of sheltered instruction methods. It uses a variety of sheltering strategies in a unified, structured way. Research using a control group design has compared ELL students in classes whose teachers had been trained in implementing the SIOP to a control group class taught by teachers not trained in the SIOP model. ELL students in classes whose teachers had been trained in implementing the SIOP outperformed control group students. (See Echevarria & Short, 2003, for more information on the research.)

Cognitive Academic Language Learning Approach (CALLA): A program model based on cognitive learning theory, CALLA integrates content-area instruction with language development activities and explicit instruction in learning strategies (Chamot & O'Malley, 1994). CALLA emphasizes active learning, in which students are given the skills and opportunities to take an active role in their own learning. Developed by Anna Uhl Chamot of George Washington University and J. Michael O'Malley, CALLA is being implemented in approximately 30 school districts in the United States and in several other countries. Chamot and O'Malley (1996) report that some studies in certain districts show ELL students in "high implementation CALLA classrooms performed significantly better" (p. 271) than ELL students in low-implementation classrooms on the use of procedures such as problem solving. They do, however, acknowledge that more research and formal program evaluations are needed. In chapter 7, we discuss how CALLA can be integrated into classroom instruction. (For more information see *www.gwu.edu/~calla/*.)

REFERENCES

Chamot, A.U., & O'Malley, J. M. (1994). *The CALLA handbook: Implementing the cognitive academic language learning approach.* Reading, MA: Addison-Wesley.

Chamot, A.U., & O'Malley, J. M. (1996). The Cognitive Academic Language Learning Approach (CALLA): A model for linguistically diverse classrooms. *The Elementary School Journal, 96,* 259–273.

Echevarria, J., & Short, D. (2003). The effects of sheltered instruction on the achievement of limited English proficient students. Washington, DC: Center for Applied Linguistics. Retrieved April 20, 2003, from www.cal.org/crede/si.htm.

Echevarria, J., Vogt, M., & Short, D. (2000). *Making content comprehensible for English language learners: The SIOP model.* Boston, MA: Allyn & Bacon.

Genesee, F. (Ed.). (1999). *Program alternatives for linguistically diverse students* (Educational Practice Report No. 1). Santa Cruz, CA: Center for Research on Education, Diversity & Excellence. Retrieved April 20, 2003, from *www.cal.org/crede/pubs/edpractice/EPR1.pdf.*

Linquanti, R. (1999). *Fostering academic success for English language learners: What do we know?* San Francisco, CA: WestEd. Retrieved February 21, 2003, from *www.wested.org/policy/pubs/fostering/.*

Rennie, J. (1993). *ESL and bilingual program models* [ERIC Digest]. Washington, DC: ERIC Clearinghouse on Languages and Linguistics. Retrieved April 17, 2003, from *www.cal.org/ericcll/digest/rennie01.html.*

Source: Instructional Methods and Program Models for Serving English Language Learners: An Overview for the Mainstream Teacher (http://www.nwrel.org/request/2003may/instructional.html). Used with permission.

Contact us:
Mail - NWREL, 101 SW Main Street, Suite 500, Portland, OR 97204
Telephone - (503) 275-9500 or (800) 547-6339

Research in Focus: Bilingual Education

From 1985 to 2001, Wayne Thomas and Virginia Collier conducted a comprehensive study of the long-term achievement of ELL students in a variety of educational programs across the nation. Their findings indicate that enrichment 90-10 and 50-50 one-way and two-way developmental bilingual education (DBE) programs (or dual language, bilingual immersion) are the only models that assist students to attain the 50th percentile in both the primary language and English across the curriculum, and to maintain that level of high achievement or reach even higher levels through the end of schooling. They also found that these programs report the fewest dropouts.

The largest number of dropouts in their study came from the group of ELLs whose parents refused language support services. Their reading and math achievement decreased significantly by grade 5 compared to students who participated in language support programs.

ELLs exiting language support programs initially outperform students in bilingual programs when tested in English. By middle school, however, students in bilingual programs match the level of achievement of students schooled only in English, and by high school, their achievement levels actually surpass the students from English-only programs.

Thomas and Collier found that the strongest predictor of achievement for ELLs is the amount of formal primary language schooling. That is, the greater the number of years of instruction in the primary language, the higher the achievement in English.

They concluded that, in order to close the achievement gap between ELLs and native English speakers, language support programs must be well implemented, not segregated, and provide support for 5–6 years. Even the most effective language support programs they examined were able to close only half of the achievement gap in 2–3 years.

Source: From Thomas & Collier, 2002.

EFFECTIVE PRACTICES

The National Research Council review of the research on the education of English language learners identified several factors reflective of effective schools and classrooms (August & Hakuta, 1997). They include:

Select one of these factors and discuss with a partner why it is important for ELLs.

- Teacher, student, and families hold high expectations for achievement
- Differentiated instruction, adapted to meet individual needs and language proficiency levels
- Differentiated assessment that informs instruction and provides feedback to students
- Valuing home culture
- Use of native language
- Curriculum that teaches the basics as well as higher-order skills
- Explicit teaching of learning strategies

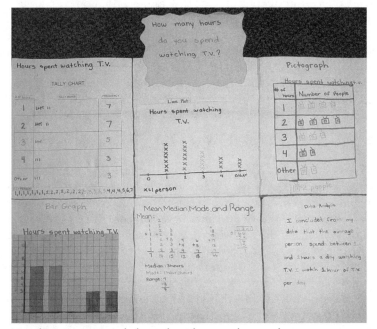

Visual representations help students learn and remember
Doug Fisher

- Opportunities for student-to-student interaction
- Opportunities for practice

Further discussion of these factors is woven throughout the chapters in this book.

A more recent review of the research focused on the attainment of literacy in English. In 2002, the U.S. Department of Education's Institute of Education Sciences convened a panel of experts to synthesize the research on the development of literacy in language-minority students. In 2006 this panel published six major findings about what we know (and don't yet know) regarding learning to read and write in a new language (August & Shanahan, 2006):

What might be the implications of these findings on your teaching?

1. Effective literacy programs provide explicit and comprehensive instruction in the key components of reading—phonemic awareness, phonics, fluency, vocabulary, and text comprehension.
2. Effective literacy programs include a focus on developing oral proficiency in English.
3. First-language proficiency is advantageous but not vital to literacy development in English.
4. Individual differences are a significant factor in developing literacy in English.
5. Existing assessments do not adequately assess strengths and weaknesses to guide either placement or instruction.
6. Home language experiences can positively affect literacy development.

We will discuss the implications of these findings and those of the National Research Council throughout the book. Before we do, however, let us lay the foundation and build a common frame of reference for that discussion. The ideas in this book rest on two important principles: First, that learning is a social act that takes place within an optimal zone of development known as the Zone of Proximal Development. And second, that there are certain classroom conditions that promote learning. Both of these principles hold true for all students. As we examine them, however, we will focus on their specific application for ELLs.

THE ZONE OF PROXIMAL DEVELOPMENT

Russian psychologist Lev Vygotsky believed that learning takes place at a level just beyond what learners can do independently, a level just far enough beyond their linguistic and conceptual understanding to require them to stretch their skills. He called it the Zone of Proximal Development (ZPD) (Vygotsky, 1978). If instruction is aimed at the level where students can already work independently, there is no room for growth. By the same token, if it is aimed at a level too far above what they can do on their own, the gap is too wide, frustration sets in, and no learning occurs. In other words, there is a difference between the *actual developmental level* (tasks that a child can complete on his or her own) and the *Zone of Proximal Development* (tasks that a child can complete successfully only with the help of an adult or a "more capable peer"). Central to this theory is the idea that learning is a social act. If learning only takes place within the

Zone of Proximal Development, where the learner requires assistance, it follows that learning only takes place through interaction with others. While Vygotsky believed that learning requires a teacher or a more capable peer, current socio-cultural theory expands on this notion. We now recognize that learning certainly occurs through interaction with more knowledgeable or experienced peers or a teacher, but that it also takes place as we interact with a less capable peer, or even as we engage in self-talk (Frey & Fisher, 2006).

It is important to note that instruction in the Zone of Proximal Development requires that the "other person" provide scaffolding—nonintrusive intervention, information, or instruction—and not simply complete the task for the learner. The Zone of Proximal Development is, of course, ever expanding as the student becomes able to work independently at higher and higher levels, and the teacher gradually releases increasing responsibility for learning (see Figure 1.2).

We need to be cognizant of our students' strengths and needs so that we can design learning tasks that will move them continually outside their independent zone into the Zone of Proximal Development, where the level of the work required is just beyond what they can accomplish on their own. While practice and enjoyment take place in the independent zone, learning takes place in the Zone of Proximal Development. Recognizing your students' Zone of Proximal Development is the foundation of differentiated instruction. And recognizing that learning is a social act is the foundation of instructional planning, planning for lessons that encourage and require collaboration, discussion, and interaction.

> Think of a time when you learned something more easily and at a deeper level as you interacted with someone else.

Figure 1.2   Zone of Proximal Development

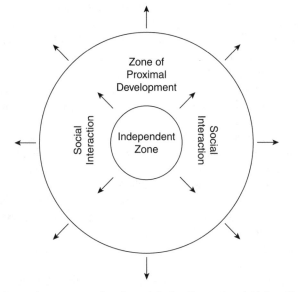

Each zone is ever-expanding through instruction and social interaction.

Spotlight on Instruction

The Application of ZPD

Ms. Allen, a bilingual fifth-grade teacher, calls five of her students to her teacher center for guided instruction. The rest of the students in her class are working collaboratively in mixed ability groups at learning centers. At one center, students are reading the Spanish version of the popular Harry Potter series and meeting in their book club to discuss character development. At another center, students are peer editing their responses to a writing prompt on character analysis. At the listening center, students are listening to a recorded book (in English) and following along with the text. Ms. Allen records the books herself so that she can pause her reading and speak directly to her students. At the independent reading center, students are engaged in free voluntary reading time. And finally, at the media center, a group of students are completing an author study on Mem Fox, using the Internet and a graphic organizer to analyze the different characters that this author uses in her books.

The group of students at the teacher center were purposefully selected based on the assessment information Ms. Allen has collected. She knows that this temporary group consists of students who are experiencing difficulty in making connections between the texts they are reading, other texts, their lives, and the world at large. Ms. Allen meets with purposefully selected groups of students each day during her language arts block. For this group, she has reduced the difficulty level of the text and uses questions to scaffold their understanding.

Ms. Allen: So, last time we met we looked at the cover and talked about the first chapter of our book *Shiloh* (Naylor, 1991). We also talked about the types of connections that readers make with books as they read. Do you remember?

Miriam: Yeah, I thought about myself. I got a dog, but my dog is my own.

Ms. Allen: Nice, you've made the connection between the text and your own life. I'll give you a minute to think about some other connections. Joe?

Joe: I gotta dog. He's black and tough. He can rip apart . . .

Ms. Allen: Amazing, another connection between the text and your own life. So, Joe, I'll give you the same question—can you think of other connections? Miriam, thoughts you'd like to share?

Miriam: I guess that I was remembering that book . . . you know . . . the other book . . .

Ms. Allen: Hmmm. Another book. A book about a dog? You aren't going to tell me about Walter from last year, are you?

Miriam: Yeah!! *Walter the Farting Dog* (Kotzwinkle & Murray, 2001). I loved that story.

Ms. Allen: Interesting. I was wondering about the connection—is it just because there were dogs in both books? Are there other connections between the two books? I think we have to dig a little deeper on this one. Who were the owners? What did they do? Sandra?

Sandra: My papa tell me no hit a dog.

Ms. Allen: I agree with your papa. I don't think that Judd should hit Shiloh. Did you talk with your dad about the book and why some people might hit their pets?

And so the guided instruction lesson continues with Ms. Allen slowly developing her students' understanding of the various types of text connections they can and should make as they learn to comprehend texts. She knows that these skills will, with enough practice, transfer into students' personal repertoires and habits.

CONDITIONS OF LEARNING

The other theoretical basis of the Differentiated Approach comes from research on language acquisition conducted by Brian Cambourne (1988). Cambourne observed toddlers interacting with others around them as they acquired their native language. In his observations he consistently found certain conditions to be present. He postulated that these conditions promote language learning in school just as they promote language learning at home. These conditions have since been recognized as important to all learning, not just language learning. In Table 1.10 you will find each condition explained in relation to English language learners, as well as ideas for classroom application.

As you read the chapters that follow, keep these conditions in mind and look for ways to apply them in your classroom.

As you do so, remember the plea of the Indian father, "What you say and what you do in the classroom, what you teach and how you teach it, and what you don't say and don't teach will have significant effect on the potential success or failure of my child" (Lake, 1990, p. 53).

What evidence of each of these conditions can be found in your classroom? Write an example that demonstrates what you do to create each condition.

Table 1.10

Conditions of Learning	
Condition	**Classroom Application**
Immersion Students are immersed in print, print, print—books, signs, charts. For ELLs, immersion refers to immersion in all four domains of language—listening, speaking, reading, and writing. Since ELLs have had far less exposure to English than their native-English-speaking peers, they need time to practice their receptive skills of listening and reading in addition to the productive skills of speaking and writing.	• Fill your classroom with environmental print such as charts, word walls, and labels. • Read aloud to students. • Incorporate listening, speaking, reading, and writing into all lessons. • Provide lots of books, magazines, books on tape, and readings that address grade-level content at a variety of reading levels.

(continued)

Table 1.10   (continued)

Condition	Classroom Application
Demonstration Students see ample demonstrations or models of concepts and skills. Since ELLs cannot rely solely on language to make meaning, they may need to have even more examples and demonstrations, as well as more explicit modeling than their native-English-speaking peers.	• Read Alouds and other demonstrations accompanied by Think Alouds (talking aloud about your thinking process as you model the activity). • Fishbowl activities: A group of students model the activity and other students observe critically before doing it themselves. • Display examples of finished products.
Engagement Active involvement in learning is crucial to comprehension and retention of concepts and skills. Tasks should be relevant and at an appropriate level—challenging yet within the learner's range of ability. A safe environment allows students to feel secure enough to take risks. A low-anxiety environment is particularly important for ELLs who may fear ridicule of their errors in English.	• Establish an environment in which students feel secure in taking risks. • Have an authentic purpose for each lesson. • Provide multiple levels of assignments and support to enable students to participate successfully.
Expectation It seems almost unnecessary to say that we must hold high expectations of our students. Evidence of high expectations can be a very subtle behavior, however. We must examine our beliefs and actions closely to be sure that we clearly communicate to our students that they can achieve at increasingly higher levels. It is sometimes difficult to maintain high expectations of students who cannot understand or express themselves clearly in English. A lack of language proficiency does not equate to a lack of ability to think critically and comprehend difficult concepts.	• Always keep the grade-level standards in mind. • Use flexible grouping configurations that are not always based on ability. • Be sure that questions and activities require higher-level thinking even for students at earlier levels of language proficiency. • Find ways to provide access to grade-level concepts and texts through scaffolds such as graphic organizers, accessing prior knowledge, modeling, visuals, etc.
Responsibility Students take increasing responsibility for their own learning. Just as we talk about the importance of "ownership" for teachers in the educational reform process, we recognize the importance of students' having "ownership" in	• Encourage reflection. • Provide opportunities for self-assessment. • Talk to students about the importance of reflection and self-assessment.

the learning process. Learners who understand their own role in the learning process are likely to be more engaged, gain deeper understanding, and retain more. This is especially critical for ELLs who may already feel disempowered by virtue of not understanding the language and culture.	• Encourage critical thinking. Don't rely on right-wrong answers. • Provide student choice of assignments. • Provide a gradual release of responsibility in tasks.
Employment (Practice) Students have many opportunities to practice and apply new concepts and skills in meaningful ways. For ELLs, practice includes opportunities to practice language as well as content.	• Provide opportunities for students to work together on tasks that give each student a clearly defined role and require them to talk in order to complete the task. • Provide real-life applications when possible.
Approximation Student responses that approximate the standard are accepted and celebrated. Especially when learning a new language, mistakes are part of the process. ELLs must feel free to take risks in their efforts to communicate.	• Create an environment in which it is not only acceptable to take risks, but encouraged. • Talk to students about how we learn, that approximation plays a role in all learning—learning to walk as a toddler, playing a sport, etc. • Display student work.
Response Feedback is specific, focused, ongoing, and from multiple sources—peers as well as teachers. For ELLs this means that we must address language form as well as meaning.	• Allow time for individual conferencing. • Provide opportunities for students to review one another's work. • Address errors in language as appropriate developmentally.

Source: Adapted from "Conditions of Learning," from The Whole Story: Natural Learning and the Acquisition of Literacy in the Classroom *by Brian Cambourne, 1988, Scholastic. Used with permission of Brian Cambourne.*

EFFECTIVE STRATEGIES FOR TEACHING ENGLISH LANGUAGE LEARNERS: ELD AND SDAIE

In our work with teachers and administrators, we often hear the comment that effective strategies for ELLs are effective strategies for all students. We agree. The same strategies we use in sheltered instruction are effective with a wide range of students. There are, however, unique considerations in their application to English language learners. These considerations are based on understanding the process of second language acquisition, factors that influence language acquisition, and how our students' diverse cultural and linguistic backgrounds impact learning. The differences in application of the strategies lie in

Figure 1.3   Comparing ELD and SDAIE

ELD		SDAIE
• Develop proficiency in English • Develop foundation language for various content areas	**Purpose**	• Develop knowledge in content areas • Develop academic language and vocabulary related to the content area
• Focus on forms, functions, and fluency • Varies based on student's English proficiency level • Includes survival language, social language, academic language	**Content**	• Grade-level content with focus on key concepts • Curriculum not "watered down"
• All English • Students are expected to use English to communicate in student-to-teacher and/or student-to-student interactions	**Language of Instruction**	• English, though primary language, may be used for clarification when necessary

the amount and type of scaffolding (support and guidance) that we provide, as well as in the focus on language development.

The Differentiated Approach to teaching English language learners includes the two components of a comprehensive program—English Language Development (ELD) and sheltered instruction or Specially Designed Academic Instruction in English (SDAIE). Although there has been some debate regarding the distinctions between sheltered instruction and SDAIE, in our minds they have the same purpose and use the same strategies, so we will use the terms interchangeably throughout this book. Figure 1.3 contains a diagram comparing and contrasting ELD and SDAIE.

SHELTERED INSTRUCTION OR SPECIALLY DESIGNED ACADEMIC INSTRUCTION IN ENGLISH?

In the late 1980s, when we first began our work with English language learners, our students were called "LEP," or "Limited English Proficient," and our classrooms were called "sheltered." The language we use, or the labels we give students and programs, reflects our culture, our belief systems. When we use the labels "LEP" or "sheltered," we reflect a belief that our students are deficient or limited and therefore in need of shelter from the rigors of "regular" classroom instruction. In the mid 1990s, the labels began to change, reflective of the change in the culture. Our students became "English language learners," indicating an affirmative belief that learning a language is a developmental process. And our classrooms now provided "SDAIE," or "Specially Designed Academic Instruction in English." This change in terminology was based on the recognition that sheltered classrooms that were meant to support access to the core curriculum for ELLs in reality often provided a watered-down curriculum with low expectations for student achievement. The very term, *Specially Designed Academic Instruction in English*, connotes high standards and rigor, along with consideration of language proficiency. Unfortunately, while the change in name reflected a change in beliefs, it did not necessarily reflect a change in practice. And even where it did, student achievement still did not rise significantly (Rumberger & Gándara, 2005).

We would suggest that this lack of progress is, in part, due to a lack of focus on the academic language that is vital to the comprehension and expression of complex academic concepts. When teachers pay more attention to comprehensible input and to making lessons engaging for their students than they do to developing academic language and academic learning strategies, students may not learn to read academic text and become independent learners. Alternatively, when teachers focus on the grade-level content using only grade-level texts, without providing comprehensible input or engaging lessons, students may not learn the content. Jim Cummins has suggested that, within the context of academic language learning, we rethink our understanding of comprehensible input. He offers the term *critical literacy* to describe the process of helping students understand academic text (Cummins, 1996). We know that comprehension expands as we make connections to prior knowledge, as we analyze language, ideas, or events, and then create a new product using our developing understanding. In other words, as we discuss further in chapter 2, learning takes place through both input and output. Students deepen their understanding as they organize and express their thoughts either orally or in writing. This output requires not only instruction in the new content, but also explicit instruction in the language needed to express those ideas and in the strategies we use for learning.

See chapter 2 for a detailed discussion on comprehensible input.

So, while we recognize the controversy over terminology, we will continue to use both terms, *sheltered instruction* and *SDAIE,* using a definition that includes three components:

- Making the **content** comprehensible and engaging
- Teaching the **academic language** that allows students to express their understanding
- Developing independence in using effective **learning strategies**

ESL, ESOL, OR ELD?

Abdurashid Ali, in response to a researcher's question about his ESL class, said, "English isn't my second language. It's my fifth. It bothers me that people think I speak only two languages."

As you saw in Figure 1.3, which highlighted the differences between English Language Development (ELD) and SDAIE, ELD refers to instruction *in* English and *of* English, instruction specifically focused on developing proficiency in the English language for non-native speakers. In many parts of the nation, you will hear the term *English as a Second Language (ESL),* and around the world you will hear the term *English for Speakers of Other Languages (ESOL).* We prefer the terms ELD or ESOL because they recognize that many of our ELL students have already mastered two, three, or even more languages. We will, however, use the term ESL at times to refer to a specific course title.

BILINGUAL EDUCATION AND ACHIEVEMENT IN ENGLISH

"[By high school] . . . students in bilingual programs . . . achievement levels actually surpass the students from English only programs" (Thomas & Collier, 2002). We are not surprised by the findings of this study. We believe that being bilingual offers a distinct advantage in life—more career opportunities are available to those who can communicate in two languages. We believe that being bilingual enriches life—entire new worlds of people and ways of understanding are opened up to those who speak two languages and understand two cultures. And we believe that being bilingual may lead to enhanced cognitive flexibility as the brain learns different ways to express the same concepts (Hakuta, 1986). Well-designed bilingual programs use each language—native and target (English)—to reinforce learning in the other language. They allow students to keep pace with grade-level concepts and skills as they learn English. The most effective bilingual programs weave together three different approaches to teaching language and content. They:

1. Use the primary language to develop literacy and teach grade-level concepts and skills.
2. Teach English, using a balance of language acquisition theory and explicit instruction to develop proficiency in both everyday and academic English.
3. Use sheltered English (SDAIE), increasing the amount over time, to teach grade-level concepts and skills as students gain more competence in English, while continuing to develop listening, speaking, reading and writing, and grade-level content in the primary language.

A tall order, given that they have the same amount of time for instruction as those who teach only in English. Our purpose in this book is to focus on the second and third approaches described above—approaches that are found across all programs, whether bilingual, native language support, ESL, or content-based. We will examine principles and strategies of a Differentiated Approach to teaching English and teaching *in* English. It is not within the scope of this book to describe how bilingual teachers can use the primary language for instruction. Rather we will focus on the teaching *of* and *in* English and ask those of you who plan to teach in a bilingual program to conduct additional inquiry into how the Differentiated Approach can fit into a dual-language model.

Application to Practice

Reflection

1. In your mind, what are the five most important ideas discussed in this chapter? Why are they important?
2. Which of these ideas are reflected (or will be) in your classroom? How are they (can they be) reflected?
3. What is something you have a question about?

Case Study: *Target a Student*

Before you continue reading this book, select your target student.

Think of a student in your classroom who is currently classified as an English language learner. (If you are not a classroom teacher, you may want to identify a student from a classroom where you can observe regularly as you read this book.)

Choose a student who is representative of the population with which you are most concerned. This may be a student who is new to English, or one who has attended U.S. schools for several years but is not making adequate progress, or perhaps one who exhibits some other behaviors that concern you. As you read this book and apply the ideas in your classroom, you will be asked to observe the effects of your instruction on your target student. Is he/she engaged? Comprehending? Developing language and understanding of content? In short, what is working for this student, what isn't working, and why?

Select a student to observe throughout your reading of this book.

Why did you select this student?

References

August, D., & Hakuta, K. (1997). *Improving schooling for language-minority children: A research agenda.* Committee on Developing a Research Agenda on the Education of Limited-English-Proficient and Bilingual Students, Commission on Behavioral and Social Sciences and Education, National Research Council. Washington, DC: National Academy Press.

August, D., & Shanahan, T. (2006). *Developing literacy in second-language learners: Report of the National Literacy Panel on Language-Minority Children and Youth.* Mahwah, NJ: Lawrence Erlbaum.

Cambourne, B. (1988). *The whole story: Natural learning and the acquisition of literacy in the classroom.* New York: Scholastic.

Cummins, J. (1996). *Negotiating identities: Education for empowerment in a diverse society.* Los Angeles: California Association for Bilingual Education.

de la Luz Reyes, M., & Halcón, J. J. (Eds.). (2001). *The best for our children: Critical perspectives on literacy for Latino students*. New York: Teachers College Press.

Frey, N., & Fisher, D. (2006). *Language arts workshop: Purposeful reading and writing instruction*. Upper Saddle River, NJ: Merrill/Prentice Hall.

Fry, R. (2003). *Hispanic youth dropping out of U.S. schools: Measuring the challenge*. Washington, DC: Pew Hispanic Center.

Gutiérrez, K. (2002). Studying cultural practices in urban learning communities. *Human Development, 45*, 312–321.

Hakuta, K. (1986). *Mirror of language: The debate on bilingualism*. New York: Basic Books.

Kotzwinkle, W., & Murray, G. (2001). *Walter the farting dog*. Berkeley, CA: North Atlantic Books.

Lake, R. (Medicine Grizzlybear) (1990). An Indian father's plea. *Teacher Magazine, 2*(1), 48–53.

Moll, L. C., Amanti, C., & Neff, D. (1992). Funds of knowledge for teaching: Using a qualitative approach to connect homes and classrooms. *Theory into Practice, 31*, 132–41.

Moll, L. C., & Arnot-Hopffer, E. (2005). Sociocultural competence in teacher education. *Journal of Teacher Education, 56*, 242–247.

National Clearinghouse for English Language Acquisition. (2004). *The growing numbers of limited English proficient students: 1991/92–2001/02*. Washington, DC: Author.

National Clearinghouse for English Language Acquisition. (2005). *The growing numbers of limited English proficient students: 1993/94–2003/04*. Washington, DC: Author.

National Council of Teachers of English. (2006). *NCTE position paper on the role of English teachers in educating English language learners (ELLs)*. Retrieved from the World Wide Web on May 11, 2006 from: *http://www.ncte.org/about/ over/ positions/category/div/124545.htm*.

Naylor, P. R. (1991). *Shiloh*. New York: Bantam Doubleday Dell.

Rumberger, R., & Gándara, P. (2005). *How well are California's English learners mastering English?* University of California Linguistic Minority Research Institute Newsletter, Vol. 14, No. 2. Santa Barbara, CA.

Scarcella, R. (2000). *Effective language instruction for English learners*. Presentation for Standards-Based Evaluation and Accountability Institute for English Learners. California Department of Education. Santa Barbara, CA.

Scarcella, R. C. (2003). *Accelerating academic English: A focus on the English learner*. Oakland, CA: University of California Press.

Slavin, R. E., & Calderón, M. (Eds). (2001). *Effective programs for Latino students*. Mahwah, NJ: Lawrence Erlbaum Associates.

Thomas, W., & Collier, V. (2002). *A national study of school effectiveness for language minority students' long-term academic achievement*. Retrieved from the World Wide Web June 30, 2005 from: *http://www.crede.org/research/llaa/ 1.1_final. html*. Center for Research on Education, Diversity & Excellence. Santa Cruz, CA and Washington, DC.

Van Hook, J., & Fix, M. (2000). A profile of immigrant students in U.S. schools. In J. Ruiz-de-Velasco & M. Fix, with B. C. Clewell (Eds.), *Overlooked and underserved, immigrant students in U.S. secondary schools* (pp. 9–33). Washington, DC: The Urban Institute.

Vygotsky, L. (1978). *Mind in society.* Cambridge, MA: Harvard University Press.

2 Language Acquisition: Dimensions of Proficiency

Charles Gupton/Corbis/Bettmann

The old woman remembered a swan she had bought many years ago in Shanghai for a foolish sum. This bird, boasted the market vendor, was once a duck that stretched its neck in hopes of becoming a goose, and now look!—it is too beautiful to eat.

Then the woman and the swan sailed across an ocean many thousands of li wide, stretching their necks toward America. On her journey she cooed to the swan: "In America I will have a daughter just like me. But over there nobody will say her worth is measured by the loudness of her husband's belch. Over there nobody will look down on her, because I will make her speak only perfect American English. And over there she will always be too full to swallow any sorrow! She will know my meaning, because I will give her this swan—a creature that became more than what was hoped for."

But when she arrived in the new country, the immigration officials pulled her swan away from her, leaving the woman fluttering her arms and with only one swan feather for a memory. And then she had to fill out so many forms she forgot why she had come and what she had left behind.

Now the woman was old. And she had a daughter who grew up speaking only English and swallowing more Coca-Cola than sorrow. For a long time now the woman had wanted to give her daughter the single swan feather and tell her. "This feather may look worthless, but it comes from afar and carries with it all my good intentions." And she waited, year after year, for the day she could tell her daughter this in perfect American English.

Focus Questions

1. What are the key principles of language acquisition?
2. What does it mean to be proficient in a language?
3. How do I make sure my students understand my instruction?
4. How do the principles of language acquisition impact classroom instruction for students at different levels of proficiency?
5. What are major factors that influence language acquisition?

Roughly one million immigrants arrive in this country each year in search of jobs, education, and a new home for their families (Ruiz-de-Velasco, Fix, & Clewell, 2000). They bring with them their language, their culture, their background and experiences, entering a new world with a new language and a new culture to learn. They arrive with the highest hopes and dreams for their children and the desire for them to learn "perfect American English." As educators, it is important to understand the process of acquiring a new language and becoming part of a new culture so that we can provide the supports our students need to achieve. This chapter will examine four primary principles of language acquisition and the major factors that influence that process. Our goal is to provide a foundation of knowledge upon which you can lay your teaching skills and strategies, enabling you to make informed decisions about your curriculum and instruction.

Accessing Prior Knowledge: Acquiring a Second Language

Complete the anticipation guide in Figure 2.1 to access your prior knowledge about this topic.

Four Principles of Language Acquisition

There are many similarities between first- and second-language learning. How do infants acquire their first language? They receive immense amounts of input from the people around them. They hear the same language over and over again, all day, and over months and years. They see many clues around them to help connect the words to actions, things, and ideas. No one minds if they make mistakes as they learn to speak. Parents often model the correct way to express a thought simply by restating it. Babies are rewarded with praise and encouragement for their efforts. They use language to communicate with others about the world around them all day long. And there is always a real-life purpose for the communication.

Figure 2.1   Second Language Acquisition Anticipation Guide

Read each statement. Mark "A" if you agree or "D" if you disagree. Tell why.

A	D	Statement	Justification
		Young children learn a second language more easily than older children or adults.	
		A student who sounds fluent in English no longer needs English language development.	
		Proficiency in the primary (first) language helps second-language acquisition.	
		The more English you are exposed to, the more quickly you will learn English.	
		Instruction in content areas (math, science, etc.) should not begin until the student has reached proficiency in English.	
		Math, science, and social studies teachers are also language teachers.	
		Students should be encouraged to use their primary language in a sheltered classroom.	

Learning a second language is not so very different. It also requires:

- *Comprehensible input*—English language learners need to hear comprehensible language all day long.
- *Contextualized instruction*—Part of what makes language comprehensible is the context or the clues provided.
- *Low-anxiety environment*—Students need to feel safe enough to make mistakes and take risks.
- *Meaningful engagement*—Students need to use language with others for authentic purposes.

Four principles of language acquisition

The differences come into play when the second-language learning takes place in school, where individual attention is infrequent, and grade-level content must be learned at the same time as language. Then it becomes essential that we provide explicit, focused language instruction, along with scaffolds (support) to make content learning accessible to students who are still learning language. Within the school environment, we also expect students to be able to use academic language to talk and write about academic concepts. This level of language requires more than comprehensible input, contextualized instruction, a safe environment, and meaningful engagement. It requires explicit instruction in the forms and functions of academic language (e.g., see Dutro & Moran, 2003). We will discuss this further in chapter 6.

What makes second-language learning different from first language learning?

WHAT IS LANGUAGE PROFICIENCY?

Before we examine the ways in which these four principles of language acquisition support language and content learning, let's examine the end goal. What does it mean to be proficient in another language?

BICS and CALP

Jim Cummins (1979) defined two levels of language proficiency: Basic Interpersonal Communication Skills (BICS) and Cognitive Academic Language Proficiency (CALP).

BICS refers to the ability to communicate about everyday subjects and needs, the language used to talk with friends, shop, eat at a restaurant, or even tell a teacher why a homework assignment isn't done. It is language learned and used in highly contextualized situations where there are many clues to aid in comprehension. The speaker or listener need not rely solely on language to construct meaning. Familiarity with the situation (background knowledge) and clues such as facial expressions, pictures, and real objects all provide a context that supports understanding.

Who are your ELLs who speak English fluently yet do not do well on writing assignments or on state standardized tests? What are the differences and similarities between their conversational language and their writing?

CALP, on the other hand, refers to academic language, the type of language used in the classroom for lectures, discussions, reading, lab reports, oral presentations, and so forth. These academic tasks provide little in the way of context or clues and generally involve abstract concepts. Students must rely on language to make meaning.

Research in Focus: Dimensions of Language Proficiency

During the 1970s and 1980s, a Canadian linguist, James Cummins, did extensive research on how people acquire language. The majority of his studies were done in Quebec centering around the French-English immersion programs. One of the first observations made by Cummins was that there are two dimensions of language: conversational and academic. The terms used to describe these dimensions are BICS (Basic Interpersonal Communication Skills) and CALP (Cognitive Academic Language Proficiency).

When children first begin to speak and eventually enter school, they arrive with BICS in their primary language. This is the language used at home, on the playground, knowledge of basic survival communication. When we chat with our friends about the events of the weekend, we are using BICS. When your child tells you about the soccer game, that is also BICS. It is expected that children entering school at the kindergarten level come with a fully developed BICS, basically, a receptive and expressive vocabulary of about 2500 words.

With that dimension at a functioning level, the school can proceed to expand and build upon that knowledge to develop CALP, the academic dimension of language that is necessary for school success. CALP is used to explain cell structure, to summarize a reading selection, write a research paper on habitats, to take any academic test.

Therefore, if a student has BICS in one language, learns to read in that language, and then uses that language in thinking and analyzing, the student develops relatively clear relationships between speech and print and between language and thought.

Thus, for a student to be both socially and academically successful in a language, these two dimensions need to be developed. In short, the degree of success that a student will experience in school is positively associated with the extent of the development of both BICS and CALP.

$$BICS + CALP = academic\ success$$

Source: The American School in Japan, http://www.asij.ac.jp/elementary/parent/mosaic/Research.htm. Used with permission.

Understanding the difference between BICS and CALP is critical to knowing our students. We hear some of our students talk at lunch or on the playground, and they sound very nearly fluent. They talk in class easily, yet they have difficulty reading. And when we look closely at their writing, we can see many errors that sound like someone who is still learning English. Particularly in secondary schools where we have many English language learners who have attended school in this country for several years, we see many students who sound very fluent. Often, however, they are lacking the academic language required to be successful in school. As educators, we must be aware of our students' skills in all four domains of language—listening, speaking, reading, and writing—in order to ensure that we continue to provide instruction aimed at developing full proficiency in English. (We will take an in-depth look at developing academic language in chapters 6 and 7. In this chapter our focus is on developing an understanding of how language is acquired.)

Cummins has since reframed our understanding of language proficiency and added a third dimension—discrete language skills (Cummins, 2003). These discrete skills include phonological, literacy, and grammatical knowledge. They are developed alongside conversational fluency (BICS) and academic language proficiency (CALP), through direct instruction and formal and informal practice in reading, writing, listening, and speaking. Recent methods of second-language instruction have often neglected this third dimension of language proficiency in the belief that students would acquire these skills over time as they used language. Remember the letter from Van in chapter 1? Clearly she was able to express her wishes about a relatively academic topic related to her education and learning. We can make the assumption that she can also communicate about more social topics. When we read her writing, what we find missing is accuracy—plurals, capitalization, subject-verb agreement, word forms—along with the sociolinguistic and strategic competence needed to express ideas appropriately for the audience.

The concept of BICS and CALP has traditionally been explained through the analogy of an iceberg (see Figure 2.2). The tip of the iceberg, the part that we can see, is BICS, that conversational fluency that we often mistakenly assume equates to the ability to understand and participate in grade-level academic work. The far greater portion of the iceberg lying beneath the water where we cannot see it is CALP, the academic language needed for successful participation in that

Figure 2.2   BICS and CALP

grade-level academic work. Building on this analogy, we have added a ship, representing the third dimension of language proficiency, those discrete language skills and strategies necessary to navigate the waters of both conversational and academic contexts. It is our contention that direct instruction of such skills as letter/sound relationships, decoding, and conventions of language, along with opportunities to practice them in authentic contexts, will accelerate the development of language proficiency. We caution that this does not mean a return to a grammar-based approach to language instruction, but rather a balanced approach that addresses conversational fluency, academic language, and the specific skills required to comprehend and produce language accurately.

Communicative competence

What does it mean to be "communicatively competent"?

Another way of thinking about what it means to be fully proficient in a language was suggested by Hymes (1972), who coined the term "communicative competence." Communicative competence refers to the ability to know when, where, and how to use language in a variety of contexts or situations (see Figure 2.3 for a visual representation of this information). The ability to communicate effectively is a complex skill that is comprised of different aspects—grammatical, sociolinguistic, discourse, and strategic (Canale, 1983).

How might you help students develop each type of competence?

Grammatical Competence. This is the aspect of competence that we often think of first when we think of what it means to be proficient. It refers to accuracy, the ability to use the language code correctly—vocabulary, sentence structure,

Figure 2.3   Communicative Competence

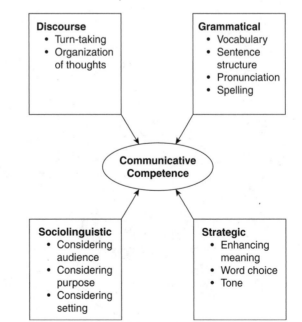

pronunciation, or spelling. For many years, language instruction, whether in English or other languages, was grammar-based, focusing primarily on this one of four aspects of competence. Of the four aspects, grammatical is perhaps the least bound by cultural norms.

Sociolinguistic Competence. Sociolinguistic competence refers to the ability to vary language according to the situation. It entails using language appropriately in different settings, understanding how language expression changes depending on the social status of participants (e.g., teacher vs. peer), the purpose of the communication (e.g., making a request), or the situation itself (e.g., classroom vs. playground).

Discourse Competence. Discourse competence refers to the way in which we organize our thoughts to communicate. It relates to the logical organization of an essay as well as to the logical progression and give and take of a conversation. This logical organization of thought varies from culture to culture as well as from discipline to discipline.

Strategic Competence. Strategic competence is the ability to manipulate language to achieve a goal. Both verbal and nonverbal communication may be involved. Strategic competence is generally used to either clarify or enhance meaning. When a speaker forgets a word or doesn't have the specific vocabulary to express an idea, gestures or paraphrasing can help to make meaning clear. Word choice, tone, or volume of voice may enhance the message and help the speaker (or writer) achieve the desired outcome. Persuasive speech or writing is an example of when strategic competence is likely to be useful.

Reaching this level of competence in English requires focused, explicit instruction as well as many opportunities to practice language in authentic situations. Just as infants engage in language learning all day long, so our students need language development to be a focus all day long. We cannot expect them to reach high levels of language proficiency when the only attention paid to learning language takes place during a 20-minute pull-out session, an hour-long English as a Second Language (ESL) class, or even embedded within a three-hour literacy block. Language development must occur throughout the entire day, integrated into the content. Instructional activities must be planned so that they integrate language learning with content learning. Language instruction must also be a subject area in and of itself, a time when we teach students how to use language and give them multiple opportunities to practice using language in ways that require them to think critically. Compare the following two tasks. Which one requires a higher level of thinking? Which one requires a higher level of linguistic competence?

Task 1: Tell your partner five things you did this morning before coming to school. Write them in sentences.

Task 2: Rewrite each sentence in the past tense: Sheryl talks to Elizabeth. Aida walks to school. Jorge rides his bike.

Spotlight on Instruction

Structured Note-Taking

As Mr. Bonine begins his science instruction, he reads aloud a book related to the content that his students will be exploring. He knows that this short Read Aloud will provide his students with vocabulary in context and will help to build his students' background knowledge.

Mr. Bonine also provides his students with a structured note-taking guide to help them record their observations during the lab. This tool provides a level of support for his students in completing the tasks. It also provides students with some of the academic language he expects them to know and use in their lab reports.

Name _____　　　Date _____

Section 2 Genetics—The Study of Inheritance (continued)

Main Idea	Details
Heredity *I found this information on page _____ .*	**Synthesize** *information about heredity by describing how traits are passed from parent to offspring.* _____ _____ _____ _____ _____
What determines traits? *I found this information on page _____ .*	**Analyze** *hybrid and pure traits by filling in the blanks.* Each gene of a gene pair is called a(n) _____ . If a gene pair contains different _____ for a trait, that trait is called a(n) _____ . If a gene pair contains identical _____ for a trait, that trait is called _____ .
I found this information on page _____ .	**Identify** *whether the dominant or recessive form of the trait will be expressed in each case.*

Alleles	Form of the Trait Expressed
two dominant alleles	
one dominant allele, one recessive allele	
two recessive alleles	

I found this information on page _____ .	**Summarize** *how environment can affect the expression of traits.* _____ _____ _____ _____

32　*The Role of Genes in Inheritance*

A sample note-taking guide
Science Noteables, Douglas Fisher, 2007, Glencoe/McGraw-Hill

Both tasks provide practice in the past tense form of language. The first task also requires students to use other vocabulary to describe events in their own lives and to think about what makes a complete sentence.

THE FOUR PRINCIPLES OF LANGUAGE ACQUISITION APPLIED

The four principles of language acquisition are the foundation of instruction for English language learners. They are reflected in all instruction throughout the day. Through providing a safe environment with ample support for making meaning and daily opportunities for students to be actively involved in learning, we can help our students develop language proficiency and facilitate learning of grade-level content in language arts, math, social studies, science, or other subjects. These principles also provide a structure for thinking about differentiating instruction—students at different levels of proficiency in English require different supports to make input comprehensible, provide context for new concepts, lower their anxiety level, and make activities meaningful.

Principle 1: Comprehensible input

The first step in developing language proficiency is to provide comprehensible input (Krashen, 1985). If students don't understand what they are hearing or reading, we cannot expect them to then produce comprehensible language at progressively more complex levels. Comprehensible input is exactly what the term sounds like—ensuring that students understand (comprehend) what they are listening to and reading (input). It is required for virtually everything that goes on in a classroom: discussions, lectures, readings, and assignments.

Providing comprehensible input requires teachers to think about how they:

- Make their speech comprehensible
- Make new information comprehensible
- Make text comprehensible
- Make directions for assignments comprehensible

Making Speech Comprehensible. Have you noticed that when you hear a language that is unfamiliar to you, it is often difficult to distinguish one word from another? Each phrase or sentence can sound like one long word. When Carol was just beginning to learn Spanish, one of the first things she learned to say was *"más despacio, por favor"* (more slowly, please). She noted that even as her language proficiency progressed, she would still sometimes find herself translating each Spanish phrase into English before it made sense. Unfortunately, by the time she finished translating the first thing that was said, the speaker would be a few sentences farther along. If there was any one part she didn't understand, she would frequently find it difficult to understand what followed because she missed vital pieces of information. A slower rate, pauses now and then, and some repetition of ideas would have helped Carol to keep up, especially as she was learning this new language.

As you read about these principles, think about students at different levels of language proficiency— beginning, intermediate, and advanced. How will you apply these principles differently for students at these different levels?

Listen to your language in the classroom. Do you speak rapidly? Do you pause between thoughts? Is your language academic, yet with enough explanation for ELLs to understand? How do you know if they understand? Tape-record yourself and listen for ways in which your language supports understanding.

Differentiating instruction: What strategies might you use for students at each level of proficiency to make your speech comprehensible?

Repetition can be an effective way of providing multiple opportunities to make meaning. Carol's friend Renee is one of those people who make the same statement several different times in a conversation. Perhaps it's her way of stressing importance, perhaps it's her way of thinking aloud. Regardless of her intent, she's exactly the type of person a new language learner wants to listen to in the new language. Renee's redundancy provides the listener additional opportunities to catch her meaning. If the listener doesn't understand a word or phrase stated in one manner, he or she may be able to get it in the reiteration. These repetitions also provide time to process the language and catch up.

Doug's friend Adam speaks very slowly when he wants to make a point. Although he has his own reasons for this, the way that Adam varies the speed of his speech provides the listener time to think and respond.

So what can classroom teachers do to give students the time they need to process the language itself and make the content of the language comprehensible? **Slowing down** the rate of speech slightly and **pausing** between thoughts gives learners time to process what they've heard and catch up. Using **gestures** helps to reduce the reliance on language alone. If you've ever traveled in a country where you were learning the language, you probably remember communicating many ideas through gestures—pointing to the item you wanted to purchase, listening to directions to the train station, and watching the speaker point to the right. **Avoid idioms** and slang or directly teach them. Simple expressions like "let the cat out of the bag" can cause an English language learner to lose the flow of the discussion. One of the most important ways in which we can give students the opportunity to understand is to amplify our language, as opposed to merely simplifying it. When we restate ideas in many different ways, we can facilitate comprehension for those who didn't understand the first time we said something. We can include additional supporting information or simply explain the concept in another way. We provide **redundancy** of both language and ideas, allowing students to hear the language and vocabulary over and over again (multiple exposures), at the same time as clarifying the ideas through further explanation. Often, when working with ELLs, we tend to simplify our language, using simple vocabulary and simple language structures. In effect, we are watering down our speech and, in the process, our content as well. Simplifying ideas and language can be like reading the Cliffs Notes to a Steinbeck novel instead of reading the novel itself. It's virtually impossible to get the flavor of Steinbeck by reading those Cliffs Notes. All of our students need to get that flavor—it's a matter of presenting it in ways that make it comprehensible.

List the techniques detailed here that make speech comprehensible. Put a check by the ones that you do.

don't overdo teach (handwritten annotation)

Making New Information Comprehensible. Connecting new ideas to prior experiences and learning helps students make sense out of the new material. When Carol was learning Spanish, she would listen to the Tijuana radio stations as she drove to work every day. As long as they were reporting on events that had taken place in San Diego, were of national concern in the United States, or were events that had been covered in the newspaper that morning, she could follow along fairly well. As soon as they began to report the news from Mexico City, however, she was lost and found herself changing the station

We will discuss background knowledge in greater depth in chapter 7 as it is a key factor in making content comprehensible to ELL.

to listen to jazz. Her background knowledge regarding the news helped her to understand the formal, complex language of a news report. The same level of language was rendered incomprehensible when she had no prior knowledge of the subject, and her response, not so dissimilar to that of many of our students, was to tune out.

Making Text Comprehensible. Much of the material we expect our students to read is dense, academic text above their reading level. Even the literature can contain unfamiliar language or make reference to unfamiliar places, experiences, or customs. In order to make the text comprehensible for students who are learning English, we must first analyze the text to determine what challenges it might present, and then plan supports that will help students make meaning as they read. Using visuals, realia (real objects), graphic organizers, and discussions before, during, and after reading are examples of ways in which we can alleviate the complex language demands of text. A picture of a covered wagon allows students to see the living conditions of the westward movement. They can connect their own understanding to the picture and thereby to the reading or discussion. A graphic organizer describing the life cycle of a frog can assist students in seeing how each phase connects to the others, and they can use this knowledge as they read or listen to the explanation. In chapter 7, we will discuss these supports and others in greater depth as part of developing academic language and helping English language learners reach grade-level standards.

Differentiating instruction: What strategies might you use for students at each level of proficiency to make text comprehensible?

Using realia helps students learn content and vocabulary
Doug Fisher

Spotlight on Instruction

Making Directions for Assignments Comprehensible

Ms. Schwartz, a tenth-grade history teacher, writes her daily agenda on the board and explains the tasks for the day. She then asks one of her students, "What are we going to do first?"

Marco replies, "Review the steps of Reciprocal Teaching," reading from the board.

"What did Marco say we are going to do?" Angie asks Yolanda.

Ms. Schwartz repeats this process rapidly with each of the parts of the daily agenda. Her students have now taken on the responsibility of knowing what they are to do, and she no longer has to answer that age-old question, "What are we supposed to do?"

Think of a task you recently assigned your students. What were your instructions to them? Did they all know what to do? How did you know?

Differentiating instruction: What strategies might you use for students at each level of proficiency to make directions comprehensible?

Making Directions for Assignments Comprehensible. Often what prevents ELL students from participating is simply that they did not understand the directions for the task. Understanding and following directions can be a stumbling block for anyone who is not proficient in the language, as those of us who have ever asked for directions in a foreign country can attest to. Words and phrases such as "circle," "underline," or "find the one that does not fit," though simple enough words, carry a great deal of the meaning. If you miss one of the words, you miss the entire idea. It is critical that we make our directions clear and explicit, and that we check for comprehension by having students explain in their own words what they are expected to do.

Giving directions visually as well as orally, demonstrating the task, using clear language, and checking to be certain students understand are crucial to assure that students can participate fully in classroom activities. Consider the advice of Rosa, a fifth-grade ELL student. When asked what would help her in

Using visuals can help students understand the directions
Diana Yemha

school, she replied, "if teachers explain more and give more examples." English language learners may require more explanation and more modeling or demonstrations than students who can understand the language easily.

Principle 2: Contextualized instruction

Read the following sentence. Before reading on, visualize the situation in which this scene might have taken place and note what you think this statement is referring to.

"Oh Bill, I missed you!" she cried.

Stop. Really think about this and visualize the scene. Once you have this in mind, continue reading.

Then she aimed and fired again. (Pritchard, 2004).

If you responded as we did when we first read these statements, you might have thought that *she* had not seen Bill in a while and was happy to see him (though an English language learner might read the word *cried* and, not recognizing the multiple meanings, think that she was unhappy). The first statement, however, takes on a completely different meaning when provided with the context of the second sentence.

As teachers, we have a great deal of knowledge about our content. We read and write at high levels. We understand the math, science, or social studies concepts that we teach. As good readers, with background knowledge about a subject, we are able to understand what we read. We usually can place new learning or information into a context that helps us create meaning. When we don't know the context, though, as we saw with *Bill* it is not only more difficult to make meaning, but we may actually develop misunderstandings. Many of our ELLs bring neither the reading skills nor the background knowledge required to understand the complex grade-level concepts with which they are presented. One way we can compensate for this lack of background skills or knowledge is by providing context for new information.

Cummins (1981) identified two intersecting continua (four quadrants) of support for comprehension and level of cognitive difficulty. These continua highlight how language is used in situations that range from context-embedded (many clues to meaning) to context-reduced (few clues), as well as in situations that are cognitively undemanding (easy) to those that are quite demanding cognitively (hard). We can use Cummins's four quadrants to think about the level of support or context provided for various academic tasks (see Figure 2.4). The tasks on the top half of the quadrant in Figure 2.4 are easy. Those on the bottom would be considered difficult. The tasks on the left-hand side of the quadrant provide lots of clues, whereas those on the right provide only language as a clue to meaning.

- *Quadrant A*—Quadrant A contains tasks that are relatively easy and offer support through visuals, demonstrations, and so on. When playing a game, for example, you can participate by watching others and doing what they do—an easy task, made accessible by watching a demonstration.
- *Quadrant C*—In quadrant C, the tasks are also easy, but provide little support other than through language. Talking on the telephone to set a lunch date does not tax the brain, but, as those among us who have ever

Think of a time when not understanding the context of a situation caused you to misunderstand what you were seeing, hearing, or reading.

Differentiating instruction: Think of a task you might ask students to complete. How can you vary the level of context you provide for students at different levels of proficiency?

Figure 2.4   Comparing Context and Cognitive Demands

Cognitively Undemanding

A	C
• Participating in an art class • Playing a game in PE • Playing with friends at recess • Following directions after watching them modeled	• Writing a list • Talking on the telephone • Copying from the board • Filling in a worksheet
B	**D**
• Listening to a lecture with a graphic organizer • Reading a textbook with graphics— pictures, charts, maps • Writing an essay after discussion, reading, organizing information on a graphic organizer • Participating in a lab experiment • Working with manipulatives in math	• Listening to a lecture • Reading a text book • Writing a persuasive essay • Writing a lab report • Solving a word problem in math • Taking standardized tests

left axis: Context-embedded   *right axis:* Context-reduced

Cognitively Demanding

Think of the most recent activity or assignment you used with your students. Which quadrant did it reflect? What context, clues, or supports did you provide?

What is a Quadrant D type of task that you might ask your students to do? What context or clues could you provide that would support them as they complete the task?

---

talked on the phone in a language we were still learning can attest to, this task is made far more difficult by virtue of the fact that the only way to make meaning is through words. There are no facial expressions or gestures to look to for support.

- *Quadrant B*—In Quadrant B, we find those tasks that require higher-order thinking skills, but also include many supports for making meaning. Students usually watch a demonstration of a lab experiment before they are asked to perform one on their own. They are usually working with a partner, with real-life objects, and have others in the class whom they can watch and mimic.
- *Quadrant D*—Quadrant D includes tasks that require students to use higher-order thinking skills where they must rely solely on language in order to understand and communicate. These are tasks required on standardized tests and in most classes at the university level.

Obviously, all of our students must be able to perform the type of tasks in Quadrant D. For our English language learners, however, reliance on language alone can often be a challenge, leaving them unable to participate successfully. So what does this mean for our instruction? How do we prepare students for cognitively demanding, context-reduced tasks?

The answer lies in Quadrant B. This is what sheltered instruction is— cognitively demanding academic content with lots of supports. The activities in which we engage our students must require them to analyze, hypothesize, synthesize, evaluate, and use all the other thinking skills we find on Bloom's taxonomy (Bloom, Mesia, & Krathwohl, 1964). At the same time, when students are not fully proficient in English, we must contextualize learning in order to help them make meaning. Many of the techniques presented in our earlier discussion of comprehensible input—visuals, demonstrations, hands-on activities—can help to provide that context for students.

Our goal is for our students to participate successfully in grade-level academic tasks, to be able to listen, speak, read, and write independently. We can get them there through providing contextual supports and gradually removing the supports as they become more proficient in English, more able to rely on language alone. We can get them there through the type of instruction (SDAIE) described in Quadrant B.

Principle 3: Low-anxiety environment

Language acquisition is enhanced when students are engaged in meaningful activities and their anxiety level is low. Students must feel comfortable enough to risk producing imperfect language. This is especially critical for older students. When learning a new language, it is virtually impossible to express yourself in a manner commensurate with your age. Even adults will make numerous mistakes and be relegated to using simple language with incorrect grammatical structures. Add to this the importance of peer approval for adolescents, and it is easy to understand why some of our students are reluctant to speak up in class. As teachers, we must take responsibility for creating an environment in which students know that all their attempts to participate will be encouraged, accepted, and celebrated.

Classroom environments must provide a balance between safety and comfort, and enough stress to push performance. If you are in an interview situation, talking about your experience and your philosophy of education, you may find it difficult to remember everything you wanted to say. Having the same conversation over coffee with your friends at school, you might easily talk for hours about the same topic. However, in the discussion with your friends, you will probably use a far more casual register of language, avoiding higher-level academic language even though talking about an academic topic. Students who are in the process of learning English must be able to speak within the comfort and safety of friends, and yet participate in activities that require them to use more explicit, formal language.

Differentiating instruction: Think of a task you might ask students to complete. What might you do differently for students at different levels of proficiency to help them feel comfortable as they complete this assignment?

Principle 4: Meaningful engagement

The purpose of language is communication. Learning a language simply for the sake of learning a language may be interesting for linguists and others whose linguistic intelligence is their strong suit (as in Gardner's [1985] theory of multiple intelligences), but for most of us, it is no more than a tool for communication. It follows, then, that as a tool, it is best learned in the process of other learning. If you have ever tried to learn another language on your own, with no

Differentiating instruction: How might meaningful activities look different for students at different levels of language proficiency?

one to use it with, you may have found that you easily forgot most of what you had studied. When learners are engaged with language in meaningful ways, they have built-in motivation to use a language through the need to communicate, opportunity to practice, and immediate feedback they receive regarding the comprehensibility of their communication.

This means that instructional activities must include daily opportunities for authentic use of language, perhaps best accomplished through student-to-student interaction where students must listen and speak in order to accomplish a task. They may be exchanging information, expressing an opinion, or solving a problem. The tasks provide meaningful application of the concepts and skills just taught, and ideally, they are of interest or personal relevance to the student.

ADDITIONAL FACTORS THAT INFLUENCE LANGUAGE LEARNING

The four principles of language acquisition we described are meant to be used as a guide to planning instruction. They are the aspects of language learning over which the teacher has control. There are other factors that also influence language acquisition over which the teacher has no control, personal factors that vary from individual to individual. Awareness of these factors can assist teachers in better understanding their students, recognizing the natural developmental progress, and adjusting their instruction based on that knowledge about their students.

Primary language

Find a student in your class who is proficient in their primary language and one who is not. What differences do you see in their English proficiency?

Perhaps one of the most important factors is the level of proficiency the student has in the primary language. Concepts and skills that children have already learned in their primary language form the foundation for learning in a new language. If they have already learned to read and write in their home language, they can readily attach new vocabulary, language structures, and organizational patterns in order to learn to read and write in another language. They have already gained the deeper understandings of making meaning from text and can focus on the surface aspects that differentiate one language from another.

When we listen to ELL students speak, or when we read their writing, we often see evidence of other ways in which their primary language influences their use of English. Recall the letter from Van. As you analyzed her writing, you might have noted errors such as "I get A in English," an error that we would not be likely to find in the writing of a native English speaker, even one with poor writing skills. This is an example of a structure that Van has brought with her from Vietnamese to English. Some languages, Chinese, Hmong, and Vietnamese, for example, have no indefinite articles. They may either leave out the article, as Van did with "[an] A," or they may substitute another word as in *I bought one car* as opposed to *I bought a car*. Even though we may not speak the student's language, when we see repeated errors such as these, we can recognize that the student may be transferring his or her own language structures, and we can call attention to them so that the errors do not fossilize and become more difficult to correct.

Just as we see students transfer structures from their primary language that are incorrect in English (negative transfer), we also see elements of the primary language that affect second-language learning in a positive manner (positive transfer). In Spanish, for instance, there are many words that are very similar to English words. Called *cognates*, words such as *independence (independencia), circle (círculo),* and *mathematics (matemáticas)* are easily recognized and can facilitate comprehension, particularly when teachers are aware of them and ask students to notice them as well. Many of them tend to be academic words, which can make learning some of the more difficult vocabulary that much easier (see Teacher Tools at the end of the book for a list of common cognates between Spanish and English).

Another way in which we can take advantage of a student's knowledge of the primary language in order to assist in learning English is by providing opportunities to compare and contrast similarities and differences between the two languages. Obviously, this strategy is most useful when the teacher has some knowledge of the student's primary language, but even without that, it can be beneficial to ask students to think about how something is said in their own language. They can then compare how it is said differently in English.

Age

Infants are born with the capacity to hear the sounds of all languages. As they grow, however, and are exposed to the sounds of only one, perhaps two languages, they begin to lose that capacity. The younger the child, the more ability remains, allowing them to hear sounds of a new language. Hearing the sounds, of course, leads to the ability to pronounce them more accurately. So young children learning English can sound like native speakers of English. Young children are not expected to use a high level of language in order to sound like native speakers their age. The language they must learn is generally simple, concrete, and full of context.

If older students can acquire a new language more rapidly through use of metalinguistic skills, what does this imply for language instruction?

Older students, on the other hand, must be able to make themselves understood at much higher levels of language and in relation to much more complex ideas. They may take the same amount of time as a 5-year-old to sound like a 5-year-old. The problem is that after that amount of time, the 5-year-old will sound like others his own age, but the 13-year-old will still sound like a 5-year-old. One advantage that older students have, however, is their greater experience with language and their greater ability to use cognitive strategies such as comparing/contrasting, memory devices, questioning, or accessing prior knowledge. Their knowledge of the world as well as their knowledge of language can accelerate their learning of a new language. Although they may continue to have more difficulty with pronunciation than young students, there is a body of research that shows adolescents and adults achieve higher levels of proficiency more rapidly than young children (Snow & Hoefnagel-Hoehle, 1978).

Personality

How can you encourage a shy ELL to participate in oral language tasks?

Personality traits such as shyness, risk taking, and self-confidence can influence the language acquisition process. Students who are shy likely will not participate in as many opportunities to practice language. They may rely on written language more than spoken language in order to learn. Students who are risk takers are not afraid to make mistakes, an unavoidable occurrence when learning a new language. They will therefore be more likely to speak up, practice language, and receive more feedback. Generally speaking, personality influences the rate at which students acquire language, not the level they will eventually achieve.

Motivation

Discuss with a partner: Is motivation a trait or state?

There usually is no debate over the idea that students who are motivated will achieve at higher levels than those who are not. The critical issue for teachers, though, pertains to how we perceive motivation. Do we believe that this discussion belongs in the previous section on personality, that it is a character trait? Or do we believe that it is a state that can change based on the situation, that it is a temporary condition that can be influenced by instructional methods and materials? If we believe the former, it absolves us of responsibility as teachers. If we believe the latter, it requires us to examine our instruction, designing activities that engage our students.

Another issue regarding motivation stems from students' perception of their need to learn English. Some of our immigrants arrive in this country with the expectation that they will soon return to their homeland. They may believe that they will be here only long enough to wait out a war and therefore won't need to become proficient in English. Other students may see their future here as limited due to their legal status. Without documentation they cannot see how they will be able to begin a career that requires proficiency in English or a high school diploma. These are not situations that we can change, but we do have a responsibility to prepare our students so that they will have options when they leave us. We must encourage them to take the most advantage of their education now, regardless of what they believe may happen in the future.

Application to Practice

Reflection

1. Select 3 of the ideas in this chapter that you think are most important and reflect on how you will incorporate them into your teaching.
2. Return to the Anticipation Guide on page 34. Have you changed any of your answers? Can you add anything to your justifications?

Case Study: *Investigate Your Target Student*

1. Begin to collect information on your target student. Look for such information as:

- English proficiency level
- Primary language proficiency level
- Prior schooling
- Math skills
- Years enrolled in U.S. schools
- Circumstances of arrival
- Strengths
- Areas of need

2. Examine a student writing sample. Look for aspects of language that the student grasps and those aspects that still need to be addressed. Look for those errors that a native English speaker would not make.

Planning and Instruction: *Using What You Know about Your Students*

- Consider your case study student. What additional information do you need to collect to effectively teach this student?
- How might this information influence your planning and instruction?

References

Bloom, B., Mesia, B., & Krathwohl, D. (1964). *Taxonomy of educational objectives: The affective domain & the cognitive domain*. New York: David McKay.

Canale, M. (1983). From communicative competence to communicative language pedagogy. In J. Richards & R. Schmidt (Eds.), *Language and communication* (pp. 2–27). New York: Longman.

Cummins, J. (1979). Cognitive/academic language proficiency, linguistic interdependence, the optimum age question and some other matters. *Working Papers on Bilingualism, 19,* 121–129.

Cummins, J. (1981). The role of primary language development in promoting educational success for language minority students. In *Schooling and language minority students: A theoretical framework*. Sacramento, CA. California State Department of Education.

Cummins, J. (2003). Reading and the bilingual student: Fact and friction. In Garcia, G. (Ed.), *English learners: Reaching the highest level of English literacy* (pp. 2–33). Newark, DE: International Reading Association.

Dutro, S., & Moran, C. (2003). Rethinking English language instruction: An architectural approach. In G. Garcia (ed.), *English learners: Reaching the highest level of English literacy* (pp. 227–258). Newark, DE: International Reading Association.

Gardner, H. (1985). *Frames of mind: The theory of multiple intelligences.* New York: HarperCollins.

Hymes, D. (1972). On communicative competence. In J. Pride & J. Holmes (Eds.), *Sociolinguistics* (pp. 269–293). Harmondsworth, UK: Penguin Books.

Krashen, S. (1985). *The input hypothesis: Issues and implications.* New York: Longman.

Pritchard, R. (2004). *Differentiating instruction to develop strategic readers and learners.* Presentation for San Diego State University Reading/Language Arts Conference. San Diego, CA.

Ruiz-de-Velasco, J., Fix, M., & Clewell, B. (2000). *Overlooked and underserved: Immigrant students in U.S. secondary schools.* Washington, DC: The Urban Institute.

Snow, C., & Hoefnagel-Hoehle, M. (1978). The critical period for language acquisition: Evidence from second language learning. *Child Development, 49,* 1114–1118.

Swain, M. (1995). Three functions of output in second language learning. In G. Cook & B. Seidlehofer (Eds.), *Principle and practice in applied linguistics: Studies in honour of H. G. Widdowson* (pp. 125–144). Oxford, UK: Oxford University Press.

Tan, A. (1989). *The joy luck club.* New York: G. P. Putnam's Sons.

3 Purposeful Planning: Equal Access for All

Liz Moore/Merrill

"Would you tell me please, which way I ought to walk from here?"
"That depends a good deal on where you want to get to," said the Cat.
"I don't much care where . . ." said Alice.
"Then it doesn't matter which way you walk," said the Cat.
" . . . so long as I get somewhere," Alice added as an explanation.
"Oh, you're sure to do that," said the Cat, "if you only walk long enough."

(Lewis Carroll, Through the Looking Glass and What Alice Saw)

Focus Questions

1. How can you use both ELD and content standards to plan differentiated instruction?
2. How does the concept of universal design help to differentiate instruction and facilitate access to the core curriculum for English language learners?
3. What are the key features of an effective lesson plan?
4. How does the framework for English language learners support development of language proficiency and achievement in the content area?
5. What do you need to consider in order to plan for frontloading a lesson?

ACCESSING PRIOR KNOWLEDGE: PREVIEWING TEXT

Take a minute to review all of the headings in this chapter. Based on the title of this chapter and the main headings you have read, what do you think this chapter will be about? What do you already know about this topic? Discuss your experience in planning instruction with a peer. What has worked for you and what still challenges you?

PLANNING INSTRUCTION THAT MATTERS

If we are not careful, we may end up like Alice in Wonderland, getting "somewhere." That somewhere may not be where we should be or need to be with our students. Thoughtful planning and understanding where we want to be at the end of the lesson, unit of study, or school year allows us to take steps to move students along in their literacy and language development. Current research suggests we must consider the outcomes we expect and then plan backwards from our students' current performance level.

You may be asking yourself, "How is this different from the lesson planning that my teachers have done over the years?" Let's look inside Carol's classroom during her first years of teaching. This is an opportunity to consider traditional planning. We will then consider what we know today and how lesson planning can and should be done.

TRADITIONAL PLANNING: A VIEW FROM CAROL'S CLASSROOM

When I taught Spanish, each September the school would give us a lesson plan book to make a schedule of activities for each day. Each page of the book was divided into 21 boxes, each box representing one period (55 minutes) for one day. My notes often looked like this:

1. Warm-up: *¿Qué hiciste anoche?* (What did you do last night?)
2. Review past tense
3. p. 29: whole class
4. pp. 30–33: partners
5. Homework: pp. 34–36

Essentially, the publishers of the textbook had done most of my planning for me. They had determined what I would teach, in what order I would teach it, how I would teach it, and how I would assess it. Of course, I made modifications and added my own activities to the curriculum, based on my professional knowledge of language acquisition and learning and what I knew about my students. I adjusted my pacing according to my students' needs. I even skipped around in the textbook if I felt that some parts of the text fit better in other chapters than the ones determined by the authors. But the reality was that the way I decided what to teach was by following the scope and sequence of the textbook. This was in the days before we had content standards to guide instruction, and at the time, it seemed a reasonable way to plan, teach, and assess.

THE ROLE OF STANDARDS

Find the content standards for your state on the state Department of Education Web site. How does your instruction correlate to the standards?

How do you know what third graders should know and be able to do? How about students earning credit in algebra? As communities, we set standards. These standards guide our thinking about what students should know and be able to do at each grade level.

Although there are many critics of a standards-based education system (e.g., Kohn, 2004), the rationale for using standards to plan our lessons is to ensure that we hold all students to high expectations and that we maintain some level of consistency in the educational system. Can you imagine if every teacher in every school were required to determine what to teach? Every time a student moved schools, lessons could be repeated or there might be huge gaps in knowledge. Table 3.1 provides a comparison between a traditional system and one based on standards.

So, standards are where we begin our lesson planning. We begin with the end in mind—where we want students to be, what we want them to know and be able to do when we complete our instruction. For English language learners, some states have identified benchmarks or modified expectations that can be used to guide instruction. These English language development standards are aligned to the English language arts standards but are modified based on the current language proficiency of students. If your state does not have ELD standards, look at those from California or Texas, or the newly revised standards from TESOL (Teachers of English to Speakers of Other Languages). The California ELD standards found at *www.cde.ca.gov/re/pn/fd/documents/ englangdev-stnd.pdf* and the Texas standards found at *www.tea.state.tx.us/rules/ tac/chapter128/index.html* are useful in planning. We highly recommend that you look at the TESOL standards, newly revised in 2005 by a team of educators

Table 3.1

Comparing Traditional and Standards-Based Planning	
Traditional Planning	**Standards-Based Planning**
• Select a topic from the curriculum.	• Select appropriate standards from among those students need to know (based on assessment).
• Plan instructional activities.	• Design assessments that require students to demonstrate the essential knowledge or skill.
• Give a test.	• Plan learning opportunities students will need in order to gain that knowledge or skill.
• Give grade.	• Plan instructional opportunities to ensure that each student has adequate opportunities to learn.
• Move to the next topic or chapter.	• Use data from assessment to give feedback, re-teach, or move to the next level.

Source: Gay Burns, Resource Teacher, 2000. Used with permission.

Standards are accessible for students
Doug Fisher

from around the country, as they reflect a broader academic focus than do many state standards. The revised TESOL standards now provide a clear bridge between English language proficiency and the academic standards in the content areas of language arts, mathematics, science, and social studies. In addition to describing standards for the use of language in social and academic settings, they

For more detailed information on teaching learning strategies, see chapter 7.

incorporate the use of learning strategies to extend communicative competence, academic content knowledge, and sociolinguistic and sociocultural competence.

The TESOL standards can be found at *http://www.tesol.org/s_tesol/seccss.asp?CID=113&DID=1583*.

To plan and deliver standards-based instructional lessons, we must recognize two significant trends in education: Understanding by Design and universal design.

UNDERSTANDING BY DESIGN

According to Wiggins and McTighe (*http://www.grantwiggins.org/ubd.html*), *Understanding by Design* (1998) is based on the following key ideas:

Think about the last unit of study you taught. Which of these ideas was reflected in your planning? How?

- A primary goal of education should be the development and deepening of student understanding.
- Students reveal their understanding most effectively when they are provided with complex, authentic opportunities to explain, interpret, apply, shift perspective, empathize, and self-assess. When applied to complex tasks, these "six facets" provide a conceptual lens through which teachers can better assess student understanding.
- Effective curriculum development reflects a three-stage design process called "backward design" that delays the planning of classroom activities until goals have been clarified and assessments designed. This process helps to avoid the twin problems of "textbook coverage" and "activity-oriented" teaching, in which no clear priorities and purposes are apparent.
- Students and schools achieve performance through regular reviews of results (achievement data and student work) followed by targeted adjustments to curriculum and instruction. Teachers become most effective when they seek feedback from students and their peers and use that feedback to adjust approaches to design and teaching.
- Teachers, schools, and districts benefit by "working smarter" through the collaborative design, sharing, and peer review of units of study. (n.p.)

When we plan instruction that includes English language learners, we must also be clear about our expectations for student learning and how to scaffold and differentiate instruction based on language proficiency. In other words, we should not plan simple lessons or rely on a number of instructional tricks or strategies. Instead, we should determine the outcomes of our lessons via the standards, determine what evidence we will accept that students have achieved the expectations, and then determine the different kinds of supports we will use for students at varying levels of proficiency.

Although most standards documents provide you with a clear set of content objectives, or what students need to know, many do not provide guidelines for two other kinds of objectives that are critical in the teaching of English language learners—language and social.

Research in Focus: Standards for Effective Teaching

Based on their research and research reviews, Tharp, Estrada, Dalton, and Yamauchi (2000) proposed five standards for effective pedagogy. They note that these standards are important for improving achievement for all students, but are especially critical for students from diverse ethnic, cultural, linguistic, or economic backgrounds. The five standards are:

- *Standard I*—Teachers and students producing together facilitates learning through joint productive activity among teachers and students.
- *Standard II*—Developing language and literacy across the curriculum develops competence in the language and literacy of instruction across the curriculum.
- *Standard III*—Making meaning: Connecting school to students' lives contextualizes teaching and curriculum in the experiences and skills of students' homes and communities.
- *Standard IV*—Teaching complex thinking challenges students toward cognitive complexity.
- *Standard V*—Teaching through conversation engages students through dialogue, especially the instructional conversation.

We believe that every lesson, regardless of the content being taught, needs to have specific language and social objectives that can be infused. For example, when we teach the content of this book to teachers, our language and social objectives include the following:

Think of a lesson you taught recently. How did it provide students opportunities to develop language skills? How about social skills?

Language Objectives

- Demonstrate understanding of key vocabulary associated with teaching and learning language (e.g., comprehensible input, transfer, communicative competence, ELD, SDAIE, etc.).
- Demonstrate ability to use vocabulary and language effectively to express opinions, ask questions, explain ideas and procedures, and so on, in a range of settings and class arrangements (e.g., small group, whole class discussions, presentations, etc.).

Social Objectives

- Participate effectively in small working groups (in class and with work groups).
- Contribute and constructively critique one another's work.
- Maintain a professional attitude throughout the development of lessons/units (e.g., arrive on time to every work meeting and class session, come prepared for tasks, complete assignments in a timely fashion, etc.).
- Actively participate in all class activities and discussions.
- Prepare and deliver a planned oral presentation with a partner.

While our content is focused on teaching about lesson planning, we also want our students to develop their understanding of language and to practice social skills. Regardless of whether you are teaching a kindergarten unit on "life on the farm," persuasive writing to seventh graders, or quadratic equations in algebra, language and social objectives should play a role in your thinking about lesson planning.

Information on assessment is presented in chapter 4.

The process we advocate in this book is to first determine what you want your students to know and be able to do in terms of content, language, and social goals and objectives. At that point, you are ready to collect assessment information to determine what your students already know and can do.

Only then are you ready to develop connected lesson plans that close the gap between what students should know and be able to do and what they already know and are able to do.

As you can see, Understanding by Design differs significantly from traditional lesson planning. As you might have guessed, though, for English language learners this is not sufficient planning. When planning instruction for a diverse group of learners, we must also consider universal design, or planning that incorporates the learning needs of all students.

Spotlight on Instruction

Language and Social Objectives

Ms. Grant, a high school physics teacher, is planning her instructional unit on momentum. She knows that she will have to frontload for her students, especially her English language learners, and spends time identifying vocabulary that they will need to know to be successful in the unit. In addition to providing content instruction, Ms. Grant also knows that her students need focused instructional time on language and social interactions.

As she plans her unit of study on momentum, Ms. Grant identifies a range of language tasks that her students can complete, including vocabulary development, journaling about experiments, discussing research findings with peers, reading for information, and identifying sources of information on the Internet. Language functions they will need to use include hypothesizing, describing outcomes, and comparing and contrasting. Ms. Grant also provides her students with social interaction opportunities such as working in groups or teams, turn-taking during experiments, asking for assistance, and maintaining an operational working environment.

Although these may not seem directly related to teaching physics, Ms. Grant knows that developing language and social objectives will ensure that her students are successful learners who can transfer their learning to new environments and tasks.

UNIVERSAL DESIGN

Universal design was first conceived in architectural studies when businesspeople, engineers, and architects began making considerations for physical access to buildings. The idea was to plan the environment in advance to ensure that everyone had access. As a result, the environment would not have to be changed later for people with physical disabilities, people pushing strollers, workers who had injuries, or others for whom the environment would be difficult to negotiate. The Center for Universal Design (*www.design.ncsu.edu/cud*) defines universal design as "the design of products and environments to be usable by all people, to the greatest extent possible, without the need for adaptation or specialized design."

Universal design and access in education

Researchers, teachers, and parents in education have expanded the considerations of built-in adaptations and inclusive accommodations from architectural space to the educational experience, especially in the area of curriculum.

In 1998, the National Center to Improve the Tools of Educators (NCITE), with the partnership of the Center for Applied Special Technology (CAST), proposed an expanded definition of universal design focused on education:

> In terms of learning, universal design means the design of instructional materials and activities that allows the learning goals to be achievable by individuals with wide differences in their abilities to see, hear, speak, move, read, write, understand English, attend, organize, engage, and remember.

Components of Universal Design and Access in Education. The original work on universal design was based on seven principles. These seven principles and an explanation of each are provided in Figure 3.1. As they apply to education and schooling, the concept of universal design and access suggests:

How are these components reflected in your planning and instruction?

- *Inclusive classroom participation:* Curriculum should be designed with all students and their needs in mind. For example, understanding the needs of English language learners and students who struggle with reading requires that vocabulary be specifically taught and reinforced.
- *Maximum text readability:* In universally designed classrooms that provide access for students, texts use direct language, clear noun-verb agreements, and clear construct-based wording. For English language learners, this assumes that assessments provide information regarding student achievement in the content that is not affected by limited proficiency in the language. In addition, multiple texts are used such that individual differences in reading can be addressed.
- *Amenable to accommodations:* In universally designed classrooms, texts can be easily translated, read aloud, or otherwise changed to meet the needs of students in the classroom. In addition, assessments should provide students with multiple ways of demonstrating their content knowledge while also ensuring that they have practice with thinking in terms of multiple-choice tests. Again, for English language learners, this allows teachers to determine what students actually know rather than what they can express.

Figure 3.1   Principles of Universal Design *(Source: Copyright © 1997 NC State University, The Center for Universal Design)*

Principle One: Equitable Use: The design is useful and marketable to people with diverse abilities.
1a. Provide the same means of use for all users: identical whenever possible; equivalent when not.
1b. Avoid segregating or stigmatizing any users.
1c. Provisions for privacy, security, and safety should be equally available to all users.
1d. Make the design appealing to all users.

Principle Two: Flexibility in Use: The design accommodates a wide range of individual preferences and abilities.
2a. Provide choice in methods of use.
2b. Accommodate right- or left-handed access and use.
2c. Facilitate the user's accuracy and precision.
2d. Provide adaptability to the user's pace.

Principle Three: Simple and Intuitive Use: Use of the design is easy to understand, regardless of the user's experience, knowledge, language skills, or current concentration level.
3a. Eliminate unnecessary complexity.
3b. Be consistent with user expectations and intuition.
3c. Accommodate a wide range of literacy and language skills.
3d. Arrange information consistent with its importance.
3e. Provide effective prompting and feedback during and after task completion.

Principle Four: Perceptible Information: The design communicates necessary information effectively to the user, regardless of ambient conditions or the user's sensory abilities.
4a. Use different modes (pictorial, verbal, tactile) for redundant presentation of essential information.
4b. Provide adequate contrast between essential information and its surroundings.
4c. Maximize "legibility" of essential information.
4d. Differentiate elements in ways that can be described (i.e., make it easy to give instructions or directions).
4e. Provide compatibility with a variety of techniques or devices used by people with sensory limitations.

Principle Five: Tolerance for Error: The design minimizes hazards and the adverse consequences of accidental or unintended actions.
5a. Arrange elements to minimize hazards and errors: most used elements, most accessible; hazardous elements eliminated, isolated, or shielded.
5b. Provide warnings of hazards and errors.
5c. Provide fail-safe features.
5d. Discourage unconscious action in tasks that require vigilance.

Principle Six: Low Physical Effort: The design can be used efficiently and comfortably and with a minimum of fatigue.

6a. Allow user to maintain a neutral body position.

6b. Use reasonable operating forces.

6c. Minimize repetitive actions.

6d. Minimize sustained physical effort.

Principle Seven: Size and Space for Approach and Use: Appropriate size and space is provided for approach, reach, manipulation, and use regardless of user's body size, posture, or mobility.

7a. Provide a clear line of sight to important elements for any seated or standing user.

7b. Make reach to all components comfortable for any seated or standing user.

7c. Accommodate variations in hand and grip size.

7d. Provide adequate space for the use of assistive devices or personal assistance.

Spotlight on Instruction

Planning for All Students

Ms. Owen's second-grade students are focused on their social studies lesson, "People Who Make a Difference." When Ms. Owen planned this unit of study, she knew that she needed to address a wide range of language backgrounds and proficiencies. The students in her class each have different funds of knowledge, interests, and skills. Rather than focus on one person who made a difference and then develop alternatives for her three students who have the least fluency in English, Ms. Owen (with the help of the school librarian) identified over 45 books focused on people who have made a difference. Ms. Owen knew that the text readability had to vary widely, that a range of cultures and ethnicities needed to be represented, and that students needed different ways to share what they had learned about the topic. She also wanted to focus on some nontraditional "heroes" who were less well known or not covered in her social studies textbook. Some of the books she selected included:

- Cohn, A. L., & Schmidt, S. (2002). *Abraham Lincoln.* New York: Scholastic.
- Johnson, A. (2005). *A sweet smell of roses.* New York: Simon & Schuster Books for Young Readers.
- Krakow, K. (2001). *The Harvey Milk story.* Ridley Park, PA: Two Lives.
- Krull, K. (2003). *Harvesting hope: The story of Cesar Chavez.* San Diego: Harcourt.
- Krull, K. (2004). *The boy on Fairfield Street: How Ted Geisel grew up to become Dr. Seuss.* New York: Random House Books for Young Readers.
- Sis, P. (2003). *The tree of life: A book depicting the life of Charles Darwin, naturalist, geologist, and thinker.* New York: Farrar Straus Giroux.
- Winter, J. (2005). *The librarian of Basra.* Orlando, FL: Harcourt.

Ms. Owen also understood that simply providing her students access to different texts and then asking them to complete the same tasks would not be consistent with universal design or differentiated instruction. To ensure that each of her students would have an opportunity to use what they know and what they have learned, Ms. Owen provided a range of options for her students including oral presentations, posters, impersonations, poems, raps, I-movies, and partner projects. The common features of the lesson were the focus on content standards, the embedded social and language objectives, and an essential question that all students could answer—What is a hero?

Second graders at work
Doug Fisher

Differentiated Instruction Is a Key to Access. To differentiate instruction, teachers must acknowledge students' differences in background knowledge, current reading, writing, and English language skills, learning styles and preferences, interests, and needs, and react accordingly.

There are a number of general guidelines for differentiating instruction, including:

For more information on differentiating instruction, see chapter 8.

Think of a unit of study you have recently taught. Which of these guidelines was reflected in your planning? Select one guideline and brainstorm how you might incorporate it next time.

- *Link assessment with instruction:* Assessments should occur before, during, and after instruction to ensure that the curriculum is aligned with what students do and do not know. Using assessments in this way allows you to plan instruction for whole groups, small groups, and individual students.
- *Clarify key concepts and generalizations:* Students need to know what is essential and how this information can be used in their future learning. In addition, students need to develop a sense of the big ideas—ideas that transcend time and place. We will discuss the importance of focusing on key concepts further in chapter 7 as we look at how to make grade-level content accessible to English language learners.

- *Emphasize critical and creative thinking:* The content, process, and products used or assigned in the classroom should require that students think about what they are learning. Although some students may require supports, additional motivation, varied tasks, materials, or equipment, the overall focus on critical and creative thinking allows for all students to participate in the lesson. This is especially critical for English language learners as it is all too easy to relegate them to tasks that require only low-level thinking simply because they do not yet possess the language skills to express their complex thoughts.
- *Include teacher- and student-selected tasks:* A differentiated classroom includes both teacher- and student-selected activities and tasks. At some points in the lesson or day, the teacher must provide instruction and assign learning activities. In other parts of the lesson, students should be provided choices in how they engage with the content. This balance increases motivation, engagement, and learning.

DAILY LESSON PLANNING

Thus far in this chapter, we have focused on unit plans or plans for major topics or themes. Planning in this way ensures that you have outcomes in mind as well as assessments, materials, and instructional arrangements. A sample unit planning format is provided in Figure 3.2.

Once you have outlined your overall goals and objectives for a unit of study, you have to consider how each daily lesson plan will connect with the whole and how each day will build to the point that students can demonstrate mastery of the standards (e.g., Hunter, 1994).

Figure 3.3 includes a sample daily lesson plan. While there are many different forms of daily lesson plans, they share common features.

Let's explore some of the common features of lesson plans.

> The Teacher Tools section at the end of the book provides you a number of lesson planning formats.

Research in Focus:
Designing Effective Lessons

As Cawelti (2003, p. 19) noted,

> Using earlier research on learning to formulate her approach, Hunter (1984) taught thousands of teachers and administrators such principles as focusing students' attention for a new lesson through anticipatory activities, clearly stating the purpose of each lesson, and providing opportunities for guided and independent practice. A trained psychologist, she synthesized findings from earlier research and developed a useful language for teaching with a model similar to the direct instruction approach that others developed. Few individuals have produced the large impact Hunter had in formulating and helping teachers apply effective lesson design.

Figure 3.2   Unit Lesson Plan

Class: _____   Unit of Study: _____

Date: _____   Teacher: _____

Standards, Objectives, and Expectations:

Assessments:

Materials:

Instructional Arrangements:

Projects, Homework, and Assignments:

Figure 3.3   Sample Lesson Plan Format

Subject: _____   Grade Level: _____

Date: _____   Duration: _____

Language and Social Objectives:

Content Standards:

Anticipatory Set:

Instruction:

Guided Practice:

Independent Practice:

Assessment and Closure:

Reflection:

Common features of lesson plans

Objectives and Standards. As we have discussed previously, every lesson should be aligned to the content standards for the grade level you are teaching. In addition, the specific language and social objectives you hope to accomplish should be part of every lesson.

Purpose. Setting a clear purpose for the lesson helps ensure that we stay focused throughout the lesson—that the questions we ask, the vocabulary and background we build, the class discussions lead toward the desired outcome. It also lets students know how this particular lesson relates to what they have learned before, why they are learning this concept or skill, and what they are supposed to get out of the lesson. At the end of the lesson, students can review what they have learned in relation to the purpose. Making the purpose of the lesson clear to students is critical to building schema, helping them to see where this new learning fits into the big picture of that subject area, how it relates to other subject areas, or simply to life. This is a step we often skip, believing that as long as we (the teacher) know why this lesson is important, we need not take up valuable class time in talking about the purpose. When we do not state the purpose clearly for our students, we leave them to their own devices to determine what information is important to focus on. When they know the purpose of the lesson, it guides their listening, their speaking, their reading, and their writing and helps them to attach new information to the framework stored in their brain.

Anticipatory Set. This is the opening for the lesson. The anticipatory set should invite students into the content and provide them with an overview of the topic they will be studying. In addition, the anticipatory set should activate students' background knowledge. In doing so, students are ready to learn.

Instruction. During this phase of the lesson, the teacher models or instructs students. This instruction should extend what students already know and challenge them to think about the content in a new way. This is often the most teacher-directed phase of the lesson and is used for sharing information with students.

Guided Practice. In guided practice, the teacher leads students through the steps necessary to accomplish the goals of the lesson. Thus the level of teacher support is reduced as students use what they have been shown during the instruction phase and apply it with assistance from others, including the teacher. This is an opportunity to provide English language learners with any additional scaffolding and instruction they may need.

Independent Practice. In this phase, the level of teacher support is reduced even further. Students are asked to use the information from the lesson on their own. Independent practice does not mean that students must work alone. Students can work in pairs or small groups as they apply their new knowledge. During this phase, the teacher moves around the room, reteaching as necessary

---

Think of a lesson you are about to teach. What can you say or do to make your purpose clear to your students?

The anticipatory set provides an excellent opportunity to activate and build background knowledge.

so students reach mastery. ELL students at the earlier levels of proficiency may spend far more time with teacher-led instruction and guided practice than in independent practice.

Assessment and Closure. We often think of assessments as culminating experiences at the end of a unit of study, which you see on the unit lesson planner, but there must also be daily assessment opportunities so that the teacher can plan future instruction. In addition, each lesson requires closure so that students can transfer their thinking and behavior to new activities.

Reflection. Time is allotted for students to reflect on their learning and for you, the teacher, to reflect on the success and challenges you experienced. Student reflection provides them the opportunity to determine what they have learned in relation to the lesson objectives and what they still need to learn. It also fosters students' sense of responsibility for their own learning. Your reflection, like your students', should be done fairly soon after the lesson. The reflection allows for future planning as well as considerations about engagement, motivation, and interest.

Discuss with a partner: How can you build in opportunities for students to reflect on their learning?

A FRAMEWORK FOR TEACHING ENGLISH LANGUAGE LEARNERS

In the last chapter, we discussed what teachers needed to know about the language acquisition process. Now let's examine how this fits into the daily schedule.

The literacy block or the English class provide an excellent opportunity for students to develop some of the academic language proficiencies they need. Students need to develop language proficiency in the content areas as well. As such, language instruction must be integrated into content area lessons throughout the school day. As teachers plan these content lessons, they must not only think about what math, science, social studies, art, foods, or physical education concepts they want their students to learn, they must also think about the language required in order to comprehend and express these ideas. Key questions to ask include:

Select a lesson you are planning to teach. Answer these questions in relation to that lesson.

1. What are students being asked to do? Write an essay, contrast habitats in a science class, participate in a group discussion, analyze a math problem?
2. What language structures are required for the task? Will they need to form questions, state a hypothesis, describe a sequence of events?
3. What vocabulary is essential in order to complete the task? This includes (a) content-specific vocabulary such as *character, beaker, equation, democracy*, and so on; (b) functional vocabulary, or words that help to perform the required language function—*if . . . then* for cause and effect, *larger than* for compare/contrast, *first, then, finally* for sequencing; and (c) high-use general academic vocabulary across disciplines such as *analyze*.

Consistent with our theme of understanding where you want to get before you start the journey, we will now turn our attention to planning the school day so that these wonderful and amazing lessons you've developed can fit together into an instructional framework. We have adapted the work of Dutro and Moran (2003) and identified the ways in which language and content can be organized to ensure that our English language learners have access to the curriculum as well as the language instruction they need. Figure 3.4 provides a visual of this instructional framework. This framework requires an understanding of and a commitment to three interrelated plans.

First, English language learners require English language development instruction that is differentiated. As Dutro and Moran (2003) note, "language instruction requires teaching English, not just teaching *in* English or simply providing opportunities for students to interact with one another in English" (p. 228). As such, differentiated English language development must become a curriculum, just like math, science, music, or art.

Second, English language learners need frontloading instruction to make meaning of the content. While frontloading has been described and defined in a number of ways, the common features indicate that English language learners need the teacher to analyze both the text and the task for language and vocabulary requirements. We will explore this in greater detail in chapter 7.

Frontloading can also be thought of as activating background knowledge, prior knowledge, and language (e.g., Marzano, 2004). In doing so, students are prepared for new ideas and can better relate to the genre, technique, themes, characters, events, topic, data, or whatever is the focus of the lesson. Frontloading applies to oral, written, visual, and multimedia texts, from the commonplace readings students do, to reading for information, to the literary canon. In other words, there are a number of strategies and activities that help readers get into texts at deeper levels than would have happened if the reading were done cold.

Third, English language learners require that we integrate language and content every chance we can. Isolated skills instruction will not likely help our English language learners to master the complex new language. More information on integrating language and content will be presented in chapter 7.

Using the information from this chapter, you will be able to plan effectively. You know that you must design lessons around content standards as well as language and social objectives. You know that you should start with the end in mind, use assessment data to inform your instruction, and consider all of your learners in advance of the lesson. You have also explored an instructional framework that will allow you to teach language and content, regardless of your grade level or subject taught. You're ready to think more deeply about curriculum and instruction. But first, in the next chapter, we'll focus on assessment.

Investigate how students at your school receive ELD instruction.

Frontloading refers to the teaching you do before reading that will assist the reading.

Figure 3.4 Instructional Framework

Instruction for English Learners: Developing English Language Proficiency and Content Knowledge*

Focused ELD	Literacy	Math	Science/Health Studies	Social	Art/Music Electives	PE

Purpose:
- Develop solid language foundation

Planning:
- Group students for instruction according to language proficiency level
- Link to literacy instruction

Content:
- Follow scope and sequence of language skills in variety of functional contexts
- Use ELD standards

FRONTLOADING LANGUAGE

Purpose:
- Ensure access to content instruction taught in English by preteaching for upcoming language demands.

Planning:
- Analyze text and task for language and vocabulary requirements.
- Preteach to small groups as necessary.

Content:
- Determined by language and content demands of upcoming task. Teach language structures and vocabulary needed to comprehend, talk, and write about the content of a lesson.

INTEGRATING LANGUAGE AND CONTENT

Purpose:
- Expand language proficiency within the context of instruction and through authentic situations throughout the day.

Planning:
- Identify appropriate points during lesson to incorporate language and vocabulary instruction.
- Include opportunities to practice academic language.

Content:
- Language required to comprehend, talk, and write about the topic or content of a lesson.
- Unanticipated language needs as they arise.
- Language skills as developmentally appropriate.

KEY PRINCIPLES OF INSTRUCTION

- State clear purpose.
- Access prior knowledge.
- Connect to prior learning.
- Provide models/demonstrations.
- Contextualize new information.
- Develop vocabulary—content-specific (brick) and functional (mortar).
- Provide opportunities for student-to-student interaction.
- Provide opportunities for authentic practice.
- Teach learning strategies: metacognition.
- Use multiple methods of assessment.
- Provide primary language support for learning as appropriate.

*This model does not address instruction in the primary language. It does apply, however, to instruction in English within a bilingual classroom.

Source: Adapted from Dutro, S., & Moran, C. (2003). Rethinking English language instruction: An architectural approach. In G. Garcia (Ed.), English learners: Reaching the highest level of English literacy (pp. 227–258). Newark, DE: International Reading Association.

Spotlight on Instruction

Frontloading Language and Background Knowledge

Ms. Javier started her middle school humanities class by asking a question, "What do you need to be a survivor?" Together, they made a list of words that related to the question, including *food, help, a place to sleep, courage, water,* and many others. They talked in partners about the words and why these particular words were important to survival.

Neil Waldman

Ms. Javier knew that she would be introducing the book *Hatchet* (Paulsen, 1987) later in the period, but wanted to frontload her students to ensure that they received the most benefit possible from her shared reading of the text. She knew that starting with an essential question would provide her students with a purpose for the reading as well as an opportunity to bring their own experiences to bear on the reading (Cushman, 1989). She also knew that she needed to activate and build her students' background knowledge and vocabulary. In particular, she wanted to be sure that her students knew about plane crashes, the location and terrain of Canada, what a hatchet is, and how a heart attack affects an individual.

As a class, her multilingual students discussed the ideas and terms, sometimes switching between English and their heritage language, and sometimes asking questions while completing visual representations such as visual maps and illustrations of the key terms. When she was satisfied that her students understood these ideas, she began reading:

> Brian Robeson stared out the window of the small plane at the endless green northern wilderness below. It was a small plane, a Cessna 406—a bushplane— and the engine was so loud, so roaring and consuming and loud, that it ruined any chance for conversation.

(Paulsen, 1987, p. 1)

Application to Practice

Reflection

1. What are the five most important ideas discussed in this chapter? Why are they important?
2. What is one key idea you want to implement in your classroom? How will you do this?
3. What is something you have a question about?

Case Study: *Frontloading*

Which of the components of universal design would help your target student learn? How will you incorporate these principles into your planning?

Planning and Instruction: *Creating Standards-Based Lessons*

Using both the content standards and the English language development standards, plan a unit and the daily lessons that comprise the unit using the forms from this chapter or at the end of this book. As we work through this book, you'll revise the unit to increase students' opportunities to interact with one another.

References

Cawelti, G. (2003). Lessons from research that changed education. *Educational Leadership, 60*(5), 18–21.

Cushman, K. (1989). Asking the essential questions: Curriculum development. *Horace, 5*(5), 1–5.

Dutro, S., & Moran, C. (2003). Rethinking English language instruction: An architectural approach. In G. Garcia (Ed.), *English learners: Reaching the highest level of English literacy* (pp. 227–258). Newark, DE: International Reading Association.

Hunter, M. (1984). Knowing, teaching, and supervising. In P. L. Hosford (Ed.), *Using what we know about teaching* (pp. 169–192). Alexandria, VA: Association for Supervision and Curriculum Development.

Hunter, M. (1994). *Mastery teaching: Increasing instructional effectiveness in elementary and secondary schools, colleges, and universities.* Thousand Oaks, CA: Sage.

Kohn, A. (2004). *What does it mean to be well educated? And more essays on standards, grading, and other follies.* Boston: Beacon Press.

Marzano. R. J. (2004). *Building background knowledge for academic achievement: Research on what works in schools.* Alexandria, VA: Association for Supervision and Curriculum Development.

Paulsen, G. (1987). *Hatchet.* New York: Aladdin.

Tharp, R. G., Estrada, P., Dalton, S. S., & Yamauchi, L. (2000). *Teaching transformed: Achieving excellence, fairness, inclusion, and harmony.* Boulder, CO: Westview Press.

Wiggins, G., & McTighe, J. (1998). *Understanding by design.* Alexandria, VA: Association for Supervision and Curriculum Development.

4 Assessment: Guide to Purposeful Planning

David Mager/Pearson Learning Photo Studio

If you don't inspect it, you might as well not expect it.

—American proverb

Measure twice; cut once.

—American proverb

Parts of this chapter were adapted from Frey, N., & Fisher, D. (2003). Linking assessments and instruction in a multilingual elementary school. In C. Coombe & N. Hubley (Eds.), *Assessment practices* (pp. 63–74). Waldorf, MD: Teachers of English to Speakers of Other Languages.

Focus Questions

1. What are the various reasons we assess students?
2. How can we assess our students' oral language development?
3. What are ways that we can assess our students' reading and writing development?
4. How can we use our assessment to plan instruction that is differentiated for students at different levels of language proficiency?
5. What are ways to differentiate assessments? How does differentiated assessment support instructional planning?
6. What does it mean to say that "assessments are the connection between what is taught and what is learned"?

ACCESSING PRIOR KNOWLEDGE: IQ TEST

Let's pause for a minute and take a test. Are you nervous? Do you think people will judge you as a result of your answers? Let's begin.

Intelligence Test Instructions: Write down each answer. It makes a difference! You will be allowed 10 minutes to complete the test. Write your answers in the spaces provided. Are you ready? What is the time? Start.

1. Some months have 30 days, some months have 31 days. How many months have 28 days? _____
2. If a doctor gives you 3 pills and tells you to take 1 pill every half hour, how long would it be before all the pills have been taken? _____
3. I went to bed at eight o'clock in the evening, wound up my clock, and set the alarm to sound at nine o'clock in the morning. How many hours' sleep would I get before being awoken by the alarm? _____
4. Divide 30 by half and add 10. What do you get? _____
5. A farmer had 17 sheep. All but 9 died. How many live sheep were left? _____
6. If you had only one match and entered a COLD and DARK room, where there was an oil heater, an oil lamp, and a candle, which would you light first? _____
7. A man builds a house with four sides of rectangular construction, each side having a southern exposure. A big bear comes along. What color is the bear? _____
8. Take 2 apples from 3 apples. What do you have? _____
9. How many animals of each species did Moses take with him in the Ark? _____

Talk with a partner about how the test made you feel.

10. If you drove a bus from Chicago with 43 people on board and stopped at Pittsburg to pick up 7 more people and drop off 5 passengers and stopped at Cleveland to drop off 8 passengers and pick up 4 more and eventually arrived at Philadelphia 20 hours later, what's the name of the driver?

The answers to this test are found at the bottom of the page. How did you do? How do you feel about your performance? Is there anything that you could do differently next time you take a test like this?

TESTING AND ASSESSMENT—WHY?

Discuss the two American proverbs that we quote to start this chapter. What do they say about the thinking in this country?

The results of standardized tests are commonly used to allocate resources, determine teacher pay, award school vouchers to students attending "failing" schools, and decide whether a student may graduate from high school. In this climate of accountability, testing is assuming an increasingly important role in the structure of the curriculum and in the amount of instructional time dedicated to it. Yet the efficacy of any single assessment to determine such a wide scope of variables seems unlikely.

Although there may be a tendency to overgeneralize what test scores can reveal, the purposes of assessment extend beyond the single dimension of testing large numbers of students to provide broad measures of group achievement (Lipson & Wixson, 1997). Lapp, Fisher, Flood, and Cabello (2001) categorize the purposes of assessment as follows:

- Diagnosis of individual student needs and decision making regarding placement;
- Provision of accountability information;
- Evaluation of programs; or
- Assessment to inform instruction.

It is this last purpose that serves as the focus for this discussion. In an era in which the broadly collected data from standardized tests are being used to make far-reaching educational decisions about large groups of students, it is vital that teacher-based assessments also be recognized for their contribution to what is

---

1. All of them. Every month has at least 28 days.
2. 1 hour. If you take a pill at one o'clock, then another at 1:30, and the last at two o'clock, they will be taken in 1 hour.
3. 1 hour. It is a wind-up alarm clock, which cannot discriminate between A.M. and P.M.
4. 70. Dividing by half is the same as multiplying by 2.
5. 9 live sheep.
6. The match.
7. White. If all walls face south, the house must be on the North Pole.
8. 2 apples. I have 3 apples. You take 2. What do you have?
9. None. It was Noah, not Moses.
10. YOU are the driver.

known about an individual student. Far more than standardized test results, which often do not arrive until the following school year, teacher-based assessments are the tools educators rely on as they design instruction.

Teacher-based assessments are those selected and administered by the classroom teacher in order to determine what instruction needs to occur next. Astute classroom teachers possess a wealth of information about their students' knowledge of literacy, language, and content and evaluate students' performance to gauge progress and guide future instruction (Gottlieb, 2006). Wise practitioners recognize the value of such assessments as a rich source of data. These assessments can be either formal or informal. Tables 4.1 and 4.2 provide information about the types of assessments teachers use. You'll note that there are a number of different types of formal and informal assessments that we can use to plan our instruction.

You will remember from chapter 1 that the findings of the National Literacy Panel indicate that most existing assessments do not do an adequate job of assessing students' strengths and weaknesses for placement or instructional purposes. The panel also found that teacher judgment was not always a reliable method of identifying ELL students in need of intensive reading instruction. These findings suggest that when teachers examine specific criteria, rather than relying solely on their opinions about students, they are more able to make effective placement and instructional decisions (August & Shanahan, 2006). Thus the role of purposefully designed teacher-based assessments becomes vitally important in designing effective instruction for English language learners.

Table 4.1

Formal Assessments		
Type	**Purpose**	**Administration**
Standardized, Norm-Referenced	Yields a student's academic performance ranking compared to a normed sample of students	• Schedule; determined by state and local agencies; often yearly • Tests are usually timed and have strict protocols
Standardized, Criterion-Referenced	Measures a student's performance compared to a set of academic skills or objectives. Scores are reported as the proportion of correct answers	• Tests may be timed or untimed • May be administered annually or more frequently

Source: Adapted from Fisher, D., & Frey, N. (2004). Improving adolescent literacy: Strategies at work. *Upper Saddle River, NJ: Merrill/Prentice Hall. Used with permission.*

Table 4.2

Informal Assessments		
Type	**Purpose**	**Administration**
Observation	Gathers information about a student's academic, behavioral, or social skills used in an authentic setting	Teacher records observational data in anecdotal notes, journals, or daily logs
Portfolio	Provides evidence of a student's academic growth through the collection of work samples	Student and teacher select representative samples of student work for display in a binder or other organizer
Inventory	Documents student's use of specified skills during a single observation	A commercially or teacher-produced form of observable behaviors is completed by the teacher
Conference	Involves the student in direct feedback to the teacher in a one-to-one discussion	Often scheduled by the teacher at regular intervals to gauge progress on more complex academic behaviors such as reading comprehension
Self-Assessment	Allows the student to engage in reflective learning and think about learning	Students assess their own academic performance using an age-appropriate checklist of indicators
Survey	Collects student feedback about interests, prior knowledge, or motivation about a topic	Student completes a commercially or teacher-produced survey of items

Source: Adapted from Fisher, D., & Frey, N. (2004). Improving adolescent literacy: Strategies at work. *Upper Saddle River, NJ: Merrill/Prentice Hall. Used with permission.*

STUDENT ORAL LANGUAGE OBSERVATION MATRIX (SOLOM)

A commonly used assessment for planning instruction for English language learners is based on observing a student's oral language proficiency. Before we consider other types of assessments, let's turn our focus to this important measure.

The administration of the SOLOM to a student who is learning English as a new language allows teachers to observe the interaction between oral language proficiency, termed Basic Interpersonal Communication Skills (BICS), and the cognitive academic skills (CALP) required for proficiency in

Refer to chapter 2 for a discussion of BICS and CALP.

reading and writing. The analysis of the SOLOM informs teachers about the students' strengths and weaknesses in oral English. The SOLOM is designed to assess authentic oral language used for real, day-to-day classroom purposes and activities. The SOLOM can be found in Appendix 4.1 at the end of the chapter.

Administering the SOLOM

To ensure that the SOLOM is as useful as possible, observe the student in several different authentic classroom activities in which he or she is interacting with the teacher and/or classmates, such as a cooperative group task. Each observation should last for about five minutes. On each occasion, mark the rankings on the matrix (Appendix 4.1) according to your impressions of the child's use of English.

You may wish to audio record one or more of your sessions to go back and confirm your impressions or to look for certain patterns of errors or usage. You will rate the child's language use on a scale from 1 to 5 on each of these traits: comprehension, fluency, vocabulary, pronunciation, and grammar. Cross-check your ratings from the different contexts in which you observed the child for consistencies or variations that may indicate different levels of proficiency according to language function or purpose.

Scoring the SOLOM

The SOLOM yields ratings for English language proficiency. These phases can be equated to the Beginning, Early Intermediate, Intermediate, Early Advanced, and Advanced proficiency levels. Alternatively, these levels are known as Entering, Beginning, Developing, Expanding, and Bridging.

See chapter 1 for more information on proficiency levels.

- Beginning/Entering = 0–5
- Early Intermediate/Beginning = 6–10
- Intermediate/Developing = 11–15
- Early Advanced/Expanding = 16–20
- Advanced/Bridging = 21–25

Using the SOLOM

The "Spotlight on Instruction: Assessing Oral Language" box relates a discussion with a student. As you read what the student said, think about each of the traits identified on the SOLOM: comprehension, fluency, vocabulary, pronunciation, and grammar. Remember that the SOLOM is an observational instrument and should not be administered as an interview. This excerpt, taken from one discussion with a student, will provide you some ideas about the use of the SOLOM, but would not be sufficient for planning instruction. The SOLOM should be administered by a teacher who knows the student well enough to make judgments about the student's level of language across academic situations.

What do you do now to assess your students' oral language?

Spotlight on Instruction

Assessing Oral Language

Ms. Fernandez assessed an eight-year-old third grader named Patrick. Patrick came to the United States from the Philippines and had been enrolled in U.S. schools for just under two years. He received minimal instruction in English at school in the Philippines. Overall, Patrick does not participate in whole group activities: He listens to his teacher, but he does not participate. Ms. Fernandez noted the following:

I observed Patrick on three different occasions. On the first observation, I observed Patrick during a writing lesson. In this observation, I modeled to the class how to pre-write a three-paragraph essay about a vacation. I explained the whole process to the class. Everyone finished the pre-write except Patrick. Given this, I sat with Patrick and explained the directions a second time. Patrick was asked to pre-write a three-paragraph essay about a vacation he took. When asked about previous vacations he took, Patrick stayed quiet. Patrick took a recent vacation to the Philippines, so I knew that he had something to write about. I had to facilitate the conversation by continuously asking Patrick questions about his recent vacation.

For the second observation, I observed Patrick in line at the beginning of the school day. Patrick was talking to his classmates and asking another teacher questions. For the third observation, I observed Patrick during a comprehension check on a grade-level reading passage called *Bruno*. In this observation, Patrick was to retell what he had read.

According to the SOLOM rating scale, Patrick is currently in the Intermediate or Developing level of English language development. In all three observations, Patrick scored 60%. Observations 1 and 3 were academic settings that both yielded the score of 60%. Interestingly, observation 2 was conducted in a social environment and Patrick still scored 60%. Patrick's oral language proficiency is consistent in both social and academic settings.

Out of the five traits, Patrick is strongest in comprehension. He needs further instruction and development in the areas of fluency, vocabulary, pronunciation, and grammar. In comprehension, Patrick understands everyday conversations with some repetitions. For instance, in observation 1, Patrick needed the directions for the writing prompt explained twice because he did not understand them. However, in the other observations, he did not need anything repeated because he understood it the first time.

In the area of fluency, Patrick's language is limited. In the first observation, Patrick was asked if he took any vacations. Patrick did not respond to the question; he remained silent. He only responded when asked specific questions like, "What did you do on your vacation? Did you go shopping? Did you visit someone?" Furthermore, in observation 2, Patrick's conversation with his classmates was limited and he uttered only a few words. For example, when trying to express that two children looked the same (it was Twin Day), he said, "Her the same [pointed to one girl] and her the same [pointed to the other girl]."

In terms of vocabulary, Patrick's usage is poor; he often uses the wrong words. For example, in observation 1, when asked why he took a vacation to the Philippines, Patrick replied, "Take me to my real house." Patrick could not express that the reason for his trip was to visit his previous home.

Patrick often has trouble pronouncing words. For example, when responding to questions in observations 1 and 3, Patrick had to repeat his responses because the class could not understand him.

In grammar, Patrick regularly makes errors. These errors are consistent with his overall language development. For example, when asked about what he read in a reading passage titled *Bruno* in observation 3 (matrix 3), Patrick replied, "About one boy with six years old has a dog his older now so about building dog house." In addition, in observation 1, when asked what he did when he arrived in the Philippines, Patrick replied, "Family and cousins are picking me up."

According to my observations and from viewing him every day in class, Patrick's fluency limits his ability to participate in whole group activities. Importantly, he wants to participate. He often blurts out questions and comments during Read Alouds, but some of these are irrelevant. For example, during one Read Aloud he said, "What are we do for PE?" On another occasion, the class was discussing the need for permission slips for a fundraiser and Patrick blurted out, "What is permission?" Overall, Patrick does gain comprehensible input from academic instruction, but some things have to be repeated. Patrick is smart; he is strong in math and in social studies.

Based on my analysis, Patrick needs more help with his oral language skills. He needs explicit instruction with grammar and pronunciation. I would improve his grammar and pronunciation by having him pair up with students who have nearly perfect grammar and pronunciation when doing partner work in class; these students will expose Patrick to the correct usage of grammar and pronunciation in the English language. Furthermore, I would give Patrick positive corrective feedback. I would correct Patrick's oral language in a positive way; for example, if Patrick said, "Lunch I eated pizza," I would say, "Oh, you mean you ate pizza for lunch." In the area of vocabulary, Patrick needs to have his own personal dictionary to have with him at all times. In addition, he needs to read widely, participate in Read Alouds, and receive intentional vocabulary instruction so that his word knowledge increases. I plan to teach him new vocabulary words each day and have him add them to his personal dictionary. In fluency, I plan to improve Patrick's fluency by having him do repeated readings, pair him up with a buddy for buddy reading, and have him participate in Reader's Theater: These activities will increase Patrick's fluency. Overall, one-on-one instruction, exposure to and instruction in the correct usage of the English language, positive intervention, and fluency activities will help Patrick move into the higher stages of language proficiency.

SAMPLE ASSESSMENTS OF READING AND WRITING

We recommend that the SOLOM be used for every English language learner. The use of the SOLOM allows teachers to focus on language development across social and academic settings. In addition to the SOLOM, teachers must collect reading, writing, and content assessment information to plan their instruction. We will discuss interactive writing charts, running records, KWL charts, reader response logs, writing samples, and content assessments in the sections that follow. Although each of these are presented in a specific grade level, it is important to note that these assessments can be used across grade levels and with students at different proficiency levels.

Mr. Klein, a kindergarten teacher, uses a daily teaching event to gather evidence of his students' understanding of writing. Second-grade teacher Ms. Antonio uses guided reading to assess her learners. Ms. Ying, a fifth-grade teacher, examines her students' work in science to determine to what extent they are utilizing their literacy strategies. Mr. Robertson uses a content assessment, in this case a multiple choice test, to determine student learning and plan instruction. Ms. ElWardi uses a writing sample to determine the next steps for instruction of one of her students at the Intermediate level of language proficiency.

Like all good teachers, they gather information, interpret it, and then act upon it. Their view of teaching as a recursive process has been influenced by their work in a master's degree program that focuses on action research in the classroom (Stringer, 1999). As with action research, these teachers use assessments to set goals and purposes, collect data, and interpret results for the purpose of informing instruction. Although separating these dynamic phases from one another in the classroom is virtually impossible, examples of their application are discussed below. Let's look inside these classrooms and observe how teachers link assessment and instruction in ways that yield meaningful data that can be utilized to guide instructional decisions.

Interactive writing charts

The students in Mr. Klein's kindergarten classroom scurry to the carpeted area to take their places. The teacher has just directed them to meet in the Writers'

What are some ways you assess your students' reading, writing, and content knowledge?

Assessment information can be stored in binders for easy access
Doug Fisher

Corner. The children know that this daily event is an opportunity to discuss and write about their lives. It is also a chance to participate, for Mr. Klein rarely misses a chance to involve all his students in the activity. Hakly and Marcos gather the markers, whiteboards, and wipes that their classmates will share. Margarita gets the pointer, translucent tape, and clothespin Mr. Klein will need. Soon they are all seated, anxiously awaiting the first question. Mr. Klein takes his seat next to the chart stand, looks around at each of the students, and in a conspiratorial tone announces, "I have a secret to share . . ."

This kindergarten teacher uses his daily classroom instructional activities to gather important assessment data on his students. Mr. Klein's Writers' Corner is more commonly known as interactive writing (McCarrier, Pinnell, & Fountas, 2000). This instructional tool calls for teacher and students to begin by discussing the purpose and content of what is to be written. They then "share the pen" as the teacher facilitates the group's writing on chart paper, assisting the students in letter formation, letter-sound relationships, cumulative word analysis, concepts about print, syntax, and semantics. Mr. Klein views this time as an opportunity to witness the evolving skills of his young writers, and he keeps a clipboard of student observation sheets nearby to record important data for later analysis (see Figure 4.1).

On this day, Mr. Klein has identified four students for *observational data collection*. He will be noting the progress of Luis, Vu, Kelly, and Mubarek in three areas: oral language development, print conventions, and letter formation. He will note evidence of the extent of their oral language skills during the group discussion of Mr. Klein's secret: A surprise guest will be arriving the next day to answer questions about the new aquarium in the classroom. The teacher's goal for this activity is to capture the students' questions about the fish in the tank, as well as their care and feeding. The students will use this class chart to guide their discussion the following day. As Mr. Klein leads this interactive writing session, he notes whether Vu's contributions to the discussion are on topic. When Kelly is called to the chart to write, the teacher observes the student's use of spacing and other print conventions. Mr. Klein requires all the children to write the message on their whiteboards at the same time it is being recorded on the chart. Not only does this keep the students engaged, but it allows him to assess Luis's letter formations when he proudly holds up his whiteboard. Mubarek, who arrived from Somalia only two weeks earlier, is just now beginning to participate in the routines of the classroom. Mr. Klein notes Mubarek's use of language to negotiate the sharing of the marker and whiteboard with his partner.

How can you organize to keep track of your observations in order to recognize patterns and growth?

Running records

"Hector, Eduardo, Carmelita, and Mercedes, please join me at the reading table." It's a Tuesday morning in Ms. Antonio's second-grade biliteracy class, and four students are about to participate in a guided reading lesson. Importantly, each child is leaving a *different* center activity. Ms. Antonio believes in heterogeneously grouping students for most instruction, while reserving homogeneous grouping for specific teacher-directed activities like guided reading.

See chapter 8 for an in-depth discussion of grouping for specific purposes.

Figure 4.1   Interactive Writing Observation Guide

Student: _____ Date: _____
Writing Topic: _____

	Proficient	Attempted	Not Evidenced	Not Available
Letter Formations (Record letters)				
Concepts of Print				
Spacing				
Directionality				
Capitals				
Oral Language				
Uses language to represent ideas				
Grammatically correct				
Predicts and recalls				
Uses accurate vocabulary				
Interacts with peers				
On topic				
Inquires				

"It just didn't make any sense to me to limit the number of children each student gets to work with. I used to rotate them all through the centers in their reading groups, but I noticed that some students just didn't progress like I thought they would."

This teacher uses the Center Activity Rotation System (Flood & Lapp, 2000), commonly known as CARS, to organize her literacy block. This classroom organizational system was first introduced to her through the ongoing professional development available at her school, when teachers had identified through a needs assessment that they would like more information on grouping and management. Because she regroups her students frequently, she needs to assess them often.

Interactive writing sample completed on chart paper
Doug Fisher

Research in Focus: Grouping—Heterogeneous or Homogeneous?

Ability grouping of students is one of the oldest and most controversial issues in elementary and secondary schools. Hundreds of research studies have examined the effects of the two most common variants: between-class and within-class ability grouping. Between-class grouping refers to a school's practice of forming classrooms that contain students of similar ability. Within-class grouping refers to a teacher's practice of forming groups of students of similar ability within an individual class.

In theory, ability grouping increases student achievement by reducing the disparity in student ability levels, and this increases the likelihood that teachers can provide instruction that is neither too easy nor too hard for most students. The assumption is that ability grouping allows the teacher (1) to increase the pace and raise the level of instruction for high achievers, and (2) to provide more individual attention, repetition, and review for low achievers. The high achievers benefit from having to compete with one another, and the low achievers benefit from not having to compete with their more able peers.

One of the main arguments against ability grouping is that the practice creates classes or groups of low achievers who are deprived of the example and stimulation provided by high achievers. Labeling students according to ability and assigning them to low-achievement groups may also communicate self-fulfilling low expectations. Further, groups with low performance often receive a lower quality of instruction than other groups. Slavin (1986) sees as the most compelling argument against ability grouping its creation of academic elites, a practice that goes against democratic ideals.

Slavin (1986) examined the research evidence on grouping and recommends that the following elements be included in successful grouping plans:

- Students should identify primarily with a heterogeneous class. They should be regrouped by ability only when reducing heterogeneity is particularly important for learning, as is the case with math or reading instruction, or focused English language development.
- Grouping plans should reduce student heterogeneity in the specific skill being taught, not in IQ or overall achievement level.
- Grouping plans should allow for frequent reassessment of student placement and for easy reassignment based on student progress.
- Teachers must vary the level and pace of instruction according to student levels of readiness and learning rates in regrouped classes.
- Only a small number of groups should be formed in within-class ability grouping. This will allow the teacher to provide adequate direct instruction for each group.

Source: ERIC Clearinghouse on Elementary and Early Childhood Education, Urbana, IL. Used with permission. (*http://www.ericdigests.org/pre-927/grouping.htm*)

The four second graders take their seats at the reading table. Ms. Antonio distributes copies of *Alexander y el Dia Terrible, Horrible, Espantoso, Horroroso* [*Alexander and the Terrible, Horrible, No Good, Very Bad Day*] (Viorst, 1989). The students eagerly reach for the now-familiar book, which they have read before in both English and Spanish. "Please begin reading softly to yourself, and I'll listen. Remember that you're not reading together, just at your own pace." Ms. Antonio leans in to listen to Mercedes, and asks her to read just a little bit louder. As the student reads, Ms. Antonio completes a running record to document her reading behaviors (see Figure 4.2). Later, when she analyzes the record, she realizes that Mercedes is self-correcting more frequently. She also completes a running record on Hector, who reads the entire text correctly.

Ms. Antonio relies on running records to analyze the strategies her learners are applying to their reading (Fountas & Pinnell, 1996). She completes a running record on each student in four-week intervals, then regroups readers based on their instructional level and their need for instruction in the use of specific strategies.

After listening to the students read, Ms. Antonio brings out fifteen 3-by-5 vocabulary cards in English and Spanish, featuring words from the story. The teacher and her students begin arranging the words in a variety of open sorts,

Figure 4.2   Excerpt from Two Running Records

Name: Hector   Date: 2/5

Text: *Alexander, Who Used to Be Rich Last Sunday* by Judith Viorst

✓   ✓   ✓   ✓   ✓   ✓   ✓   ✓   ✓   ✓   ✓
Last   Sunday,   when   I   used   to   be   rich,   I   bet   that

✓   ✓   ✓   ✓   ✓   ✓   ✓
I   could   hold   my   breath   til   300.

Name: Mercedes   Date: 2/6

Text: *Alexander, Who Used to Be Rich Last Sunday* by Judith Viorst

✓   ✓   ✓   ✓   ✓   ✓   ✓   ✓   ✓   ✓
Last   Sunday,   when   I   used   to   be   rich,   I   bet   that
                                    was|SC

✓   ✓   ✓   ✓   ✓
I   could   hold   my   breath   til   300.
can | SC   bread|SC

using categories the students have determined. They sort the words by word families, as well as by words with similar conceptual values. Ms. Antonio writes anecdotal observations about each child's knowledge of the various ways that words can be manipulated.

KWL charts and response logs

Ms. Ying circles the classroom, listening in on the excited conversations of fifth graders in the process of being stumped, amazed, and otherwise dumbfounded. "Look at this one!" says Orian as she holds up a "magic eye" painting for her group members. "The Statue of Liberty's in there—can you see it?" At another learning center, four students are trying to beat "Poggendorf's Illusion," visual puzzle first created by Johann Poggendorf in 1860 and now featured on the *www.sandlotscience.com* Web site. Another small group of students is using Eric Carle's (1998) book *Hello, Red Fox* to test the theory of color reversal by gazing at the seemingly mis-colored images in the book, then shifting their focus to a blank white sheet of paper, where a correct image appears before their eyes.

"Cool!" whistles Miguel. Ms. Ying smiles to herself. The introduction to her new science unit on illusions and perception is already a success.

After the students have explored many of the illusions set out by Ms. Ying, she signals an end to exploration and transitions to the next task. "I'm very curious about your conversations. We're going to begin a science unit called 'More Than Meets the Eye.' Let's write your thoughts and questions down so we can begin to discover the answers to them." She then moves to the large KWL chart posted at the front of the classroom (Figure 4.3).

Ms. Ying has created an observational event in order to elicit student responses for the purposes of informing future instruction. The KWL (what do we *k*now/ what do we *w*ant to know/ what have we *l*earned) chart (Ogle, 1986) serves a dual purpose in this science classroom—it assists students in organizing their prior knowledge and "wonderings," as well as being an assessment tool to determine prior knowledge and areas of future instruction.

"What do you already know about illusions?" prompts Ms. Ying. "Those magic eye paintings are illusions!" calls out Orian, gesturing to the posters on the table at the back of the room. Patrick chimes in, "Magicians perform illusions!

Figure 4.3   KWL Chart for "More Than Meets the Eye"

It can be helpful for ELLs to have an opportunity to brainstorm with a partner first.

What do we **know** about illusions?	What do we **want** to know?	What have we **learned?**
• Magic eye paintings are illusions	• Do they work on everybody?	
• Magicians do them	• Could we invent new ones?	
• They play tricks on your brain	• What happens in your brain when you see an illusion?	
• They are very fun	• Do your eyes get mixed up, or your brain?	
• There are optical illusions	• Are there other illusions?	
• Some illusions are used in art	• Why do some animals use camouflage and others don't?	
• Animals use illusion to hide (camouflage)	• Why don't humans use camouflage?	

I saw them on TV!" Naushad wrinkles his forehead. "But do they work on everyone? Does everyone get tricked?" Ms. Ying, who had been recording student responses in the first column of the chart, turns to face the class. "That sounds like a question to me. I'm going to write that in the 'want to know' column."

Ms. Ying used the information on the KWL chart to plan her instruction for the unit. She was surprised that some of the students were familiar with the phrase *optical illusions* and pleased to hear of their curiosity regarding the biological basis of these visual puzzles. Her unit of instruction extended over two weeks and included a detailed look at the relationship between the eye and the brain. Students researched optical illusions and constructed their favorites for a "More Than Meets the Eye" gallery walk at the end of the unit. However, the KWL chart was not finished yet. Further assessment information was also done at the end of this unit using this KWL chart. The last phase, "what have we learned," was done first in small groups, then completed in a class discussion. Ms. Ying recognized that this instructional event served the multiple purposes of reinforcing new knowledge and providing her with a window on the progress of the class.

Teacher-created tests

Mr. Robertson, a middle school science teacher, wanted to know what his students had learned from their study of electricity. Language development is important to Mr. Robertson and he uses a number of language assessments, including the SOLOM, to plan his instruction. In addition, as a content teacher he wanted to assess students' mastery of the content. The type of assessment selected is based on the purpose of the assessment. As we will discuss further in the section on implementing an assessment system, teachers start with the goal of the assessment to determine which kind of assessment to use.

Given his goal of assessing content knowledge, Mr. Robertson planned a multiple-choice test that included a writing prompt. On a specific day, the entire class took the required test. However, Mr. Robertson knew that he had to scaffold the test items for his English language learners. One of the questions from the test and the version that was modified for a student at the Intermediate level of English proficiency can be found in Figure 4.4. You'll see that the item was restructured visually, the number of words was reduced, and that information was presented in such a way that students' content knowledge was required while the language demands were reduced.

What are some ways you can scaffold assessments to allow students at different levels of English proficiency to demonstrate their content knowledge?

Table 4.3 provides a list of content assessment examples and strategies teachers can use to scaffold the assessment for English language learners.

Using writing samples

Mrs. ElWardi uses her students' writing as a source of information to plan instruction. She often asks her students to complete quickwrites on a given topic. The responses she gets from her students allow her to plan whole class, small

Figure 4.4   7th Grade Science Test

---

8. Suppose you were performing experiments to determine some properties of an electromagnet. You had available several batteries, a switch, a compass, several washers, a nail, and a long piece of wire that you could wrap around the nail in a coil. Which one of the following would likely **not** be an experimental conclusion?
   A. The greater the number of batteries added to the circuit, the greater the number of washers the electromagnet would be able to lift.
   B. If the two wires connected to the positive and negative ends of the battery were reversed, the compass needle would deflect (rotate) in the opposite direction.
   C. If additional turns of wire were wrapped around the nail, the strength of the electromagnet would increase.
   D. If the tip of the nail were moved closer and closer to the compass, the compass needle would deflect (rotate) less and less.

---

8. You will perform experiments to determine the properties of an electromagnet.
   Materials:
   - batteries
   - switch
   - compass
   - several washers
   - nail
   - long piece of wire to wrap around nail

   Which of the following would be an experimental conclusion?
   A. An electromagnet with more batteries lifts more washers.
   B. The compass needle rotates in the opposite direction when you reverse the wires connected to the positive and negative ends of the battery.
   C. The strength of the electromagnet increases when you wrap more wire around the nail.
   D. The compass needle rotates less when you move the nail closer to the compass.

---

group, and individualized instruction. For example, during a unit of study on migration and immigration, students were asked to write about who they are and where they are from. The prompt read, "Who am I?" She provided her students five minutes to respond. San, a student from Vietnam, wrote:

What are two of the greatest areas of need for San's writing?

> *Hi! My name is San, I was born on September 7, 1985, in Cho Lon (now Sai Gon), Ho Chi Minh City. Vietnam is a beautiful country have beaches, rivers, mountains, and hills. I lived in Vietnam from the day I birth to see the beautiful country arrive my 17 years old birthday. My family and I leave my homeland and beautiful county has traditional generation and generation came to United State with the papers reunite of domestic. Thanks to my uncle helped my family do the papers and bring together my family come to California.*

Table 4.3

Scaffolding Assessment		
Assessment Examples	**Without Scaffolding**	**With Scaffolding**
Define/describe object or concept	Write a description of the object or concept and label it	Write a *list* of the main features of the concept, or provide labels for objects in a *picture* that is *provided*
Provide examples of a concept and justify them	Provide 3 examples and explain orally or in writing why these are good examples	*Select* 3 examples from a *list provided* and explain *orally* why they were selected
Retell or summarize text	Write 5 main ideas from an article and give examples	Complete an *outline* or a *semantic map*
Write a word problem	Create a problem from own numbers; give equation, story, and question	Complete a word problem *given examples* and *an outline* of a sample problem
Summarize a science experiment	Write a summary of procedures in a science experiment following scientific principles	*Complete* a summary *given a list* of procedures in science experiments, including questions, materials, a plan, observations, and conclusions, or *demonstrate* the steps **using actual materials.**

Source: Adapted from: Fig. 7.1, p. 167 from Authentic assessment for English language learners: Practical approaches for teachers *by J. Michael O'Malley and Lorriane Valdez Pierce. Copyright © 1996 by Addison-Wesley Publishing Company, Inc. Reprinted by permission of Pearson Education, Inc.*

Mrs. ElWardi uses the rubric found in Figure 4.5 to score her students' writing and to plan instruction. We will discuss writing instruction further in chapter 6, but it should be clear that this student needs help with her thesis development, grammar, and organization.

IMPLEMENTING AN ASSESSMENT SYSTEM

Calfee and Hiebert (1988, 1991) have proposed that teachers participate in three phases of teacher-based assessment: *setting goals and purposes, collecting data,* and *interpretation.* These activities closely parallel effective instructional principles (Bereiter & Scardamalia, 1996). In this model, assessment is infused into instruction rather than seen as something separate from the instructional

Think of a unit you recently taught or planned. What types of assessments did you/will you include? For what purpose?

Figure 4.5   Writing Rubric

Content/Structure/Organization
  Introduction
  - Strong introduction (hook), adequate background knowledge   5   4   3   2   1
  - Clearly stated topic/thesis   5   4   3   2   1

  Body of Information
  - Paragraphs have adequate content   5   4   3   2   1
    - (evidence, support, examples, proof)
  - Sentences state ideas clearly   5   4   3   2   1
  - Appropriate choice of vocabulary   5   4   3   2   1

  Conclusion
  - Thoughtful reflection back to thesis or topic   5   4   3   2   1

Grammar/Mechanics
  Sentences
  - Correct, comprehensible sentence structure   5   4   3   2   1
    - No fragments or run-ons
  - Varied sentence patterns (simple, complex, compound)   5   4   3   2   1

  Grammar
  - Subject/verb agreement and correct verb tenses   5   4   3   2   1

  Spelling
  - Words spelled correctly, especially "no excuse" words   5   4   3   2   1

  Punctuation
  - Proper use of periods, commas, apostrophes, quotes, etc.   5   4   3   2   1

Automatic Rewrite
  Off topic
  Lack of substance
  Serious organizational problems
  Incomprehensible writing

flow of the classroom (Frey & Hiebert, 2003). These three phases of teacher-based assessment are further described in the sections that follow.

Setting goals and purposes

The goals and purposes of gathering assessment data are influenced by the teacher's beliefs about what constitutes learning, the frequency and timing of the administration of assessment tools, and the type of information needed by the teacher. When these goals and purposes closely match the students, the link between assessment and instruction becomes clear-cut and definitive. It is when the goals and purposes do not complement the instruction that both educators and learners struggle to find meaning in these time-consuming practices. In fact, when a teacher protests that he or she "does not have time" to assess, it may actually be an instance of a poor match of assessments to students.

One of the strongest predictors of a teacher's choice of assessment tools is in the way she or he defines literacy, language, and learning. In a classroom where responses to literature are highly valued, it can be expected that much of the assessment will focus on reflection and literature circle discussions. If fluency and automaticity are emphasized in another classroom, measures of words read per minute would be frequently used. In a classroom where content reigns supreme, these types of assessments will likely be used to the exclusion of language assessments. Educators often have an easier time linking assessment to instruction when there is a menu of instruments available to match their classroom practice.

When and where an assessment is given also reflects the teacher's goals and purposes. For example, even the most carefully designed assessments are squandered if they are used infrequently and erratically. To avoid this, many teachers collect informal assessment information at regular intervals to make grouping decisions to respond to continually changing student needs. Wise practitioners recognize the value of flexible grouping patterns as a way to build community and increase learning (Flood, Lapp, Flood, & Nagel, 1992). The results of these assessments are then used to group students in a number of ways, including by interests, skills, and social development. This mix of heterogeneous and homogeneous grouping ensures that students have many opportunities to work alongside one another. Like frequency, the timing of the assessment also reveals a teacher's goals. Some choose an anticipatory activity at the beginning of a unit to provide information about the content to be taught. One example of this is the KWL chart (Ogle, 1986). Analysis of student responses on a KWL chart can alert the teacher to the specific points that need to be taught, as well as those that only require a brief review.

As with teacher beliefs, frequency, and timing, the type of information needed by the teacher also influences the selection of assessments. Teachers of emergent readers may choose assessments that yield a current analysis of each student's literacy skills so they can effectively instruct on problem-solving strategies such as chunking smaller word parts and using context. They may analyze running records to identify the strategies each reader is using but confusing. Teachers of more fluent readers may be concerned with their students' comprehension strategies. Vocabulary assessments, information webs, and extended writing responses are likely to be more common in these classrooms.

Collecting data

After determining the goals and purposes of teacher-based assessments, teachers collect the information they are seeking about their students. Running records (Clay, 1979) are an important tool because they allow the teachers to

What do your own assessment practices tell you about your goals and purposes?

In chapter 8 we discuss grouping patterns that consider language proficiency.

"Jacket cover," copyright, from And to Think That We Thought We'd Never Be Friends *by Mary Ann Hoberman. Used by permission of Random House Children's Books, a division of Random House, Inc.*

monitor progress in reading and to strategically group students for focused instruction in a skill. When Ms. Antonio discovered that three of her students were consistently having difficulty with the *th* sounds during the reading of *And to Think We Thought We'd Never Be Friends* (Hoberman, 1999) she grouped the students for reteaching. She then led them through a word study of the problem vocabulary in the story—*that, think, thwacked, thirsty, thought, they, together, there, then, thin, them, their,* and *the.* Clearly her data collection resulted in an instructional opportunity.

Ms. Ying enjoys introducing students to quality literature and facilitating their love of literature. She values the transactional nature of reading as well and understands that talking and writing about books is very important. Thus, this becomes one of her goals for assessment. She uses reading response logs that students complete as they finish their books. In addition to the title and author, the reading response log provides three sentence starters that students complete in their journals:

- I chose this book . . .
- I thought that . . .
- I want to read . . . (Dewsbury, 1994)

"Cover," copyright © 1998 by Steve Cieslawski, cover art, from A Long Way from Chicago *by Richard Peck. Used by permission of Dial Books for Young Readers, A Division of Penguin Young Readers Group, A Member of Penguin Group (USA) Inc., 345 Hudson Street, New York, NY 10014. All rights reserved.*

After reading their books and completing their reading response logs, students then conference with the teacher and discuss their responses. The teacher asks questions about the characters, plot, and setting, but also makes certain to ask inferential questions as well, such as inquiring about character motivation. Finally, the interview ends with questions about the aesthetic nature of the book, for instance, asking, "How did the story make you feel?" When asked this question after reading *A Long Way from Chicago* (Peck, 1998), Akemi cried out, "Oh! I felt so sad that those kids had to live in the country! Their grandma really took good care of them, maybe better than their momma. My grandma takes care of me all year, but we don't have chickens and pigs and stuff. We still do cooking together and make things and take walks, just like Mary Alice and her grandma." Only through this interview was Ms. Ying able to determine that Akemi truly understood the message of this book and that she had made a personal connection to the text. Ms. Ying knows that an aesthetic response to text promotes a lifelong love of reading (Sebesta, Monson, & Senn, 1995).

The methods used to collect data can be categorized into three activities: observing, interviewing, and sampling student work (Frey & Hiebert, 2003). By relying on a multifaceted approach to data collection, they ensure a more complete portrait of each student's progress.

Interpreting data

As stated earlier, it is virtually impossible to separate the phases of teacher-based assessment when done effectively, because its recursive nature propels it in a fluid fashion from setting goals, to collecting data, to interpretation and instruction, then back again to new goals. There are, however, critical features of interpretation to consider.

One is the reliability of the information gathered. On any given day, a child may be able to perform (or fail to perform) a discrete skill or task. A single performance may not indicate whether the skill has been mastered. To ensure that his assessments are reliable, Mr. Klein administers assessments on several occasions. For instance, the interactive writing assessments he uses are given approximately once every six weeks. This increases his confidence that Javier, a student whose performance may have been depressed because of an earlier conflict in the cafeteria, still has an opportunity to demonstrate what he knows about letter formation. As a wise practitioner, Mr. Klein knows the value of analyzing the context of an assessment event, not just the end product.

Validity, like reliability, must be considered with all forms of assessment. A way to increase validity in teacher-based assessment is to take care that assessments reflect the daily instructional climate (Mabry, 1999) and do not require the student to perform an artificial task. Ms. Antonio accounts for this when she uses running records because the assessment is directly tied to authentic instructional activities during her guided reading groups. The story read by the student is one used for instructional purposes, and it has been viewed once or twice before (Fountas & Pinnell, 1996). A criticism of standardized tests for reading is that they often do not reflect the daily instructional activities that take place in a classroom (Murphy, 1995). Mr. Robertson scaffolds his content assessments to be sure that he is really measuring content knowledge and not simply an artifact of language experience and development.

EFFECTIVE PRACTICES

Use daily teaching events

Assessments are often criticized because they replace instructional time in a classroom. Teachers who understand the use of assessments as instructional tools do not need to take away valuable time to conduct assessments. Instead, they use their daily teaching events to collect data. For example, Mr. Klein used his interactive writing time to collect information about four students. Ms. Antonio used her guided reading group time to collect information. Mr. Robertson used a restructured multiple-choice assessment to determine students' grasp of the

Collect some assessment data on a small group of students. Identify a common area of need for focused instruction.

Reflect on your own practice.

Rate yourself on these assessment practices.

Consistent ↔ Doesn't
happen

4   3   2   1

content. Mrs. ElWardi used her daily writing prompt—the one she uses to start class and make connections between the students' world and the things they are studying in school. The key is understanding which students will be the focus of assessment data collection for the day and which tools will produce the best, or most useful, information.

Match assessments to instructional practices

Consistent ↔ Doesn't
happen

4   3   2   1

As noted above, teachers must select tools that provide them with useful information. It would not have been helpful for Mr. Klein to use a KWL chart during his interactive writing time. It would have been equally useless for Ms. Ying to focus on the print conventions while introducing the whole class to a unit on illusions. Different assessment tools have different purposes and yield different information. Many teachers favor interactive writing charts, running records, KWL charts, and reader response logs as classroom-based assessment tools.

Use a variety of tools

Consistent ↔ Doesn't
happen

4   3   2   1

As we have noted, no one assessment tool can provide the information that teachers need to plan instruction (or make placement decisions, or determine the success of a school, for that matter). Using a variety of assessment tools allows English language learners to demonstrate their understanding in ways that do not require language skills they have not yet acquired. The composite view provided by these various assessment tools allows teachers to make generalizations about student learning and required teaching. Storing this assessment information, however, can be a challenge (e.g., see Courtney & Abodeeb, 1999). In response, several teachers have created "showcase portfolios" to hold specific pieces of student work. For example, in Ms. Ying's class, students each maintain their own showcase portfolio. There are required entries such as a beginning of the year writing sample, book logs, and KWL charts from each science unit and optional (student choice) entries such as journal entries, reading assessments, and informal inventories.

Plan instruction after assessments

Consistent ↔ Doesn't
happen

4   3   2   1

All too often teachers plan their instructional units and then determine the assessments they will use to gauge student success and determine student progress. Mr. Klein, Ms. Antonio, Ms. Ying, and Mr. Robertson use the assessment information they have about their students to plan their instruction. They know what each of their students needs to be taught next and plan instructional units that will allow them to accomplish that task. As they plan, they are also aware of opportunities to gather additional assessment information about students to make mid-course corrections. These teachers focus on what students already know and can do as the basis for instructional planning. While they acknowledge that this can be more time consuming, they believe it is an important shift—students come first in planning.

Assessments allow for instruction that is matched with student needs
Doug Fisher

Make assessments recursive

The most important lesson we have learned from these teachers is that the link between assessment and instruction is not linear. The teachers profiled in this chapter understand the recursive nature of setting goals and purposes, collecting data, and interpreting data. They know that this interpretation will result in the establishment of future goals and purposes, direct new data collection that requires interpretation. Their classrooms illustrate how teaching and learning are parts of a continuous process in which teachers use information about student learning to plan their teaching.

Consistent ↔ Doesn't
happen

4   3   2   1

CONCLUSION

The link between assessment and instruction is a central feature of effective teacher-based assessment. Policy centers (e.g., IRA, 2000; NASSP, 2000) cite the importance of a recursive process of assessment and instruction in the effort to achieve critical goals of literacy. Mr. Klein, Ms. Antonio, Ms. Ying, and Mr. Robertson demonstrate Calfee's (1994) statement that classroom teachers can apply research methods in a unique fashion, not only to measure current status but also to inform practice. They pinpoint their instruction through the use of informal and ongoing assessments.

A challenge to school districts, staff developers, and university teacher preparation personnel is to clearly link assessments with instruction. This linkage has sometimes been an afterthought in the rush to quantify students and teachers. When this occurs, assessments are perceived as separate from daily classroom life. Thoughtful practitioners, such as the teachers profiled here, view assessment as an intentional and strategic process to engage students and facilitate learning.

Application to Practice

Reflection

1. What are the advantages of planning instruction after you have planned your assessment?
2. What kind of systematic approach can you use to assess all your students in order to gain a clear picture of their understanding?

Case Study: *Using the SOLOM*

Use the SOLOM to assess your target student. As you consider the student's performance, draft a language report that includes the following information:

- The child's total score and phase of English language development
- A discussion of the child's strengths and weaknesses across the five traits
- Overall impressions of the child's ability to function in English in an academic context as well as a social interaction context

  Address issues such as:

- Did the child's level of overall language development allow him or her to participate fully in academic activities or was his or her participation impaired?
- Did you note a marked difference between the child's performance in social settings within the classroom versus his or her performance on academic tasks?
- Was the child's command of vocabulary adequate for him or her to gain "comprehensible input" from academic instruction?
- Did the child's pronunciation and/or grammar usage impede others' abilities to comprehend the child? If so, did this occur occasionally or frequently?
- What modifications in instruction and/or interpersonal communications did you observe for this child? Would you recommend different or additional accommodations based on this analysis?
- What specific instructional interventions would you recommend for this student?

Planning and Instruction: *Identifying Assessment Tools*

Write an assessment for the unit you designed in chapter 3 or for another unit you are planning. The Teacher Tools section at the end of this book provides a number of formats you can use for lesson planning.

References

August, D., & Shanahan, T. (2006). *Developing literacy in second-language learners: Report of the National Literacy Panel on Language-Minority Children and Youth.* Mahwah, NJ: Lawrence Erlbaum.

Bereiter, C., & Scardamalia, M. (1996). Cognition and curriculum. In P. W. Jackson (Ed.), *Handbook of research on curriculum* (pp. 517–542). New York: Macmillan.

Calfee, R. C. (1994). Cognitive assessment of classroom learning. *Education and Urban Society, 26,* 340–351.

Calfee, R. C., & Hiebert, E. H. (1988). The teacher's role in using assessment to improve literacy. In C. U. Bunderson (Ed.), *Assessment in the service of learning* (pp. 45–61). Princeton, NJ: Educational Testing Service.

Calfee, R. C., & Hiebert, E. H. (1991). Classroom assessment in reading. In R. Barr, M. Kamil, P. Rosenthal, & P. D. Pearson (Eds.), *Handbook of research on reading* (2nd ed., pp. 281–309). New York: Longman.

Carle, E. (1998). *Hello, red fox.* New York: Simon & Schuster.

Clay, M. M. (1979). *The early detection of reading difficulties: A diagnostic survey with recovery procedures* (2nd ed.). Exeter, NH: Heinemann.

Courtney, A. M., & Abodeeb, T. L. (1999). Diagnostic-reflective portfolios. *The Reading Teacher, 52,* 708–714.

Dewsbury, A. (1994). *Reading: Resource book.* Portsmouth, NH: Heinemann.

Flood, J., & Lapp, D. (2000). Teaching writing in urban schools: Cognitive processes, curriculum resources, and the missing links—management and grouping. In R. Indrisano & J. Squire (Eds.), *Perspectives on writing: Research, theory, and practice* (pp. 233–250). Newark, DE: International Reading Association.

Flood, J., Lapp, D., Flood, S., & Nagel, G. (1992). Am I allowed to group? Using flexible patterns for effective instruction. *The Reading Teacher, 45,* 608–616.

Fountas, I. C., & Pinnell, G. S. (1996). *Guided reading: Good first teaching for all children.* Portsmouth, NH: Heinemann.

Frey, N., & Hiebert, E. H. (2003). Teacher-based assessment of literacy learning. In J. Flood, J. M. Jensen, D. Lapp, & J. R. Squire (Eds.), *Handbook of research on teaching the English language arts* (2nd ed.) (pp. 608–618). Mahwah, NJ: Lawrence Erlbaum.

Gottlieb, M. (2006). *Assessing English language learners: Bridges from language proficiency to academic achievement.* Thousand Oaks, CA: Corwin Press.

Hoberman, M. A. (1999). *And to think we thought we'd never be friends.* New York: Crown.

International Reading Association (IRA). (2000). *Making a difference means making it different: Honoring children's rights to excellence in reading education.* Position Statement. Newark, DE: International Reading Association.

Lapp, D., Fisher, D., Flood, J., & Cabello, A. (2001). An integrated approach to the teaching and assessment of language arts. In S. Hurley & J. Tinajero (Eds.), *Assessing literacy for English language learners* (pp. 1–26). Boston: Allyn & Bacon.

Lipson, M. Y., & Wixson, K. K. (1997). *Assessment and instruction of reading and writing disability.* New York: Longman.

Mabry, L. (1999). Writing to the rubric: Lingering effects of traditional standardized testing on direct writing assessment. *Phi Delta Kappan, 80,* 673–79.

Mariotti, A. S., & Homan, S. P. (2001). *Linking reading assessment to instruction: An application worktext for elementary classroom teachers* (3rd ed.). Mahwah, NJ: Lawrence Erlbaum.

McCarrier, A., Pinnell, G. S., & Fountas, I. C. (2000). *Interactive writing: How language and literacy come together, K-2.* Portsmouth, NH: Heinemann.

Murphy, S. (1995). Revisioning reading assessment: Remembering to learn from the legacy of reading tests. *Clearing House, 68,* 235–39.

National Association of Secondary School Principals (NASSP). (2000). *NASSP board of directors position statement on standards and assessment.* http://www.nassp.org/hot_topics/ps_stand_assess.html.

Ogle, D. M. (1986). K-W-L: A teaching model that develops active reading of expository text. *The Reading Teacher, 39,* 564–70.

Peck, R. (1998). *A long way from Chicago.* New York: Puffin.

Sebesta, S. L., Monson, D. L., & Senn, H. D. (1995). A hierarchy to assess reader response. *Journal of Reading, 38,* 444–450.

Slavin, R. E. (1986). *Ability grouping and student achievement in elementary schools: A best-evidence synthesis.* Baltimore, MD: Center for Research on Elementary and Middle Schools.

Stringer, E. T. (1999). *Action research* (2nd ed.). Thousand Oaks, CA: Sage.

Viorst, J. (1989). *Alexander y el dia terrible, horrible, espantoso, horroroso.* New York: Atheneum.

Appendix 4.1 Student Oral Language Observation Matrix

Student Name: _____ Grade: _____ Age: _____ Language: _____

	1	2	3	4	5	Scores
Comprehension	Cannot be said to understand even simple conversation.	Has great difficulty following what is said. Comprehends only social conversation spoken slowly with frequent repetitions.	Understands most of what is said at slower-than-normal speed with repetitions.	Understands nearly everything at normal speed, although occasional repetition may be necessary.	Understands everyday conversations and normal classroom discussions without difficulty.	
Fluency	Speech is so halting and fragmentary as to make conversation virtually impossible.	Usually hesitant; often forced into silence by language limitations.	Speech in everyday conversation somewhat limited because of inadequate vocabulary.	Speech in everyday conversation and classroom discussion is generally fluent, with occasional lapses while student searches for the correct manner of expression.	Speech in everyday conversation and classroom discussion is fluent and effortless, approximating that of a native speaker.	
Vocabulary	Vocabulary limitations so extreme as to make conversation virtually impossible.	Misuse of words and very limited vocabulary make comprehension quite difficult.	Frequently uses the wrong words; conversation somewhat limited because of inadequate vocabulary.	Occasionally uses inappropriate terms and/or must rephrase ideas because of lexical inadequacies.	Use of vocabulary and idioms approximates that of a native speaker.	

(continued)

Appendix 4.1 Student Oral Language Observation Matrix (continued)

Student Name: _____ Grade: _____ Age: _____ Language: _____

	1	2	3	4	5	Scores
Pronunciation	Pronunciation problems so severe as to make speech virtually unintelligible.	Very hard to understand because of pronunciation problems. Must frequently repeat in order to be understood.	Pronunciation problems necessitate concentration on the part of the listener and occasionally leads to misunderstanding.	Always intelligible, though one is conscious of a definite accent and occasional inappropriate intonation patterns.	Pronunciation and intonation approximates that of a native speaker.	
Grammar	Errors in grammar and word order so severe as to make speech virtually unintelligible.	Grammar and word order errors make comprehension difficult. Must often rephrase and/or restrict self to basic patterns.	Makes frequent errors and word order errors which occasionally obscure meaning.	Occasionally makes grammatical and/or word order errors which do not obscure meaning.	Grammatical usage and word order approximate that of a native speaker.	

5

Oral Language: The Foundation of Literacy

Scott Cunningham/Merrill

We look back at the thoughts of our predecessors, and find we can see only as far as language lets us see. We look forward in time, and find we can plan only through language. We look outward in space, and send symbols of communication along with our spacecraft, to explain who we are, in case there is anyone there who wants to know.

(Crystal, 1992)

Focus Questions

1. How is social interaction important to learning?
2. What are ways to make group work most effective?
3. How can grouping students help you to differentiate instruction?
4. How do we develop students' listening skills?
5. How can we scaffold our questions to facilitate critical thinking for students at all levels of proficiency in English?
6. Why is it important to teach students to ask questions? How can we do this?

ACCESSING PRIOR KNOWLEDGE: LANGUAGE, CULTURE, AND LEARNING

Reflect on the following quote. Share your reflections with a partner and, together, complete a Venn diagram comparing and contrasting your responses.

> *"Language is our cultural tool—we use it to share experience and so to collectively, jointly, make sense of it . . . Language is therefore not just a means by which individuals can formulate ideas and communicate them, it is also a means for people to think and learn together."* (Neil Mercer, *The Guided Construction of Knowledge*)

LEARNING AND SOCIAL INTERACTION

Language, in all its forms, spoken and written, is how we make meaning of the world. Its primary function is as a tool for communication with others. It is also a means by which we learn and clarify thinking.

As we acquire our first language, we spend tens of thousands of hours first listening, and then speaking. We are immersed in oral language, listening and speaking long before we are asked to read or write. Obviously we don't have the luxury of that amount of time with our ELL students. Nor, quite frankly, is it necessary in learning a new language. Learners bring with them a wealth of knowledge about the world and about how language works that can be easily transferred to their new language. However, the principle of the sequence—listening and speaking before reading and writing—can be applied to literacy and content learning in a new language. This is not to say that students must learn to speak English before they learn to read and write

A Venn diagram is a graphic organizer that uses overlapping circles to compare and contrast two things—elements of a story, types of government, geometric shapes, chemical reaction, etc.

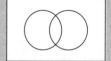

Characteristics that are unique to each thing being compared are listed in the side areas; shared characteristics are listed in the area that contains both circles.

it, but it suggests that students should talk about a topic before being asked to read and write about it. Oral language can serve as a building block for reading and writing by allowing students to develop their understanding of concepts and the related academic language through talking about them first.

The National Literacy Panel on Language-Minority Children and Youth found a high correlation between oral proficiency in English and reading comprehension skills in English. Their findings indicate that English language learners often learn word-level skills—decoding, word recognition, and spelling—but lag behind their native-English-speaking peers in text-level skills—reading comprehension and writing. They suggest that the missing link is proficiency in oral English. "It is not enough to teach language-minority students reading skills alone. Extensive oral English development must be incorporated into successful literacy instruction" (August & Shanahan, 2006, p. 5). As the panel looked at both language-minority students and monolingual English speakers who had been identified as poor readers, they found that the only significant difference in the profiles of the two groups was their oral language skills in English, suggesting that developing our ELLs' oral proficiency in English is part and parcel of developing their literacy.

The importance of developing oral language is reinforced by the National Council of Teachers of English in their position paper on the role of English teachers in teaching English language learners (*www.ncte.org/about/over/positions/category/div/124545.htm*). They clearly state that one of the key elements in effective instruction in language and literacy is the teaching of academic oral language. When students have authentic opportunities to use language within the context of various content areas, they develop the academic oral language that supports their development in reading and writing. These purposefully structured opportunities include collaborative tasks that promote peer interaction and discussion.

In chapter 1 we described the philosophical foundation upon which this book is based. Vygotsky's theory—learning is a social act that takes place in the Zone of Proximal Development—is at the heart of that foundation. Our discussion of oral language in this chapter rests on Vygotsky's belief that it is through social interaction that learning occurs. According to his view of cognitive development, as children engage in dialogue with others, they develop not only understanding of the subject, but their thinking skills as well. As they talk about the best way to solve a math problem, they are engaged in both solving the problem and thinking about the *process* of solving the problem. As they talk about a story, they arrive at an understanding of the meaning, at the same time as they participate in a *process* for constructing meaning. They are practicing and applying *strategies* for learning even as they are learning.

As English language learners engage in academic conversations, they learn grade-level concepts, develop strategies for learning, and improve their skills in English. These conversations require them to use language that is understandable to others in their group. They receive immediate feedback as they communicate

What opportunities to talk and develop oral language did your students have in your most recent lesson?

In chapter 7 we will look at developing lessons that address content, strategies, and language through the Cognitive Academic Language Learning Approach, or CALLA (Chamot & O'Malley, 1994.)

their ideas, perhaps having to restate or clarify a statement in order to make themselves understood. It is this negotiation of meaning that extends their linguistic abilities and pushes them to the next level of proficiency.

Research in Focus:
Oral Language in the Classroom

At the most basic level, oral language means communicating with other people. But when we talk about oral language development across the curriculum, we do not mean teaching children to speak, as much as we mean improving their ability to communicate more effectively. Speech is not usually simply basic communication—it involves thinking, knowledge, and skills. It also requires practice and training.

Oral language acquisition is a natural process for children. It occurs almost without effort. The ability to speak grows with age, but it does not mean that such growth will automatically lead to perfection. To speak in more effective ways requires particular attention and constant practice. Holbrook (1983) identified specific areas of oral language competence: fluency, clarity, and sensitivity. To help children achieve these levels of development is our responsibility as educators.

Many studies have indicated that oral language development has largely been neglected in the classroom, despite the fact that it is through speech that children learn to organize their thinking (Holbrook, 1983; Lyle, 1993). Most of the time oral language in the classroom is used more by teachers than by students. However, oral language, even as used by the teacher, seldom functions as a means for students to gain knowledge and to explore ideas.

Underlying this fact are two assumptions. One of these assumptions—that the teacher's role is to teach—is usually interpreted to mean that to teach means to talk. Accordingly, teachers spend hours and hours teaching by talking while the children sit listening passively. Such conventional teaching and learning is one of the obstacles preventing the real development of oral language. Children leaving these classrooms tend to carry this passivity over to their learning attitudes and tend to be "disabled" in their learning abilities, as well.

The second assumption is based on the fact that children start learning and using oral language long before they go to school. Therefore, it is assumed that the primary learning tasks for children in school are reading and writing, which are usually seen as the two major aspects of literacy.

In one investigation Stabb (1986) reported a steady decline in the use of oral language in classrooms as a major reason for the inhibition of students' abilities to reason and to forecast as they progressed from lower to higher grades. Such a phenomenon is found not only in the language arts classroom, but also in other classrooms. According to Stabb's and many other researchers' observations, classrooms are dominated by teachers talking and by workbook exercises. Researchers call this phenomenon "teachers-talk-students-listen" or "teacher-dominated."

Another result of teacher-dominated classrooms is the negative effect on children's attitudes toward learning. Operating under the two above-mentioned assumptions, teachers often fail to see that literacy learning is a continuum—an ongoing process of learning—for children. Learning before going to school and learning in school are often viewed as separate processes. Oral language, which is the major learning instrument for children before going to school, is no longer available with the onset of formal schooling. Confronted with new tasks of learning to read and write while being deprived of their major learning tool, children tend to feel depressed and frustrated. Learning begins to loom large, and schooling gradually becomes routine—exactly the situation described in Stabb's research.

After a few years students become programmed to a kind of passive learning atmosphere—the teacher talks, the students listen and do their homework. Here, learning simply means taking down whatever is given. In this type of classroom environment, students learn the basic skills of reading and writing. However, they will not learn how to think critically and how to make sound judgments on their own. Stabb (1986) speculates that we teachers often become "so involved with establishing routine, finishing the textbook, covering curriculum, and preparing students for standardized tests that we have forgotten one of our original goals, that of stimulating thought." Although Stabb's speculation sounds critical, she does provide us with a thought-provoking expansion of the relationship between oral language development and thinking abilities development.

Source: ERIC Clearinghouse on Reading English and Communication, Bloomington, IN. Used with permission. *http://www.ericdigests.org/1996-3/oral.htm.*

Comprehensible Output

As a learner, how is your understanding changed when you are provided time to talk with peers as opposed to merely sitting and listening?

You will recall that, in chapter 2, we discussed the importance of providing comprehensible input for students in order to facilitate their language development. It is clear that students must receive instruction in ways that they can understand—comprehensible input—in order to understand the concepts and strategies being taught. It has also been suggested that language output, or language that the students produce, is equally necessary for language development.

Swain (1995) suggests that when students are required to produce language, they process it at a deeper level than when they merely listen. As they clarify their meaning to make it understandable to others they must stretch their language resources, thereby developing their proficiency. When instruction incorporates opportunities for students to interact in ways that require them to use language, students not only practice the language they already control, but also are pushed to extend their skills to higher levels in order to communicate. Integrating communicative activities into daily classroom routines requires purposeful planning and explicit instruction. It also may entail reorganizing classroom structures to facilitate interaction.

Organizing for Interaction

In order to develop proficiency in language, students must practice language. We know that practice alone does not make perfect. Nothing is as simple as that.

Although a lack of practice will almost certainly ensure lack of skill, students also need monitoring and feedback along with that practice.

Most of us would think it ridiculous to teach a child to ride a bicycle by explaining how to ride a bike, and then giving a test. It would be equally absurd to have the child practice pedaling as a skill separate from riding a bike. Rather, we would put the child on the bike, likely with training wheels, in addition to a firm hand on the seat or the handlebars, and run up and down the sidewalk alongside the bike. Similarly, listening to an explanation of the past tense promotes little language development without the opportunity to apply it in meaningful contexts, without time to try out the verb forms in authentic communicative situations. Writing verb conjugations, or even repeating them after the teacher, will not develop proficiency in language any more than practice pedaling develops the ability to ride a bike.

Obviously, using the correct conjugation of a verb is an essential element of language proficiency, just as the ability to push the pedals is necessary when riding a bicycle. In and of themselves, however, neither conjugating verbs nor pedaling gets the job done. Both bicycling and communicating require the learner to practice skills as part of a whole. The ability to communicate effectively requires practice in communicating. As students engage in conversations they practice verb conjugations, gain fluency with language structures, and use vocabulary pertinent to the topic being discussed.

> Information on grammar instruction is provided in chapter 6.

Language and content

At the same time that students are developing their language proficiency through oral language practice, they can develop their content knowledge. Opportunities to talk give students much needed time to process the concepts being taught. As they engage in this "exploratory talk" (Wegerif & Mercer, 1996), students question and clarify, revise their thinking based on input from others, and develop deeper understanding. The content being learned provides not only the focus for the task, but also the authentic situation for language practice.

So how, then, do we organize in order to provide these opportunities for students to talk? In a traditional whole class activity, whether it is a lecture or a shared reading, one person talks at a time. Generally, the students alternate with the teacher. The teacher typically controls and dominates the "conversation." It is not uncommon to find that, out of an hour of instructional time, whether in elementary school or secondary, any given student will speak less than one minute (time it yourself and see). If we believe that verbal interaction is a key factor in developing language proficiency and that students learn content through these interactions, it comes as no surprise that many of our students leave our school system without having reached full proficiency in either language or grade-level content. Providing frequent opportunities for students to interact with each other around important concepts is a key factor in ensuring that ELLs attain full proficiency in English as well as grade-level standards in all subjects.

> Observe yourself as you teach (or observe another classroom if you do not have your own). How much time do you spend talking? How much time do your students spend talking? How often do students work collaboratively, either with a partner or in a small group in your classroom?

GROUPING STUDENTS

Classrooms that provide maximum opportunities for students to talk are those that are organized around a variety of grouping configurations. Students frequently work collaboratively with others, in pairs or small groups, to develop skills, complete a task, and construct meaning. When students work in pairs, half the class is talking at any given moment. Half the class is speaking, as opposed to one student at a time in a whole class structure. In a class of 32, even in groups of four, eight students will be talking at a time. And students are much less likely to talk at length than the teacher, thus giving others more opportunities to contribute.

What are the benefits to having students work in groups?

In groups, students receive more language input than in whole class activities. They hear a wider variety of language, and, because students seem to have a way of making things clear to each other, it is often more comprehensible language input. The language used within the group is contextualized and directed towards a meaningful purpose. (You will remember that having a meaningful purpose for communication is one of the principles of language acquisition.) Group work also provides the redundancy of language that supports ELLs. As ideas are expressed in different ways, English language learners have multiple opportunities to make meaning. They also have additional time to process the language required to understand and express their understanding of the content. Language output is increased when students feel more comfortable expressing themselves in a small group, take more responsibility for their learning, ask questions to clarify, and contribute their own ideas (Gibbons, 2002; McGroarty, 1992).

Productive group work is critical for student learning
Anthony Magnacca/Merrill

Effective group work

Organizing classrooms for students to work in groups effectively requires planning around some basic principles (Gibbons, 1991). We must create situations where there are not only opportunities to talk, but also reasons to communicate in order to complete the task. Gibbons (2002) suggests the following principles to guide planning:

- Provide clear and explicit instructions on how to complete the task.
- Provide explicit instruction on working in a group.
- Build in a necessity for talk in order to complete the task.
- Require a clear outcome for the group work.
- Select cognitively appropriate tasks that require critical thinking.
- Organize so that all students are involved.
- Provide sufficient time to complete the task.

Provide Clear Instructions on How to Complete the Task. When students work without direct teacher guidance, they must be able to determine what to do on their own. This means that the instructions for the task must be clear and explicit. Verbal directions may not be sufficient for English language learners whose language skills may prevent them from keeping up with the teacher. They may need to hear the directions more than once and see them in writing.

As you read about the principles of effective group work, rate yourself on each. Which ones are you best at? Which ones do you need to work on?

Rate yourself:

Consistent ↔ Doesn't happen

4 3 2 1

Spotlight on Instruction

Providing Clear Instructions

After Ms. Kania explains a task to her sheltered eleventh-grade U.S. history class she asks individual students to restate each step of the task, and then asks other students to repeat what was said. The entire process takes less than two minutes, and the students have heard the instructions three times as well as read them on the board. For more complex directions, she provides a handout students can refer to as they work. Strategies that students use frequently in their groups are outlined on charts posted around the room.

Demonstrations are also helpful for students who cannot rely on language alone for comprehension. When Ms. Allen wanted to teach her kindergarteners how to engage in partner talk, she first explained what they were going to do and why. Then she asked Abdi, an intermediate-level language learner, to come to the front of the room, where she modeled partner talk with him. Afterwards she asked the other students to tell what they had seen. She then asked Laura, another intermediate-level student, to join Abdi in a "Fishbowl" to model partner talk once more. (A Fishbowl is a structure in which a few students model an activity while other students look on and then discuss the process with the teacher.) Abdi and Laura sat in the center of the circle of children, and Ms. Allen asked them to talk to each other about what they wanted to learn to do in kindergarten this year.

Provide Explicit Instruction on Working in a Group. Mr. Hanula wanted his eighth grade algebra students to work together to create word problems. He had not had them work in groups yet and determined that he could teach them how to work in a group at the same time as practicing their math skills. Mr. Hanula first explained that they were going to work in groups, and he asked them to pay attention to how they worked together. Since they had been studying linear equations, he asked them to write a word problem using one. At this point there was no discussion of the responsibilities of each group member, or how they might work together. Once they had completed the task, he led a whole class discussion on working in groups—why people work in groups and how to make the process effective. As students talked about when it is useful to work in a group and brainstormed strategies to make sure the groups worked well, Mr. Hanula wrote their ideas on a chart.

What strategies do you think the students brainstormed?

They then brainstormed what language and vocabulary they might use to clarify understanding, express disagreement, expand on the ideas of others, and offer an opinion. Following this discussion, he asked them to create another word problem using another linear equation. This time he assigned each group member a role. One student was to record the group's work on chart paper, one was to draw an accompanying illustration, one was to ask questions to keep all group members engaged, and the fourth was to write an explanation of how they solved the problem. After they completed their word problem, Mr. Hanula asked the groups to assess their behavior using the co-created chart on effective group work. He then asked them to complete a Venn diagram comparing and contrasting the two group experiences. The consensus in the room was that, when they used a structure to work in their group, all members contributed, and they felt they learned more.

The ability to complete academic tasks in a group does not come naturally to all students. Discussion of how, why, and when we work in groups can help students collaborate effectively. It is particularly essential to be sure that the rules and roles are made explicit for students who come from another culture, where ways of interacting may be different, or for those who are not yet proficient in English and may miss the nuances of the language of interacting effectively with others.

What are other ways you can encourage participation by all students besides assigning roles?

Build In a Necessity for Talk in Order to Complete the Task. Group or partner activities are most effective when the need to communicate is built in, when there is a requirement to use oral language in order to accomplish the objective. Without a carefully planned structure, it can be all too easy for one or two members of a group to dominate, or for a group member to abstain from participation. When each partner or group member has only one part of the information needed to complete the task, the communication becomes authentic; they cannot complete the assignment without talking to their partners. Information gap activities such as a jigsaw, where each group member reads a section of text and must teach it to the others, or opinion gap activities, where students solicit an opinion from others, perhaps on a survey or questionnaire, require students to talk in order to complete the assignment. Appendix 5.1 at the end of this chapter presents some ideas for partner and group work.

Select Cognitively Appropriate Tasks That Require Critical Thinking. It is not always easy to find tasks that are suitable for students who are new to English, particularly older ones. The tasks must be challenging yet allow all students to participate, even those at earlier levels of English proficiency. When possible, it can be beneficial for students to discuss ideas in their primary language prior to completing a task in English. The use of manipulatives or pictures facilitates involvement without having to rely solely on language.

Provide a Structure That Involves All Students. When our friend Deborah was in high school, her geometry teacher had the students work in groups every day. From Deborah's point of view, as a student who wasn't very good in geometry, this worked out well. She simply made sure that she was in a group with Barry, the math whiz, and thus always had the right answers to turn in. From an instructional point of view, the structure of the assignment allowed Deborah to sit back without learning. With a different structure, her participation could have been required, and her A in geometry might have been deserved.

Providing structure for group work has two components—determining the composition of the group and designing the task. There are many ways to group students—homogeneously by English proficiency level, reading level, or primary language; heterogeneously with students of varied levels; or letting students self-select. Grouping students by having them work with whomever they sit next to may be the least effective method, unless your seating chart has been arranged for the explicit purpose of having students work together. The two key elements in grouping students are first, that it is done purposefully, and second, that it is varied. When students are discussing a difficult concept, it may help them to understand by discussing it first in their primary language. In this case, it makes most sense to place students who speak the same language and need this support in a group together. If you have differentiated an assignment by providing a selection of tasks that address the same concept at different levels of difficulty, you may want to group students by their proficiency level, giving each group a task that addresses the concept using an appropriate level of English.

> How do you decide which students work in which group?

Alternatively, you may have chosen to differentiate the assignment by providing a series of tasks at different levels of skills or language proficiency, with all tasks necessary for the group to complete its work. In this case, you can group students heterogeneously and have each group member responsible for a different part. Jigsaws, where students become "expert" on a topic they must then teach their group members, are an invaluable way to organize for the involvement of students at different levels of English proficiency. Assigning roles within a group, such as the Summarizer, Clarifier, Questioner, Visualizer, or Predictor, also provides a structure that facilitates the involvement of all students. These roles are discussed in greater detail later in this chapter.

> See chapter 8 for more information on differentation.

Provide Sufficient Time to Complete the Task. Time is the constant bane of a teacher's life. There never seems to be enough of it. At each grade level and in every subject area, we have many concepts and skills to teach our children. We may sometimes see it as more expedient to act as the "sage on the stage" and simply give students the information they need to learn the content. Having students work in groups or with partners takes more time than telling them what they need to know. However, we cannot overestimate the value of creating situations in which students construct their own meaning through the process of discussion and negotiation. In designing lessons that involve group work, we must take into account the time it takes to make sure students understand what they are expected to do, the time it will take for discussion and to complete the task, as well as the time we need to debrief the task and recap or summarize the learning. The conundrum of time can be addressed when planning is purposeful and when we realize that less is often more.

See also chapter 3 for a discussion of planning.

Language development and group work

We have discussed the importance of language practice and how group work provides students far more opportunities to practice and develop language than whole class activities. Group tasks can also provide practice in specific academic language structures that serve specific academic functions. In order to complete tasks that require comparing, describing, justifying, hypothesizing, or asking questions, students must use the relevant vocabulary and language structures. When a group task requires a particular language function, it may help English language learners if you preteach, or "frontload," the necessary vocabulary and language structures. For example, if you ask students to compare two characters in a story, they may need to use language structures such as *different from . . . , similar to . . .*, or *more than. . . .* They may need such vocabulary as *alike, however*, or *both*. Although these may seem like simple expressions, they carry a great deal of the meaning of a statement, and to an English language learner, they can be quite confusing. Teaching this vocabulary and providing sentence frames allows your English language learners to participate more fully, practicing the academic language needed to express their ideas and focusing on the concepts being discussed.

Observe your students. How can you tell if they understand what they are hearing? When they appear to be off task, could it be because they don't understand? What do they do when they don't understand?

Listening. Listening attentively is a challenge for many students. For ELL students, listening is made more difficult by lack of familiarity with the language—the sounds, vocabulary, sentence structure, and the nuances of the language. Listening, like reading, requires certain background knowledge, and, just as in reading, our ELLs may not bring with them the necessary background knowledge to make meaning of what they hear. English language development instruction should include activities that allow students to practice and improve their listening skills.

Listening is obviously a requisite part of much of what we do in the classroom. Yet, we expect students to be able to listen without providing instruction on how to listen. As students move through the grade levels and the work becomes more complex, the requirements for listening become more advanced. Students must follow multiple steps to perform lab experiments and distinguish main ideas and details from lectures and discussions about abstract concepts. Teaching listening, then, should take place over time, at increasingly more complex levels. The process of teaching listening is similar to the process of teaching any other skill—explicit teaching, modeling, guided practice, independent practice, and reflection. Since we typically listen for a specific purpose, listening is best taught when integrated with speaking, reading, and writing within the context of subject matter content.

Step 1: Explicit Teaching. You can begin by having students sit silently in the classroom, or outdoors, and note the sounds they hear. Engage students afterwards in a discussion about what they had to do to hear all the sounds—sit quietly, focus their attention, perhaps visualize. This can lead into further discussion about how the same behaviors are necessary for listening in the classroom.

Students can also learn strategies to develop listening skills. Learning to pay selective attention is one of the most important listening skills we can teach students (Chamot & O'Malley, 1994). This skill is required for a multitude of classroom tasks—solving word problems in math, taking notes from a lecture or a text, following directions for an assignment or activity. Students must learn to listen for specific information; identify key words, phrases, or ideas; and recognize linguistic markers such as *first* or *because* that signal meaning.

See chapter 7 for a detailed discussion of how to teach learning strategies such as paying selective attention.

Another central element of listening is asking for clarification. This is a two-part process that requires students first to recognize when they do not understand, and then to ask questions to get back on track. When students are new to English they are unable to understand a lot of what is going on around them. Unfortunately, some of our students get used to not understanding, and hence do not attend closely enough to recognize when they understand something and when they don't. Students must listen well enough to know when they need clarification or further explanation. They must feel comfortable enough to let others know that they don't understand, and they must know how to formulate questions that will get them the answers they seek. We will discuss questioning in the next section of this chapter.

Step 2: Modeling. You can model good listening skills for your students by doing a Think Aloud demonstrating how you determine what to focus on as you listen to a story, or how you know when to ask for clarification. You can also have a group of students sit in a Fishbowl in front of the class where they listen to a text and then participate in a class discussion. This group of students can also explain to their peers what they did as they listened.

Step 3: Guided Practice. As English language learners listen to lectures and class discussions or watch video clips, you can scaffold these activities for different levels of English proficiency. Providing a note-taking guide for reading, a lecture, or a video with some of the information filled in allows students to focus on listening rather than trying to figure out what to write and how to write it. Students at earlier levels of proficiency in English might be given an outline or a graphic organizer that has most of the information filled in, with a few gaps for them to complete. Those at higher levels of proficiency would have less information provided for them.

Ms. Allen models her thinking during a Read Aloud
Doug Fisher

Frontloading can also assist ELLs as they listen to a story or an introduction to a new unit. Taking a small group aside prior to the lesson and providing differentiated instruction on some of the key points, concepts, or vocabulary builds background knowledge and provides a context for learning. It is also an excellent way to differentiate instruction.

Step 4: Independent Practice. All of the communicative activities described in this chapter, especially those in Appendix 5.1, are designed to provide practice in listening as well as speaking. When students have a purpose for listening, it is easier for them to discern which information is relevant to that purpose. Listening practice can be built into activities that focus on the content. Young children can play a bingo game, listening to sounds and matching them with picture cards. Older students might participate in activities such as Dictogloss or a Listening Jigsaw. (See Appendix 5.1.) Listening activities can also be designed to help students of all ages work on the sounds of English. A learning center might ask students to listen to a tape recording with minimal pairs such as *ship/sheep, tree/three, van/fan*, and match the words with pictures.

During a unit on the human body, Ms. LeBaron assigned her fifth graders to work with a partner to learn the path of the blood through the circulatory system. One student described the path while the other traced it on a diagram.

Step 5: Reflection. Periodically, after students have participated in an activity that required them to use their listening skills, they should take the time to reflect on how well they listened. This can be done through a learning log, a class discussion, or a self-assessment on how well they listened and what strategies they used—asking for clarification, taking notes, sitting where they would not be distracted, visualizing, and so on.

QUESTIONING

"Questioning leads to growing understanding." —Ed Gough, biology teacher, Morse Senior High School, 2004

"It is not the answer that enlightens, but the question." —Eugene Ionesco Decouvertes

Questioning is an integral component of instruction from two perspectives—teacher questioning and student questioning. Well-designed teacher questions can lead students to respond with thoughtful answers that extend language beyond one-word answers. Student questions are part of small group and partner work as students collaborate to share information, construct meaning, and complete tasks.

Teacher questioning

In the traditional format of a class discussion, the teacher asks a question (usually one to which he or she already knows the answer); a student (usually one of a handful of students who readily volunteer to answer every question) answers the question; and the teacher evaluates the answer, letting the student know whether or not it was a "good" answer.

While this pattern, known as Initiate-Respond-Evaluate or IRE (Mehan, 1979), can be useful as a way for teachers to assess learning, it tends to be limited to "display" questions, or those which allow students to display their knowledge and often require only a one-word answer. Typically 60% of the questions teachers ask are lower-level questions that do not require critical thinking, 20% are higher-level, and 20% are procedural (Gall, 1984). When we look at those students perceived to be poor learners (a perception that includes many of our English language learners), the percentage of higher-level questions directed toward them drops significantly (Cotton, 1988).

Teacher questions can serve many purposes in addition to assessment of knowledge. Well-constructed, purposeful questions aid students in building understanding on a variety of levels. Open-ended questions challenge students to think critically, rather than trying to find the "right answer." We do not mean to suggest that factual, display-type questions have no place in promoting achievement, simply that there should be a balance of levels of questions. It is also important to remember that English language learners may be limited in their ability to express themselves in English, but that limitation is not indicative of an inability to think critically.

Make a note of the questions you ask during a lesson. Which are open-ended? Which are display questions with one correct answer?

Research in Focus:
Levels of Questions

In 1912, Stevens stated that approximately 80% of a teacher's school day was spent asking questions to students. More contemporary research on teacher questioning behaviors and patterns indicate that this has not changed. Teachers today ask between 300 and 400 questions each day (Leven & Long, 1981).

Teachers ask questions for several reasons (Morgan & Saxton, 1991):

1. The act of asking questions helps teachers keep students actively involved in lessons.
2. While answering questions, students have the opportunity to openly express their ideas and thoughts.
3. Questioning students enables other students to hear different explanations of the material by their peers.
4. Asking questions helps teachers to pace their lessons and moderate student behavior.
5. Questioning students helps teachers to evaluate student learning and revise their lessons as necessary.

As one may deduce, questioning is one of the most popular modes of teaching. For thousands of years, teachers have known that it is possible to transfer factual knowledge and conceptual understanding through the process of asking questions. Unfortunately, although the act of asking questions has the potential to greatly facilitate the learning process, it also has the capacity to turn a child off to learning if done incorrectly.

In order to teach well, it is widely believed, one must be able to question well. Asking good questions fosters interaction between the teacher and his or her students. Rosenshine (1971) found that large amounts of student-teacher interaction promotes student achievement. Thus, one can surmise that good questions foster student understanding. However, it is important to know that not all questions achieve this.

Teachers spend most of their time asking low-level cognitive questions (Wilen, 1991). These questions concentrate on factual information that can be memorized (e.g., "What year did the Civil War begin?" or "Who wrote *Great Expectations*?"). It is widely believed that this type of question can limit students by not helping them to acquire a deep, elaborate understanding of the subject matter.

High-level cognitive questions can be defined as questions that require students to use higher-order thinking or reasoning skills. By using these skills, students do not remember only factual knowledge. Instead, they use their knowledge to problem solve, to analyze, and to evaluate. It is popularly believed that this type of question reveals the most about whether or not a student has truly grasped a concept. This is because a student needs to have a deep understanding of the topic in order to answer this type of question. Teachers do not use high-level cognitive questions with the same amount of frequency as they do low-level cognitive questions. Ellis (1993) claims that many teachers rely on low-level cognitive questions to avoid a slow-paced lesson, keep the attention of the students, and maintain control of the classroom.

Arends (1994) argues that many of the findings concerning the effects of using lower-level cognitive versus higher-level cognitive questions have been inconclusive. While some studies and popular belief favor asking high-level cognitive questions, other studies reveal the positive effects of asking low-level cognitive questions. Some studies do not reveal any difference in achievement between students whose teachers use mostly high-level questions and those whose teachers ask mainly low-level questions (Arends, 1994; Wilen, 1991). Therefore, although teachers should ask a combination of low-level cognitive and high-level cognitive questions, they must determine the needs of their students in order to know which sort of balance between the two types of questions needs to be made to foster student understanding and achievement.

Source: ERIC Clearinghouse on Assessment and Evaluation, Washington, D.C. Used with permission. *http://www.ericdigests.org/1999-2/questions.htm.*

Questioning and teacher expectations

All too often, when a student is unable to give the correct answer to a question, another student is asked to respond, or the teacher will simply give the answer and move on. The following two student-teacher exchanges demonstrate how a different approach to questioning can elicit different responses. A small group of sixth-grade Beginning English language learners is looking at a picture as part of a language experience activity designed to generate language and vocabulary prior to writing about the picture.

T: Marco, what is going on in this picture?

S: (no response)

T: What are the children doing?

S: Boy.

T: Esther, can you tell us what the children are doing?

After asking the question and rewording it once, the teacher moves on to another student, perhaps feeling uncomfortable about putting the student on the spot when he is unable to come up with an answer, perhaps feeling pressured for time and wanting to maintain the pace of the lesson.

In the following exchange, the teacher persists with another student.

T: Dulce, what do you think the children in this picture are feeling?

S: (no response)

T: Look at their faces. What do you think they are feeling?

S: (no response)

T: Do you think this boy is happy or sad?

S: Sad.

How do the teacher's questions help elicit language from Dulce?

In the latter case, the teacher began with a more difficult question and then provided progressively more support when the student was unable to respond. This type of "backwards scaffolding" provides students the opportunity to demonstrate their knowledge at a higher level if they are able and allows teachers to quickly assess what students are able to do, gaining valuable information to guide instruction. In this case, the teacher found that Dulce knew the meaning of *happy* and *sad*, but either couldn't come up with the word *feelings* on her own, or didn't understand the word. Further questioning can help determine whether Dulce simply needs more exposure to and practice with words that describe feelings, or whether she needs direct instruction on the word *feeling* itself.

Teachers who know their students well can use questions to scaffold student learning, leading them to deeper levels of thinking than they might have reached on their own. Mr. Gough, a tenth-grade biology teacher, asked his students to make an observation about a mystery substance called "Ooblick." When he got no response, he asked a series of questions to help them understand what is involved in making an observation: "What does it look like?" and "What does it feel like?" With these simple questions, he suddenly had students vying to respond.

When teachers ask questions at a variety of levels, they provide models for their English language learners as they begin to ask their own questions, moving them beyond knowledge-level questions with answers that can be found in the book to questions that require analysis, synthesis, and evaluation. Again, this is not to say that we should not be asking questions at the knowledge level; students must have the basic knowledge in order to answer questions at other levels. Table 5.1 provides examples of how we can vary levels of questions to help students build meaning.

Table 5.1

Levels of Questions		
Level	**Description**	**Example**
Knowledge	Recall facts, definitions.	What is the capital of California?
Comprehension	Understand meaning.	Explain why Sacramento was selected as the state capital.
Application	Apply learning to a new situation.	What city in California would you select as the state capital today?
Analysis	Identify components. Make inferences.	Why do you believe the legislature chose to move the capital from San Jose to Sacramento?
Synthesis	Use parts to create a new whole.	Design a state capital that will be useful in the 21st century.
Evaluation	Make judgments.	Assess the suitability of the present state capital and make recommendations for future development.

Wait Time. The length of time teachers wait for a student response before asking another question, moving on to another student, or even answering the question themselves is an important consideration in effective questioning.

On average, teachers allow 1 second or less for students to respond after posing a question (Honea, 1982). For students who are still learning English, this may not be enough time for them to process the language being used, think of what they want to say, find the English words, and then formulate their response. It is clearly a difficult proposition to balance the time needed for a student to respond to a question with the need to maintain the rhythm and pace of the lesson, holding students' interest and attention. When Ms. Shirley reads the poem "I Thought I Spotted Bigfoot"(from *Monday's Troll*, Prelutsky, 1996) to her third graders and asks them what they think the author is referring to when he writes "He was utterly imposing" (p. 24), eager hands shoot up to answer. They are the usual culprits, though, the ones who are always quick to respond, and Ms. Shirley wants to give Francisco and Alejandra, her ELLs, a chance to think about their own interpretation of the poem, rather than listen to someone else's.

Instead of calling on an individual student to answer, she asks them to talk with a partner about what they think the line means. This gives Francisco and Alejandra the time to think about the meaning and to find the language to express their thinking. It has the added benefit of requiring all the students to think about the line, including those eager hand-raisers who sometimes want to participate so badly they may not have taken the time to think about the meaning before their hands shoot up. It also allows her to listen in on Francisco and Alejandra and provide them with any needed support. Other ways to maintain the pace of the lesson, while still providing sufficient wait time for English language learners, include having students write their responses, allowing students to ask a friend, or giving students a choice between two possible responses.

Used by permission of HarperCollins Publishers.

Student questioning

Marta, a fifth-grade English language learner who was reading *Shiloh* (Naylor, 1991) was asked to tell her teacher about her book. Marta described the basic story and provided details about the main characters. She said, "Marty has to lie to make Shiloh safe." When asked to explain what had happened in the last few pages, however, Marta was stumped and had to go back and reread what she had just finished. She understood the basic gist of the story, but was missing

Use a stopwatch to count from the time you ask a question until the time you begin to feel uncomfortable when the student does not respond. What do you do when you call on a student and he or she does not respond within a few seconds?

"The struggling reader thinks it's his job to answer questions. The good reader knows it's his job to ask questions" (Kinsella, 2001).

Jacket cover from SHILOH by Phyllis Reynolds Naylor. Used by permission of Bantam Books, a division of Random House, Inc.

out on much of the richness of the text because she continued reading even when she wasn't understanding what she read.

Marta is not atypical of many struggling readers, including native and proficient English-speaking children, who do not monitor their comprehension as they read. ELL students, still learning the language, may miss even more—failing to recognize subtleties of language that foreshadow coming events, or perhaps skimming over a portion of text that contains many pronouns, which can cause confusion regarding who is saying or doing what. This lack of self-monitoring becomes even more of an obstacle when reading content-area expository texts in which paragraphs are dense with ideas and every sentence may contain important information. Teaching students to stop and ask questions as they read is a critical piece of the instructional process if they are to become independent learners.

Question-answer relationships (QAR)

Taffy Raphael describes four kinds of questions that students should be asking themselves and each other (Raphael, 1986). Table 5.2 contains a summary of these types of questions.

Based on a topic or book you recently taught, write a question for each of the four types of questions.

- *Right There:* These are questions with answers that can be found directly in the text.
  "When did World War II end?"
- *Think and Search:* The answer is in the text but the student must look in different parts of the text to give a complete response to the question.
  "Name three causes of World War II."
- *Author and You:* The reader combines his or her own knowledge with information found in the text. This may involve drawing inferences.
  "How was World War II similar to World War I?"
- *On Your Own:* The answer comes from the reader's own experience and knowledge. The text may not be needed to answer the question.
  "What would you have done if you had been president of the United States when Pearl Harbor was attacked?"

How do we teach students to ask questions?

Listen to your students. What types of questions do they ask? Who is asking questions?

Just as with any other content to be taught, students require explicit teaching about the types of questions and repeated models. We follow the same steps outlined previously in this chapter in our discussion about listening.

Table 5.2

Question-Answer Relationship Comparison Chart	
QAR Strategy	**Description**
Right There	The question is asked using words from the text, and the answer is directly stated in the reading.
Think and Search	The questions are derived from the text and require the reader to look for the answer in several places and to combine the information.
Author and You	The question has the language of the text but to answer it the reader must use what he or she understands about the topic. The answer cannot be found directly in the text, but the text can provide some information for formulating an answer. The information is implied. The reader infers what the author meant by examining clues in the text.
On My Own	The question elicits an answer to come from the reader's own prior knowledge and experiences. The text may or may not be needed to answer the question.

Source: Fisher, D., & Frey, N. (2004). Improving adolescent literacy: Strategies at work. *Upper Saddle River, NJ: Merrill/ Prentice Hall. Used with permission.*

Step 1: Explicit Teaching. Teacher discusses why we ask questions as we read and explains what the different types of questions are.

Step 2: Modeling. Teacher reads a text aloud, asks questions, and tells what type of question each is. After students have an understanding of the different types of questions, the teacher asks questions and the students tell what kind of question each is.

Step 3: Guided Practice. Students practice developing the four different types of questions, using text that is at an easy level so that they can focus on the task of learning how to ask questions rather than struggling with the content of the text. This can be done in the whole class or in small groups with students at the same level. Once some students begin to get a good grasp of the different types of questions, they might be asked to model for the rest of the class using a Fishbowl technique: They sit in the center of the class, read a piece of text aloud, and formulate their questions. The other students observe and, with partners, identify each type of question.

Step 4: Independent Practice. Students can work with partners to write questions for each of the four types. Give half the class one piece of text; give the other half a different piece of text. After writing questions, students change partners and pair up with a student who has questions for the other piece of text. They then read both pieces of text and answer the questions the other has written. Once students become more proficient at questioning they can skip the first step in this practice and simply read and ask/answer questions with their partner.

Step 5: Reflection. A Think-Pair-Share activity is a good way to give students an opportunity to reflect on how questioning helped their comprehension and think about which parts they do well, which parts they still need to work on.

English language learners may require more time in Steps 1–3 because they may need more practice with the language of questions. Teachers need to make thoughtful decisions about how to pair up their English language learners—whether to allow them to work first in their primary language, to have them work with students at a similar English-proficiency level, or to pair them with fluent English-proficient students. As we discussed earlier, these are decisions that must be based on a clear understanding of student strengths and needs, as well as the purpose of the specific task.

STUDENTS HELPING STUDENTS

Before we continue, it is worthwhile to expand on the discussion of pairing students who speak the same language, often called "language brokers." This approach has benefits and potential drawbacks. Teachers often use peer support for students who are very new to the English language. Consider Marta and her needs.

Marta had just arrived from Chihuahua, Mexico. It was November, and her fifth-grade classroom was getting ready to write a letter to their principal using all their skills in persuasive writing to convince her that they should no longer have to wear school uniforms. Marta spoke no English, other than a few basic

Language brokers making meaning of the content
Doug Fisher

Figure 5.1   Using Peer Support

If your purpose is to help the student:	Select a partner who:
Adjust to their new environment	Speaks the same language or has a similar background
Use more English	Speaks English and who is patient
Learn from peers	Enjoys teaching others and is helpful
Become part of the learning community	Is outgoing and connected with other students (but change partners as often as possible to encourage relationships)

social phrases. Her teacher, Ms. Hoffman, assigned Marisol to be Marta's "buddy." Marisol, one of two Spanish-speaking students in the class, would be able to help Marta get around the school and understand the class assignments. After a few days, Ms. Hoffman noticed that Marta was sitting quietly at her desk while Marisol was working with her group on the letter to the principal. When Ms. Hoffman asked Marisol why Marta was not working with the group, Marisol complained, "Teacher, I always have to help the new students and I don't have time to do my own work."

Perhaps one of the most difficult dilemmas a teacher of English language learners faces is what to do with the new arrivals who speak no English at all. There really is no ideal way to involve students in grade-level classwork in English when they don't understand even the most basic conversation. Many teachers rely on students who speak the same language to help out, not only placing an undue burden on their bilingual classmates, but depriving the new student of valuable language-learning experiences. Just as we know that having a clear purpose for teacher-directed instruction promotes higher achievement, defining the purpose of the "buddy" work can make peer work far more effective. Figure 5.1 illustrates how you can match your purpose to your choice of buddies.

Reciprocal Teaching

In addition to using questions in the classroom, there are classwide structures that can be taught to students so that they can ask and answer questions as they read texts. The most widely researched and used classwide instructional strategy in this area is Reciprocal Teaching.

Reciprocal Teaching, developed by Palinscar and Brown (1984), combines the questioning skills students have learned through QAR with other reading strategies for making meaning from text. Students read a small portion of text and take turns asking questions, clarifying, summarizing, predicting, and visualizing. This strategy is particularly valuable for English language learners because they find support for comprehension through the small group interaction, or through discussion and clarification in their primary language.

Which of these skills can your students already do? Which need more instruction?

Question. Questioning helps to check for comprehension in addition to deepening understanding.

Clarify. Students may need to clarify unfamiliar vocabulary, a new or difficult concept, the structure of the text, or the meaning. They can assist each other by explaining, re-reading, or using outside resources such as a dictionary.

Summarize. Students integrate the ideas and identify the main points and supporting information in the text. They may use graphic organizers to help organize the information.

Predict. Students use what they have read along with their prior knowledge about the topic and the type of text to predict what they might read next. Predicting helps to set a purpose for reading as students confirm or reject their hypotheses.

Visualize. Visualizing—drawing a physical or mental image of the key ideas in the text—can be especially helpful for students who are learning English. It will not be appropriate for every section of text read, but when it fits, it not only offers meaning without reliance on language, but it requires students to think deeply about what they have read, analyzing the meaning in order to create a visual image.

How do we teach students to use Reciprocal Teaching?

Reciprocal Teaching is a perfect example of teaching from whole to part to whole. It is a complex structure that is quite likely to fail the first time it is used, unless students thoroughly understand the process. It is perhaps easiest to implement after students have become familiar with QAR and with asking different types of questions. Prior to teaching the other steps in the process, the teacher explains what Reciprocal Teaching is and how it helps comprehension. Then each of the steps of Reciprocal Teaching is taught explicitly and modeled following a similar process to that described previously for QAR. While the strategies of clarifying, predicting, and visualizing may not be as difficult for students to grasp as questioning, time spent up front on each part of the Reciprocal Teaching process will lead to a smoother implementation. Summarizing is a skill that eludes many students, even proficient readers. It may require repeated explanation, modeling, and a variety of scaffolds to help students differentiate between main ideas and details, between summarizing and retelling. Once the students have learned each part of the process and know what each step entails, they are ready to put it all together and the entire process can be modeled. The Fishbowl technique and small group instruction with the teacher monitoring and assisting as needed are effective methods to get students started.

Ms. Allen used modeling and a Fishbowl to introduce her students to partner talk earlier in this chapter.

CONCLUSION

Oral language, or oracy, provides the foundation for literacy. Opportunities to talk prior to reading prepare students for reading; during and after reading, they deepen their understanding of the key concepts. And most importantly for English language learners, talking allows them to practice the language they are in the process of learning.

Incorporating these opportunities into instruction does take time. It is much more expedient to tell students what you want them to know, or to have them read and answer the questions at the end of the chapter. The questions we must ask ourselves as we plan are:

- Is this concept worth the time to have students talk?
- Is it a key concept?
- Will they "get" it if I just tell them about it?

Not everything we do in class warrants taking the time for students to work and talk in groups. But it does seem that, on a daily basis, perhaps students should be talking at least as much as the teacher.

Application to Practice

Reflection

1. What is one strategy you feel comfortable trying out right away? Why did you choose this one?
2. Why is oral language development so important for English language learners? What will you do to facilitate the listening and speaking skills of your students?

Case Study: *Oral Language Development*

Observe your target student during a whole class, small group, and partner activity. In which configurations does he or she talk more? With whom? What might you do to elicit more academic language from this student?

Planning and Instruction: *Student Talk*

Take a lesson you have done before or are about to do, which does not currently include opportunities for students to interact. Incorporate at least one activity for student-to-student interaction. Use the lesson planning guide (Figure 5.2) in this chapter to assist in designing a lesson that accounts for grouping configuration, differentiating based on English proficiency level, identifying language and content to be taught, actively engaging all students, and integrating reading and writing.

Chapter 5

Figure 5.2   Lesson Plan: Planning for Interaction

Purpose *What do I want my students to understand, be able to do, or practice and apply?*	
Language/vocabulary needed *What language is needed to participate in the discussion?*	
Task *What is the assignment?* *How will I introduce it and make sure they understand what they are to do?*	
Talk *How have I organized the task to require students to interact?*	
Differentiation *How will I group students with different levels of English proficiency?*	
Link to literacy *What reading and writing will be required?*	
Reflection *What worked? Why?* *What would I change for next time?*	

References

Arends, R. (1994). *Learning to teach*. New York: McGraw-Hill.

August, D., & Shanahan, T. (2006). *Developing literacy in second-language learners: Report of the National Literacy Panel on Language-Minority Children and Youth*. Mahwah, NJ: Lawrence Erlbaum.

Chamot, A.U., & O'Malley, J.M. (1994). *The CALLA handbook: Implementing the cognitive academic language learning approach*. Reading, MA: Addison-Wesley.

Cotton, K. (1988). *Classroom questioning*. Northwest Regional Educational Laboratory. Retrieved December 30, 2004 from: *http://www.nwrel.org/scpd/sirs/3/cu5.html*.

Crystal, D. (1992). *The Cambridge encyclopedia of language*. New York: Cambridge University Press.

Ellis, K. (1993). *Teacher questioning behavior and student learning: What research says to teachers*. Paper presented at the 1993 Convention of the Western States Communication Association, Albuquerque, New Mexico. (ED 359 572)

Gall, M. (1984). Synthesis of research on teachers' questioning. *Educational Leadership, 42*(3), 40–47.

Gibbons, P. (1991). *Learning to learn in a second language*. Portsmouth, NH: Heinemann.

Gibbons, P. (2002). *Scaffolding language, scaffolding learning, teaching second language learners in the mainstream classroom*. Portsmouth, NH: Heinemann.

Holbrook, H. T. (1983). Oral language: A neglected language art? *Language Arts, 60*, 255–258.

Honea, J. M. Jr. (1982). Wait-time as an instructional variable: An influence on teacher and student. *The Clearing House, 56*, 167–170.

Kinsella, K. (2001). *Expository writing scaffolds for English learners in content area classrooms*. Presentation for Standards-Based Evaluation and Accountability Institute for English Learners. California Department of Education, Santa Barbara, CA.

Leven, T., & Long, R. (1981). *Effective instruction*. Alexandria, VA: Association for Supervision and Curriculum Development.

Lyle, S. (1993). An investigation into ways in which children talk themselves into meaning. *Language and Education, 7*, 181–187.

McGroarty, M. (1992). Cooperative learning: The benefits for content-area teaching. In P. Amato-Snow & M. Snow (Eds.), *The multicultural classroom: Readings for content-area teachers* (pp. 58–69). White Plains, NY: Longman.

Mehan, B. (1979). *Learning lessons*. Cambridge, MA: Harvard University Press.

Morgan, N., & Saxton, J. (1991). *Teaching, questioning, and learning*. New York: Routledge.

Naylor, P. R. (1991). *Shiloh*. New York: Bantam Doubleday Dell Books for Young Readers.

Palinscar, A. S., & Brown, A. (1984). Reciprocal teaching of comprehension-fostering and comprehension monitoring activities. *Cognition and Instruction, 1*(2), 117–175.

Prelutsky, J. (1996). *Monday's troll.* New York: Greenwillow Books.

Raphael, T. E. (1986). Teaching question-answer relationships, revisited. *The Reading Teacher, 39,* 516–522.

Rosenshine, B. (1971). *Teaching behaviors and student achievement.* London: National Foundation for Educational Research in England and Wales.

Stabb, C. (1986). What happened to the sixth graders: Are elementary students losing their need to forecast and to reason? *Reading Psychology, 7,* 289–296.

Stevens, R. (1912). *The question as a means of efficiency in instruction: A critical study of classroom practice.* New York: Teachers College, Columbia University.

Swain, M. (1995). Three functions of output in second language learning. In G. Cook & B. Seidlehofer (Eds.), *Principle and practice in applied linguistics: Studies in honour of H. G. Widdowson* (pp. 125–144). Oxford: Oxford University Press.

Wegerif, R., & Mercer, N. (1996). Computers and reasoning through talk in the classroom. *Language and education, 10*(1), 47–64.

Wilen, W. (1991). *Questioning skills for teachers: What research says to the teacher* (3rd ed.). Washington, DC: National Education Association.

Appendix 5.1 Communicative Activities

Activity	Description	How can you apply?
Barrier Games	Students sit with a barrier between them so they cannot see the other's information. Student A has a set of instructions that Student B needs in order to complete a task. Student A must convey the information orally. For example: One student has a drawing and must describe it without showing it the other student, who must draw it.	
Find the Difference	Each student has a similar picture but with some differences. Without showing their pictures they must find the difference.	
Find the Difference— Listening Comprehension	A variation on Find the Difference that focuses on teaching listening skills. Have partners listen to two recorded stories that have minor differences or read their stories to each other. They must identify those differences.	
Sequencing	Each group member has a picture that is part of a sequence (e.g., life cycle of a frog, steps in solving a math problem, sequence of a story). Without showing the picture to the rest of the group, each describes his or her picture to the others. Together they determine the logical sequence.	

Appendix 5.1 Communicative Activities (continued)

Activity	Description	How can you apply?
Find Your Partner	1. Each student has part of a statement written on a card, either the first part or the last part. They must find the student whose card completes their sentence. 2. Each group member has a picture. Two are alike, the others are similar. One of the identical pictures is marked. That student must determine, through questioning, which other picture is identical.	
Jigsaw	Each group member is given a different piece of text on a related topic. They read and discuss their text with one member from each group in the class, becoming expert on that text. They then return to their original group and each member teaches the others about their piece of text.	
Listening Jigsaw	A variation on the jigsaw that focuses on listening skills. Give students recorded information to listen to on a cassette recorder in lieu of the written information.	

Activity	Description	How can you apply?
Anticipation Guide (with justification)	The teacher writes a series of statements regarding the topic to be studied. Students read them individually and mark whether they agree or disagree. With a partner, they discuss their responses and come to consensus regarding each statement, writing a justification for why they agree or disagree. Pairs can join into groups of four and share their opinions.	
Dictogloss	Students listen to repeated readings of a text and write down as much of the text as possible, including more each time they hear it. In pairs and then in groups, they share their notes to create a text as close as possible to the original.	
Think-Pair-Share	Students are given a question to talk about, sharing their opinions or experiences.	
Literature Circles	Students who have chosen to read the same piece of literature meet in small, temporary groups to discuss what they have read. Members may take on different responsibilities in the discussion (Summarizer, Illustrator, Discussion Director, Vocabulary Enricher, etc.). Circles meet regularly and change discussion roles at each meeting. When students finish the book, they decide on a way to showcase their reading for the class.	

6 Academic Language: Building Proficiency

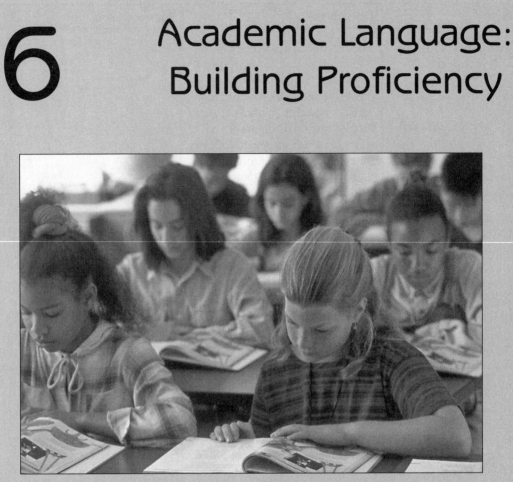

David Young–Wolff/PhotoEdit Inc.

The limits of my language mean the limits of my world.

—Ludwig Wittgenstein, Tractatus Logico-Philosophicus *(1922)*

[Teachers] must know enough about language to discuss it and to support its development in their students. Academic language is learned through frequent exposure and practice over a long period of time, from the time children enter school to the time they leave it."

—Lily Wong-Fillmore *(2000)*

Focus Questions

1. What is academic language?
2. What are the registers of language?
3. What are the components of an effective reading program?
4. What is the role of word knowledge in the performance of English language learners? How can we teach this knowledge?
5. Which instructional strategies are effective in writing instruction? How can they be differentiated for students at different levels of proficiency in English?
6. How do we differentiate error correction?

ACCESSING PRIOR KNOWLEDGE: DEVELOPING ACADEMIC LANGUAGE

What do you already know about teaching academic language? Vocabulary? Writing?

What do you want to know?

After reading this chapter, what have you learned that you will use in your classroom?

In the previous chapter, we discussed the importance of providing opportunities for our students to talk, to communicate orally, to practice making themselves understood and understanding others. Although oral language is clearly the foundation of literacy, talk alone will not lead to the level of academic language proficiency required for success in school. A large segment of our ELL population languishes at the Intermediate and even the Early Intermediate level of language proficiency. This chapter will focus on how to move students out of that Intermediate zone into full proficiency. We will examine the characteristics of academic language proficiency and identify strategies to promote its development. In other words, this chapter will link oral language with reading and writing.

ACADEMIC LANGUAGE PROFICIENCY

How would you feel about the credibility of this book if you found a number of typographical and grammatical errors? We have higher standards for written work.

Have you ever listened to a tape-recording of yourself? Did you consistently speak in complete sentences? Was every statement clear, or did you repeat and reword in order to clarify? Did you make any grammatical errors? While some of us never hesitate while speaking and organize our thoughts succinctly and clearly, many of us sometimes use a word incorrectly, use run-on sentences, or start a sentence without finishing it. Yet we are still considered proficient, even articulate, in English. The occasional errors we make while speaking are perfectly acceptable. Even in a job interview, a few errors would likely be overlooked. A few errors on the letter of application, however, might well lose you the job. This is because our standards for written English are much higher than for speaking. Proficiency in written language, then, becomes a much more challenging proposition for our English language learners than proficiency in oral communication. And, while we certainly want our ELLs to have multiple opportunities to talk in class, these opportunities cannot end with talk; they must lead into reading and writing.

WHAT IS ACADEMIC LANGUAGE?

What exactly is the difference between everyday English and English that is considered academic? What skills does academic language require that are not necessarily used in everyday language? Robin Scarcella and Russell Rumberger (2000) identify five differences (see Table 6.1). Academic English requires a far greater depth of knowledge—knowledge of language, vocabulary, and context (background knowledge.) Students must draw upon their metalinguistic abilities as they choose the words and the structures to state their ideas, as they edit their writing to express themselves more clearly and precisely. They must also be able to think critically—analyzing, evaluating, and synthesizing what they hear and read.

Table 6.1

Differences between Everyday English and Academic English		
Aspect of Proficiency	**Everyday English**	**Academic English**
Language Domains	More use of listening and speaking.	More use of reading and writing.
Accuracy	Minor errors are acceptable.	High standard of accuracy in grammar and vocabulary required.
Linguistic Functions	More reliance on narrative such as describing.	Persuading, analyzing, interpreting, hypothesizing, etc.
Cognitive Demands	Often highly contextualized.	Fewer contextual clues, must rely on prior knowledge of content and language.
Range of Knowledge	Requires smaller lexicon.	Requires knowledge of over 20,000 word forms and applicable grammatical rules.

Source: Adapted from Scarcella, R., & Rumberger, R. (2000). Academic English key to long term success in school. University of California Linguistic Minority Research Institute Newsletter, 9:4. Santa Barbara, CA. Used with permission.

LANGUAGE REGISTERS

The ways in which we express ourselves and the expectations for accuracy, vocabulary, and language structure vary with the situation—the method, the topic, and the audience. Halliday and Hasan (1976) use the terms *mode, field*, and *tenor* to describe the varying situations that influence how we use language.

Mode: Means of communication. Communication that is read, written, spoken, listened to, or viewed.

Field: Subject matter being discussed. A lecture, conversation, or piece of written text might be academic—about a short story, a mathematical formula, or the Westward Movement; or the subject might be of a more personal nature—talking about your family, making a date to meet a friend.

Tenor: Relation between the listener/reader and speaker/writer. A discussion of a short story might take place in a classroom among the students and the teacher, between friends in a book club or literature circle, or it might be in the form of a book review for class or a newspaper.

These three conditions—mode, field, and tenor—comprise the register, or the style of language. Full proficiency in a language requires that the learner be able to

What might be the differences in your language if you were discussing a student during a parent conference versus discussing the same student with your colleagues over lunch?

vary his or her language, or register, appropriately along a full continuum of situations, from personal to academic. So often our ELLs, particularly at the Intermediate level, appear to be proficient as they talk (mode) about personal topics (field) with their friends (tenor). Where they run into difficulty is when the mode of communication is writing and the field is an academic topic. Instruction at all levels, therefore, must incorporate opportunities to develop skills in writing (mode) about grade-level academic content (field) to an unfamiliar audience (tenor).

Research in Focus: Language Registers

Sociolinguists note that registers are one of the ways in which social relationships reveal themselves in language. "The concept of register is typically concerned with variations in language conditioned by uses rather than users and involves consideration of the situation or context of use, the purpose, subject-matter, and content of the message, and the relationship between the participants" (Romaine, 1994, p. 20). The more registers a speaker possesses, the more able he or she is to communicate effectively in a variety of settings. There are five generally agreed upon language registers, including (e.g., Payne, 1995):

Fixed or frozen. Fixed speech is reserved for traditions in which the language does not change. Examples of fixed speech include the Pledge of Allegiance, Shakespeare's plays, and civil ceremonies such as weddings.
Formal. At the formal level, speech is expected to be presented in complete sentences with specific word usage. Formal language is the standard for work, school, and business and is more often seen in writing than in speaking. However, public speeches and presentations are expected to be delivered in a formal language register.
Consultative. The third level of language, consultative, is a formal register used in conversations but less appropriate for writing. Students often use consultative language in their interactions in the classroom.
Casual. This is the language that is used in conversation with friends. In casual speech, word choice is general and conversation depends upon nonverbal assists, significant background knowledge, and shared information.
Intimate. This is the language used by very close friends and family. Intimate speech is private and often requires a significant amount of shared history, knowledge, and experience.

Payne (1995) argues that students often do not understand the match between the language register and the setting. She strongly advocates that teachers provide students instruction in language registers. This requires that teachers scaffold students' use of language and do not try to eliminate registers or dialects that students use in different settings. In other words, teaching students about language registers should be an additive model of education—one that encourages students to maintain their heritage language, dialect, and/or accent *and* provides them access to standard English (e.g., Brock, Boyd, & Moore, 2003).

Source: Frey, N., & Fisher, D. (2006). *Language arts workshop: Purposeful reading and writing instruction.* Upper Saddle River, NJ: Merrill/Prentice Hall. Used with permission.

Pauline Gibbons (2002) uses a science experiment to demonstrate this progression from informal, conversational language, to a more formal oral presentation, to written language, and finally, to academic text.

"Look, it's making them move. Those didn't stick."

"We found out the pins stuck on the magnet."

"Our experiment showed that magnets attract some metals."

"Magnetic attraction occurs only between ferrous metals."

How is each statement different from the previous one?

In the first statement, the students are conducting a science experiment, talking about what is happening as they work together. The second statement is taken from the oral report to the class. The third is part of the written report. And the fourth is taken from a child's encyclopedia. Notice how the level of language changes as the statements move from a shared experience, to an oral report, to written. As the children work together, they are sharing the experience and know what *it, them* and *those* refer to without explanation because the objects are right in front of them. When there is no shared context or experience, the language must be much more explicit to be understood by the listener or reader. Notice the difference between the oral report and the written one. Not only is the written text more explicit than during the shared experiment, but it also uses more academic language (e.g., *experiment, attract, metals*). The final statement, taken from the encyclopedia, is reflective of the type of text our students need to be able to read. It uses a passive voice and a label or noun for what was previously a verb—*attract* becomes *magnetic attraction.*

So how do we move students beyond the type of language that presumes a shared experience? How do we teach them to use more explicit academic language in their writing? How do we teach them to comprehend grade-level academic text when the language structures are so different from those used in everyday conversation, or even in literature?

What strategies can you use to encourage use of academic language?

In chapter 2 we discussed the importance of providing comprehensible input as part of helping students acquire language. And it is indeed a critical component of instruction. All too often, however, we assume that students will develop an understanding of the structure of English simply through hearing lots of comprehensible English, just as children are able to speak their primary language without focused instruction in grammar. Comprehensible input develops informal language, or BICS. It is explicit instruction that leads to development of academic language, or CALP. Let's turn our attention to reading first.

READING ACADEMIC LANGUAGE

Our experience and reviews of research suggest that students need purposeful, explicit instruction to become proficient users of the language. Readers must understand both the function and form of the language, or how the language is used to convey a message. This is similar to the way a doctor who knows the skeletal structure of the human body must also know how the bones and the muscles work in order to make a diagnosis and begin treatment.

The components of effective reading instruction include developing an awareness of the sounds of the language (called *phonemic awareness*) and the relationship between letters and the sounds they represent (*phonics*). In addition, the National Reading Panel (NRP) identified *fluency development, vocabulary development,* and intentional instruction in *comprehension strategies* as essential components of reading. These five essential instructional components of reading appear in Figure 6.1.

Figure 6.1   Five Essential Components of Reading (*Source: U.S. Department of Education, Office of Intergovernmental and Interagency Affairs, Educational Partnerships and Family Involvement Unit. (2003).* Reading tips for parents. *Washington, DC: Author. Used with permission.*)

Five Essential Components of Reading

Reading with children and helping them practice specific reading components can dramatically improve their ability to read. Scientific research shows that there are five essential components of reading that children must be taught in order to learn to read. Adults can help children learn to be good readers by systematically practicing these five components:

- Recognizing and using individual sounds to create words, or **phonemic awareness.** Children need to be taught to hear sounds in words and that words are made up of the smallest parts of sound, or phonemes.
- Understanding the relationships between written letters and spoken sounds, or **phonics.** Children need to be taught the sounds individual printed letters and groups of letters make. Knowing the relationships between letters and sounds helps children to recognize familiar words accurately and automatically, and "decode" new words.
- Developing the ability to read a text accurately and quickly, or **reading fluency.** Children must learn to read words rapidly and accurately in order to understand what is read. When fluent readers read silently, they recognize words automatically. When fluent readers read aloud, they read effortlessly and with expression. Readers who are weak in fluency read slowly, word by word, focusing on decoding words instead of comprehending meaning.
- Learning the meaning and pronunciation of words, or **vocabulary development.** Children need to actively build and expand their knowledge of written and spoken words, what they mean and how they are used.
- Acquiring strategies to understand, remember, and communicate what is read, or **reading comprehension strategies.** Children need to be taught comprehension strategies, or the steps good readers use to make sure they understand text. Students who are in control of their own reading comprehension become purposeful, active readers.

Based on the findings of the NRP, the U.S. Department of Education published indicators of effective literacy programs (2003). The indicators for effective reading programs are not narrow and prescriptive, but rather can be accomplished using a number of different scheduling structures. As noted in Figure 6.2, we should emphasize sustained periods of instruction, including time each day when students read silently and aloud. Quality reading programs focus on assessment for the purpose of informing instructional decisions. In addition, we must teach skills and strategies at the letter, word, and text level. We accomplish this through connections between reading and writing.

Figure 6.2 Components of a Quality Reading Program (*Source: U.S. Department of Education, Office of Intergovernmental and Interagency Affairs, Educational Partnerships and Family Involvement Unit. (2003). Reading tips for parents. Washington, DC: Author. Used with permission.*)

Components of a Quality Reading Program

- Every teacher is excited about reading and promotes the value and fun of reading to students.
- All students are carefully evaluated, beginning in kindergarten, to see what they know and what they need to become good readers.
- Reading instruction and practice lasts 90 minutes or more a day in first, second, and third grades and 60 minutes a day in kindergarten.
- All students in first, second, and third grades who are behind in reading get special instruction and practice. These students receive, throughout the day, a total of 60 extra minutes of instruction.
- Before- or after-school help is given to all students beyond first grade who need extra instruction or who need to review skills. Summer school is available for students who are behind at the end of the year.
- Reading instruction and practice includes work on letters, sounds, and blending sounds. Students learn to blend letters and sounds to form new words.
- Learning new words and their meaning is an important part of instruction.
- Students have daily spelling practice and weekly spelling tests.
- The connection between reading and writing is taught on a daily basis. Students write daily. Papers are corrected and returned to the students. By the end of second grade, students write final copies of corrected papers. Corrected papers are sent home for parents to see.
- All students have a chance to read both silently and aloud in school each day and at home every night.
- Every classroom has a library of books that children want to read. This includes easy books and books that are more difficult.
- The school library is used often and has many books. Students may check books out during the summer and over holidays.

Figure 6.3   Teaching Reading to English Language Learners (*Source: Copyright 2006 by the National Council of Teachers of English. Used with permission.*)

Strategies to Teach Reading to English Language Learners

- Use culturally relevant reading materials.
- Connect readings with students' background knowledge and experiences.
- Encourage students to discuss the readings, including the cultural dimensions of the text.
- Have students read a more accessible text on the topic before reading the assigned text.
- Ask families to read with students a version in the heritage language.
- Replace discrete skill exercises and drills with many opportunities to read.
- Provide opportunities for silent reading in either the students' first language or in English.
- Read aloud frequently to allow students to become familiar with and appreciate the sounds and structures of written language.
- Read aloud while students have access to the text to facilitate connecting oral and written modalities.
- Stimulate students' content knowledge of the text before introducing the text.
- Teach language features, such as text structure, vocabulary, and text- and sentence-level grammar to facilitate comprehension of the text.
- "Frontload" comprehension via a walk through the text or a preview of the main ideas.
- Do pre-reading activities that elicit discussion of the topic.
- Teach key vocabulary essential for the topic.
- Recognize that experiences in writing can be used to clarify understanding of reading.
- Recognize that first and second language development increases with abundant reading and writing.

Select a page or two of text that you are about to use with your students. Which words are most important to teach? Why?

In teaching English language learners, we assume that these quality program indicators are in place. Teachers must understand the components of reading instruction (Figure 6.1) as well as the components of a quality reading program (see Figure 6.2). The National Council of Teachers of English also identified specific strategies for teaching reading to English language learners (see Figure 6.3). Word learning plays a critical role in students' reading development. Students need to know a number of types of words, which we will review first. Then, we'll look inside several classrooms at instructional approaches teachers have taken to develop students' word knowledge and thus reading skills in English.

Research in Focus: Independent Reading and Vocabulary

Research on vocabulary instruction suggests that one very effective way for improving students' word knowledge is to provide students time to engage in extensive amounts of independent reading.

The amount of free reading done outside of school has consistently been found to relate to growth in vocabulary, reading comprehension, verbal fluency, and general information (Anderson, Wilson, & Fielding, 1988; Greaney, 1980; Guthrie & Greaney, 1991). Students who read independently become better readers, score higher on achievement tests in all subject areas, and have greater content knowledge than those who do not (Krashen, 1993; Cunningham & Stanovich, 1991; Stanovich & Cunningham, 1993).

Similarly, Scott and Nagy (1994) summarize the evidence on the relationship between reading and vocabulary. In their words, "to promote the goal of learning a large number of different words, independent reading should be encouraged as a regular and significant part of each school day" (p. 1242).

Vocabulary

"When I use a word," Humpty Dumpty said in a rather scornful tone, "it means just what I choose it to mean—neither more nor less." —Lewis Carroll, Through the Looking Glass

Vocabulary has been found to be one of the greatest predictors of reading comprehension, an even stronger predictor than cognitive ability (Farley & Elmore, 1992). In this section we will discuss the different types of vocabulary and look at effective ways to develop students' lexicon. As you read and think about how to incorporate explicit instruction of vocabulary into your daily teaching, remember that, while an instructional focus on vocabulary is especially important when teaching ELLs, it is only one of five components necessary for students to learn to read. Although without an adequate bank of words students will never reach proficiency in English, many other factors contribute to communicative competence.

When talking about vocabulary, we often talk about *brick* and *mortar* words (Dutro & Moran, 2003). *Bricks* refer to those content-specific words that express the big ideas we are teaching. In early grades these are often nouns such as *plant, number, pilgrim,* whereas in upper grades and secondary school, they tend to be more conceptual or words that are related to those concepts—*government,*

Look at a piece of text you are planning to use with your students. Find the brick words. Find some mortar words that your ELLs might not know.

photosynthesis, stem, equation, estimate. These are typically the words that are the focus of most vocabulary instruction. *Mortar* words are the general-utility words that we use to string the bricks together in meaningful sentences, the words that demonstrate relationships among the key words and ideas. They include prepositions and conjunctions such as *from, before, in addition to;* verbs such as *go, speak, work, circle, underline;* and general academic words such as *analyze, compare, suggest, design, establish*. (See the Teacher Tools at the end of this book for a list of some of the most commonly used general academic words.) In chapter 7, as we discuss how to integrate language and content, we will look further at how to identify important vocabulary, whether brick or mortar, and we will look at some of the ways in which vocabulary can pose specific challenges for our English language learners.

High Frequency or Sight Words. Approximately 50–75% of all words used in schoolbooks, library books, newspapers, and magazines are in the Dolch Basic Sight Vocabulary of 220 words (1936). Many of these words cannot be sounded out because they do not follow decoding rules. Table 6.2 contains a listing of the Dolch words and the approximate age/grade at which students typically recognize the words. It is important to note that the age/grade notation is based on a student's ability to sight *read* the word, not write it. It is also important to remember that the grade levels for these words were based on native English speakers. English language learners, even older ELLs, may not automatically recognize these sight words, and therefore we must teach them.

A *podcast* is a method of publishing audio files to the Internet, allowing users to subscribe to a feed and receive new files automatically by subscription, usually at no cost.

Root Words. The English language derives words from languages all over the world. Other words like *podcast* enter our language because they represent a new concept. However, most of the words in the English language are derivatives of Latin and Greek. Teaching some of the more common Latin and Greek root words gives students a transportable set of strategies to use as they encounter new words. For example, when a student knows that *therm* means *heat*, she can use that information to figure out both the spelling and meaning of *thermometer, thermal, thermos,* and *thermostat*. A list of common Latin and Greek root words can be found in Table 6.3.

Affixes. Prefixes, which come before the root word, and suffixes, which come after, are together referred to as affixes. Affixes modify the root word to further refine the exact definition. For example, in the word *disrespectful, dis-* is the prefix and—*ful* is the suffix. These basic affixes are highly transportable within the language. In fact, five basic suffixes make up more than 50% of the prefixes used, while four suffixes make up 65% of the suffixes used (Cunningham, 2002). By teaching these affixes alone within a spelling curriculum, students can utilize them to spell thousands of words. A list of these and other common affixes can be seen in Figure 6.4.

Cohesion Devices. Cohesion devices, like signal words, help link sentences together to make a comprehensive, or cohesive, whole. They are generally

Table 6.2

Dolch Sight Vocabulary Words				
Preprimer	**Primer**		**First**	**Second**	**Third**
a	all	please	after	always	about
and	am	pretty	again	around	better
away	are	ran	an	because	bring
big	at	ride	any	been	carry
blue	ate	saw	as	before	clean
can	be	say	ask	best	cut
come	black	she	at	both	done
down	brown	so	by	buy	draw
find	but	soon	could	call	drink
for	came	that	every	cold	eight
funny	did	there	fly	does	fall
go	do	they	from	don't	far
help	eat	this	give	fast	full
here	four		going	first	got
I	get		had	five	grow
in	good		has	found	hat
is	have		her	gave	hold
it	he		him	goes	if
little	into		his	green	keep
look	like		how	its	kind
make	must		jump	made	laugh
me	new		just	many	light
my	no		know	off	long
not	now		let	or	much
one	on		live	pull	myself
play	our		may	read	never
red	out		old	right	only

(continued)

Table 6.2   (continued)

Dolch Sight Vocabulary Words					
Preprimer	**Primer**		**First**	**Second**	**Third**
run	too	what	once	sing	own
said	under	white	open	sit	pick
see	want	who	over	sleep	seven
the	was	will	put	tell	shall
three	well	with	round	their	show
to	went	yes	some	these	six
two			stop	those	small
up			take	upon	start
we			thank	us	ten
where			them	use	today
yellow			then	very	together
you			think	wash	try
			walk	which	
			warm	why	
			were	wish	
			when	work	
				would	
				write	
				your	

How would you define/explain the following words to an ELL: *but, it, if?*

what we think of as easy little words, though rather difficult to define outside of a context without using words that the ELL student may not know. For example, the online dictionary, dictionary.com, defines *it* as: "used to refer to that one previously mentioned." Halliday and Hasan (1976) identified five types of cohesion devices found in English, words or phrases that typically do not cause problems for native English speakers but whose meaning may elude an English language learner, causing them to miss the main idea of the text or to write text that does not flow well. As you read the following examples, you will find the text easy to comprehend. Think about the examples in two ways. First, as a reader of text in an unfamiliar language—would

Table 6.3

Common Latin and Greek Root Words		
Root	**Meaning**	**Examples**
aer	air	aerial, aeronautical
aster/astr	star	astronomical, asterisk
auto	self	automatic, autograph
bio	life	biography, biology
chron	time	chronicle, synchronous
derm	skin	epidermis, pachyderm
fac, fact	to make; to do	factory, facsimile
fer	to carry	transfer, ferry
gram	written	grammar, diagram
graph	to write	biography, graphic
hydr	water	hydrant, hydroponics
logo	reason	logic, epilogue
meter	measure	metric, thermometer
micro	small	microscope, microwave
mono	one	monastery, monotonous
par	get ready	prepare, repair
port	to carry	airport, export
phon	sound	telephone, phonics
photo	light	photograph, photosynthesis
stat	to stand	status, station
tech	art; skill	technology, technical
therm	heat	thermometer, thermal
vid, vis	to see	video, vision

Sources: Bear, D. R., Invernizzi, M., Templeton, S., & Johnston, F. (2004). Greek word roots (p. 274). Words their way: Word study for phonics, vocabulary, and spelling instruction (3rd ed.). Upper Saddle River, NJ: Pearson Merrill/Prentice Hall. Blachowicz, C., & Fisher, P. J. (2002). The most common Latin words in the vocabulary of children (p. 196). Teaching vocabulary in all classrooms (2nd ed.). Upper Saddle River, NJ: Merrill/Prentice Hall.

Figure 6.4   Common Affixes

Prefixes		
	re-	*de-*
	dis-	*a-/an-*
	un-	*pro-*
	in-/im-	
Suffixes	*-s/-es*	*-tion/-sion*
	-ed	*-able/-ible*
	-ing	*-al*
	-en	*-ness*
	-ly	*-er/-est*
	-er/-or	*-ful/-less*

Students engaged in word study
Hope Madden/Merrill

these devices cause you to pause and reread or question to clarify meaning, slowing down your reading or listening. And second, as a writer of text in an unfamiliar language—would you be likely to use these devices? Or would you be more likely to repeat words, causing your writing to sound awkward, wordy, or redundant?

Reference. In the following text selection, the word *it* refers to *I'm sorry* the first time it is used. In the third sentence, the word *it* refers to when the main character answered the telephone two pages earlier. In this case, the same word is used as a reference to two completely different things.

I say, "Sure, Frosty. I'm sorry."

Actually I'm not really sorry, but people usually stop being mad at me whenever I say <u>it</u>.

Frosty says, "Just don't do <u>it</u> again." (Trueman, 2003, p. 37)

References are words, like *it*, that are used to refer to something else, usually something that was previously mentioned in the text. As in the passage above, that something else may have been mentioned far earlier, and the reader must be able to recall it. References are often pronouns, a part of speech that can cause difficulty for even those non-native speakers of English who are considered to be proficient. They include words such as *this, that, those, his, ours, theirs,* words that native English speakers, including those who might be considered struggling readers or writers, recognize easily.

Substitution. In the sentence that follows, the reader must recognize that the word *ones* has been substituted for the word *tulips.*

> She was saying she liked red tulips and I was saying I liked yellow <u>ones</u>. (Williams, 1982)

Common words used in substitution include *do, one,* and *the same.*

Ellipsis. Kindergarten ELL students wrote the following sentences during their interactive writing time: *We like ice cream. We like cookies. We like cake.*

They have not yet learned to use the cohesion device of ellipsis, an omission in the text, a way of expressing ideas without repeating words. If they had, they might have written:

> We like ice cream, cookies, and cake.
> Some schools require uniforms. <u>Ours</u> <u>doesn't</u>.

In the second sentence the word *school* has been omitted, as have the words *require uniforms.* This sentence actually contains two cohesion devices—the word *ours* is a substitution for *our school.* ELLs may comprehend the first sentence, but not recognize that there are missing words in the second sentence and simply skip over it, missing a significant idea. In their own writing, they may sound more like the kindergartners writing about what they like to eat—*Some schools require uniforms. Our school doesn't require uniforms*—unnecessarily redundant.

Lexical Chain.

> I'm sitting in the <u>sun</u> even though it's the <u>hottest</u> part of the day, the part that makes the streets <u>dizzy</u>, when the <u>heat</u> makes a little hat on the top of your head and <u>bakes</u> the dust and weed grass and <u>sweat</u> up good, all <u>steamy</u> and smelling like sweet corn. (Cisneros, 1991, p. 4)

Lexical chains are a type of cohesive device that enhances both style and meaning. The underlined words in this passage are linked by the idea they convey—a hot, steamy day. They give us a visual image of the writer's message and thereby help us to understand the larger meaning. It is not necessary to be

As you read this section, examine a piece of text you are planning to use. Look for examples of the types of cohesion devices discussed here. How will you know if your ELLs understand these words?

able to use lexical chains in our writing, but they certainly enhance the style and reinforce the meaning. English language learners may not have the variety of vocabulary necessary to create this type of writing.

Conjunctions.

> The light was red, so the car . . .
> Although the light was red, the car . . .
> The light was red, but the car . . .
> Because the light was red, the car . . . (Gibbons, 1991, p. 84)

How do you know what word(s) would make sense to complete the sentence?

Each of these sentences has a different meaning because of one little word—*so, although, but, because*—a little word that allows you to predict the end of each statement. Conjunctions are words or phrases that link ideas. They fall into four categories:

Additive: words that add on to the ideas
and, or also, in addition, furthermore, besides, similarly, likewise
Adversative: words that express opposite or difference
but, yet, however, instead, on the other hand, nevertheless
Causal: words that express cause and effect
so, consequently, because, for this reason
Continuative: words that continue the same idea
now, of course, after all

As we saw in the examples of the stoplight, conjunctions can carry much of the meaning in the text. Conjunctions are one type of device that allows us to predict what follows in the text. They not only join thoughts but they can provide a clue or a signal to what we should be looking for as we continue reading.

Signal Words. Signal words are examples of cohesion devices that tell us to look for a certain kind of information when we are reading. They are words that are required to construct complex sentences when we are writing or speaking.

As we discussed earlier, conjunctions such as *because, before, therefore,* and prepositions such as *under, next to, in front of,* carry much of the meaning in a sentence. For students who are unfamiliar with the language, it can be helpful to know that, when you see a certain word or phrase, *consequently,* for instance, it is a signal to look for a certain kind of information, in this case, an effect of the cause previously described. Table 6.4 lists some of the signal words that are key to both reading comprehension and academic writing.

Content Vocabulary. These are the technical words associated with specific disciplines and are typically only used in one field of study. *Senate* in social studies, *photosynthesis* in science, and *pi* in mathematics are all examples of technical vocabulary because they have only one meaning and are associated with only one content area.

Table 6.4

Cognitive Process, Language Function, and Signal Words				
Cognitive Process	**Language Function**	**Signal Words by Proficiency Level**		
		Beginning	**Intermediate**	**Advanced**
Sequencing events	• Relate steps in a process • Express time relationships, including several actions within a larger event • Give/follow multi-step directions	First Second Next Later Then	While Before Now After Finally For the past . . .	Prior to Previously Since Eventually Subsequently
Describing things	• Describe attributes • Tell or write about something	Can Has/have Is/are	Usually Often Occasionally	Tend to Generally Consists of
Describing location	• Following or giving directions in a game, procedure, movement • Directing someone to find something	Next to Around Behind Above Under	To the left, right of Between In front of In back of In the middle of Below	Located in, on Situated near Beside
Compare	• Understand and express how two or more things are similar and how they are different	Like Are the same because . . . Both _____er, _____est	Just like Are similar because . . . Compared to	Just as Are similar in that . . . By comparison
Contrast	• Understand and express how two or more things are different	But However Unlike _____er than	In contrast On the other hand Differences between	Whereas As opposed to A distinction between . . .
Identifying cause and effect	• Explain the cause of an outcome	Because Because of So	If . . . then . . . For that reason	Consequently Due to This led to

(continued)

Table 6.4   (continued)

Cognitive Function	Language Function	Signal Words		
		Beginning	**Intermediate**	**Advanced**
Summarizing	• Express why something occurred • Express the main points of a passage or story in a brief and factual way	Because But Then	In summary In short To conclude In conclusion	Consequently Therefore
Drawing conclusions	• Use evidence to draw a conclusion	Because So	Since	Consequently As a result of
Generalizing	• Make an overall statement based on evidence	All Many Most	Almost all Mostly Often	Nearly all Generally

Source: Adapted from Dutro, S. (2005). Questions teachers are asking about courses of study for secondary English language learners. The California Reader, *39(1), 45–58. Used with permission.*

Used by permission of Harcourt, Inc.

Most textbooks and curricula that you use will identify the content or technical words. Frey and Fisher (2006) developed criteria, based on their review of research, for selecting content vocabulary worth teaching. Answering the questions in Table 6.5 will allow you to differentiate your instruction based on the specific terms that your students need to know and that they will be likely to use in the future. As an example, during a fourth-grade unit on people who have made a difference, Ms. Nguyen read aloud *Harvesting Hope: The Story of Cesar Chavez* (Krull, 2003). She focused on the vocabulary words *family, fighting, conflicts, organized, cause, obstacle,* and *compassionate* because they were words that would have lasting impact through the unit. She did not focus on *coaxing, cabin,* or *announcement* because they were words used once in the book and would not likely be used again in this unit of study.

Table 6.5

Considerations for Selecting Vocabulary Words	
Considerations for Selecting Vocabulary to Teach	**Questions to Ask**
Representative	Is the concept represented by the word critical to understanding the piece?
Repeatability	Will the word be used again during the school year?
Transportable	Will the word be used in other subject areas?
Contextual Analysis	Can students use context clues to determine meaning?
Structural Analysis	Can students use structural analysis to determine meaning?
Cognitive Load	Have I identified too many words?

Source: Frey, N., & Fisher, D. (2006). Language arts workshop: Purposeful reading and writing instruction. *Upper Saddle River, NJ: Merrill/Prentice Hall. Used with permission.*

Academic Vocabulary. Averil Coxhead compiled a list of the 570 most frequent words used across a range of academic contexts. These are not words that are included in the 2000 most frequent words in English, such as *the, in,* and *about,* rather they are of general academic utility—words such as *occur, analyze, define,* and *create.* An adaptation of the academic word list can be found in the Teacher Tools at the end of the book.

In a literature selection in one high school anthology, the "Words to Know" section listed *impersonal, entity, edifice, nuance,* and *gaunt* (McDougal-Littell, 2006, pp. 242–243). Within those same two pages, we also find the words *survive, considerable,* and *perspective,* academic words included in Coxhead's list. Perhaps the authors assumed that students will already know these words, or that they are not key to understanding the selection. If we analyze the text for language use, and we know our students well, we might determine that our ELLs do not know these words and that this is an opportunity to teach vocabulary that crosses disciplines, vocabulary that students are likely to encounter in a variety of contexts. Of the words selected by the publisher as key words, only *entity* is found on Coxhead's Academic Word List. Of the other "Words to Know," *impersonal* might be a word that provides an opportunity to teach a word analysis strategy, using prefixes to help students arrive at meaning. *Edifice, nuance,* and *gaunt* are certainly words that enrich our students' lexicon; yet, given the frequency of use of the other words, given the notion that learning a word requires multiple exposures over time, given the limited amount of time that we have with our students, we must ask ourselves, "Which are the words that will be of most value?"

The complete list can be found on Coxhead's Web site at *http://www.vuw.ac.nz/lals/research/awl/index.html.*

Look at a piece of text you are planning to use. Find the general academic words that can be found across content areas.

Spotlight on Instruction

An Interactive Word Wall

Ms. Cole uses a word wall to introduce and reinforce her kindergarteners' knowledge of words. She starts with the high-frequency sight words that her students are learning. But word walls are not just for young students. We believe that every classroom should be a print-rich environment in which students can use the environmental print in their reading and writing. However, simply having a word wall is not sufficient. Students must be taught to use the word wall.

Ms. Cole devotes between five and ten minutes every day to word wall activities (Cunningham, Hall, & Sigmon, 1999). The words are added to the wall gradually—only five or so a week. The idea is to spend time teaching those words well. Word walls for younger children are often arranged alphabetically or by rime patterns. Figure 6.5 is a photograph of Ms. Cole's word wall. Word walls for older students are often arranged thematically based on the specific units of study, such as momentum, the Civil War, or fractions.

Cunningham, Hall, and Sigmon (1999) have other suggestions for using the word wall, including:

- *On the Back*—The teacher shares a number of sentences featuring word wall words, and the students write down the word wall words they hear being used.
- *Add an Ending*—Students create new words by adding a suffix to word wall words.
- *Add a Beginning*—Students create new words by adding a prefix to word wall words.

Figure 6.5 Kindergarten Word Wall *(Doug Fisher)*

- *Chant, Clap, Cheer, Write, Check*—In unison the children chant, clap, and cheer the spelling of some number of word wall words as determined by the teacher, then write the words on paper and check them against the word wall for accuracy.

Nancy Frey, teaching ninth-grade English, uses her word wall in a weekly word wall bingo game. She gives students blank bingo forms and instructs them to write words from the word wall into any of the squares they want. She then calls words until one of the students earns a bingo!

Another classwide use of the word wall is known as non-negotiable words. In every piece of student writing, the teacher expects all of the word wall words to be spelled correctly. When students submit papers with word wall words spelled incorrectly, the teacher returns the paper and asks the student to find the word wall word that is not correct.

Word learning strategies

There are at least 50 research-based ways to provide vocabulary instruction for students (e.g., Brassell & Flood, 2004; Tompkins & Blanchfield, 2004). We will review some of the more common vocabulary instructional approaches used with English language learners, understanding that there are many more and that students tire of the same instructional strategies used over and over again.

> Select one of the word learning strategies listed and think about how you might use it with your students.

Barrier Games. These are communication games in which students use their vocabulary words to describe actions to a partner. The partner cannot see what is being described and must rely on the verbal information being shared. For example, in a biology class, pairs of students may be asked to assemble their dissection trays. One student can see the correct placement of each item and the other cannot. Using content terms such as *scalpel*, *forceps*, and *probes* and direction words (mortar words) such as *near*, *next to*, or *to the left of*, one student describes to the other (who cannot see the tray) how to complete the task. Barrier games reinforce language use and interactions in the classroom (Fagan & Prouty, 1997).

List-Group-Label. This instructional strategy is designed to help students identify words based on a topic, group those words into meaningful categories, identify labels for those categories, and then find additional words or categories as they read, watch a film, or participate in an instructional unit of study (Taba, 1967). The procedure is fairly straightforward. First, students brainstorm all of the words they know associated with a specific topic. For example, what do you think about when you hear the word *revolution*? Once the list has been generated, students group the words. Finally, each group is labeled. When the list-group-label has been completed, students can add words or groups, or even relabel groups of words, based on new information they gain as they engage with the topic.

Vocabulary Journals. Students need a place to collect information about all of the words they learn. Vocabulary journals are a versatile tool for students to do just that (Graves & Slater, 1996). There are a number of vocabulary journals and formats, but English language learners will benefit significantly from journals that allow them to focus on multiple meaning words. A sample vocabulary journal page can be found in Table 6.6.

Table 6.6

Sample Vocabulary Journal			
Word	**Common Definition**	**Math Definition**	**Where I Found It**
Prime	The best	A number that can only be divided by itself and 1	Poster on the wall
Set	Put someplace	A range of numbers	p. 19
Factor	A part of	Numbers that form a product	p. 22
Balance	Even on both sides or a scale	Make the equation equal on both sides of the equal sign	Lecture
Pi	???	Ratio of the circumference to the diameter of a circle; approximately equal to 3.14	p. 30

See chapter 7 for a discussion about the components of an effective interactive Read Aloud.

Read Alouds. In addition to independent reading (see the *"Research in Focus: Independent Reading and Vocabulary"* box in this chapter), teacher Read Alouds are an effective way to build students' word knowledge (Beck & McKeown, 2001; Ulanoff & Pucci, 1999). Read Alouds are used to: (1) provide students an opportunity to listen to connected texts, often text that is more difficult than they can read alone; (2) introduce new words and concepts in context; (3) build background knowledge on a topic; and (4) introduce students to various text patterns, structures, and features. Table 6.7 contains a portion of a text and the words the teacher used to discuss the text, from *Star of Fear, Star of Hope* (Hoestlandt, 1993).

Semantic Feature Analysis. Like concept maps, which are discussed in chapter 7, semantic feature analysis charts are another instructional strategy useful for helping students understand relationships between and among words (Pittleman, Heimlich, Berglund, & French, 1991). Using a matrix students list examples of the targeted vocabulary word or key concept in the left column. Across the rows, they list characteristics of the word or concept. They then decide if each specific example has the characteristic. For example, during a fourth-grade study of geography and geographic features, the class created the semantic feature analysis found in Table 6.8.

Vocabulary Cards. To create vocabulary cards, give students a set of 4-by-6 or 5-by-7 index cards and instruct them to divide each into four quadrants

Table 6.7

Read Aloud with Vocabulary Instruction	
What the Text Said	**What the Teacher Added**
In 1942, the north of France was invaded by the German army.	1942 was a long time ago, right? Invaded. Let's see. Since it's about the army, I think that the author is telling me that the Germans took over the land of northern France.
Madam Eleven O'Clock fled to the top floor in fear.	So, when you're really afraid, do you walk slowly? No, I didn't think so. So she fled— she left very quickly.
I fell asleep cuddled up against Mama and Papa, completely worn out.	Can you just see it? Cuddled—what a great word to add—she's just there all snug with her parents, finally feeling safe. Cuddled, all close and warm. But she's worn out. That's a funny term—but it just means that she's worked very hard and is tired.

Table 6.8

Semantic Feature Analysis for Geographic Regions of the USA								
Location	**Heavily Populated**	**Soil Used for Farming**	**Developed**	**Hot**	**Wildlife**	**Boats Used for Transportation**	**Tornadoes**	**Little Water**
Valleys/ Prairies	+	+	+	+	+	−	+	?
Mountains	−	−	?	−	+	−	−	−
Coast/ Beaches	+	−	+	?	+	+	−	−
Deserts	−	−	−	+	+	−	−	+
Forests	−	+	−	−	+	+	−	−
Swamps/ Wetlands	−	−	−	?	+	+	−	−

Source: Brassell, D., & Flood, J. (2004). Vocabulary strategies every teacher needs to know. San Diego, CA: Academic Professional Development. Used with permission.

(see Figure 6.6). For example, a seventh-grade teacher selected terms related to the prefix *mal-* meaning *bad*. Students created their vocabulary word cards for *malodorous, malcontent,* and *malevolent.* They write the target word in the top left quadrant. After class instruction, they record the definition in their own words in the upper right quadrant of the card. They write an antonym or something that the word does not mean in the lower right quadrant and draw an illustration or graphic symbol representing the term in the lower left quadrant. A sample student vocabulary card can be found in Figure 6.7.

Figure 6.6   Format for Vocabulary Card

Vocabulary word	Definition in student's own words
Illustration	Antonym or what it doesn't mean

Figure 6.7   Sample Student Word Card

Constructing vocabulary cards serves several uses (e.g., Frayer, Frederic, & Klausmeier, 1969; Bromley, 2002). First, the cards allow students to analyze a word's essential and nonessential features. In addition, vocabulary word cards provide students with examples and illustrations to help them remember the word. Further, when placed on a binder ring the cards become an accessible reference. The time involved in creating each card also provides an opportunity for the students to concentrate on the meaning, use, and representation of the term, thereby increasing the likelihood that the term will become a part of their permanent vocabulary.

Word Sorts. Students sort words that are chosen by the teacher based on commonalities, relationships, or other criteria. The goal is for students to develop an understanding of the nature of words (Bear, Invernizzi, Templeton, & Johnston, 1996). Word sorts activate students' background knowledge, develop students' understanding of word relationships, and encourage students to identify patterns in words. There are two kinds of sorts. In closed sorts, the teacher provides the categories. In open sorts, students create or identify the categories that make sense to them. For example, Table 6.9 contains a closed word sort on prefixes; Table 6.10 is an open sort on endangered species from a seventh-grade science class.

TEXT STRUCTURES AND FUNCTIONS

All students need to learn the rhetorical structures associated with storytelling and the various kinds of expository, or informational, writing in English. However, some students bring to this task culturally based text structures that contrast with those expected at school. The emphasis in mainstream English stories is on getting the order of events correct and clear. This emphasis can seem so obviously right to a monolingual speaker of English that the narrative of the Latino child, which emphasizes personal relationships more than plot, or of the Japanese child, who may provide very terse stories rather than recounting all of the events, can be dismissed at best as not meeting standards, or at worst as incomprehensible.

Different cultures focus on different aspects of an episode. Understanding a child's story requires knowing what information the child considers most

Table 6.9

Closed Sort on Prefixes		
de-	**mis-**	**per-**
detach	misinform	permit
deploy	misinterpret	perspire
deodorize	mispronounce	perforate
devoid	mistake	persuade
deflate		

Table 6.10

Open Sort on Endangered Species				
Characteristics and Types	**Breeding Areas**	**Causes of Extinction**	**Flight**	**Chicks**
vultures	caves	DDT	55 mph	57 days
10 ft wingspan	cliffs	poison	15,000 ft	pip
social	boxes	shooting	primaries	6 oz
scavengers		urbanization		crop
monogamous				mice

Source: Moss, B. (2003). 25 strategies for guiding readers through informational texts. *San Diego, CA: Academic Professional Development. Used with permission.*

important; such knowledge can help teachers guide students in acquiring the story structure valued at school. Similarly with expository writing, argument structures vary considerably across cultures. There is no best way to make a point. Different ways make sense in different cultures. The topic sentences, main ideas with supporting details, and compare-and-contrast essays that are staples of English prose may be more difficult to learn for students whose prior experience includes other ways of organizing ideas. Understanding the absence of some of these concepts, or the extremely differing conceptions in literacy traditions of other languages, is important to know how to teach students accepted ways to compose both expository and narrative text in English.

WRITING FOR ACADEMIC PURPOSES

Educators, parents, and policymakers alike lament the writing performance of American students. Newspapers and professional journals suggest that writing achievement in the United States has not changed appreciably in the past several decades. For example, of the 36 states or jurisdictions that participated in the 1998 and 2002 grade 8 writing National Assessment of Educational Progress (NAEP) assessments, only 16 showed score increases in 2002 (National Center for Educational Statistics, 2003).

As you read about these approaches to teaching writing, think about which approaches are best for each level of language proficiency. How might you scaffold each approach for students at different levels of proficiency?

We believe that one of the reasons for this lack of significant progress is that many teachers are unsure of how to teach writing. In addition, we believe (and the NAEP data confirms) that students today are given more writing assignments than ever. Unfortunately, these assignments are mostly in the form of independent writing prompts with little formal instruction. As Leif Fearn notes, "we are *causing* more writing than ever before." In other words, teachers are assigning more writing but are not necessarily teaching it. The National Council of Teachers of English identified strategies for teaching writing to English language learners (see

Figure 6.8   Teaching Writing to English Language Learners *(Source: Copyright 2006 by the National Council of Teachers of English. Used with permission.)*

Strategies to Teach Writing to English Language Learners

- Provide a nurturing environment for writing.
- Use collaborative writing activities that promote discussion.
- Promote peer interaction to support learning.
- Replace drills and single-response exercises with time for writing practice.
- Provide frequent meaningful opportunities for students to generate their own texts.
- Design writing assignments for a variety of audiences, purposes, and genres.
- Provide model papers and highlight specific aspects of the paper that make it well written.
- Provide feedback on student strengths and indicate areas where the student is meeting expectations.
- Provide explicit feedback (in written and in oral response). Begin with global comments (content and ideas, organization, thesis), then mechanical errors.
- Give more than one suggestion for change—allow students to maintain control of their writing.
- Talk explicitly about citation and plagiarism. Explore the cultural values implicit in the rules of plagiarism and textual borrowing. Note that not all cultures ascribe to the same rules and guidelines. Give students strategies to avoid plagiarism.

Figure 6.8). Our classroom observations, instructional experiences, and research reviews suggest that there are at least 10 instructional strategies every teacher needs to know and use to ensure that students can and do write well.

1. Language experience approach

For our younger readers or for readers who have yet to master the conventions of print, teachers use the Language Experience Approach (LEA) to demonstrate the speech to print connection (Ashton-Warner, 1959; Dixon & Nessel, 1983). Generally, this approach requires the students and teacher to have a discussion about a topic. It is helpful if the topic stems from a shared experience such as a field trip or from a visual. Once the group agrees on a sentence from their conversations, the teacher records the sentence in writing on chart paper, a dry erase board, or in students' journals. When they have written several sentences, the teacher guides the students through organizing these sentences into a paragraph. In this way, the teacher draws upon the shared experiences of the students to compose text.

This strategy can be used with the whole class, small groups, or individual students. Regardless of the group size, the conversation and oral language development occurs first and the writing second. In this way, students see how their talk becomes writing. It is particularly valuable for ELLs and is one of the most effective strategies for those at the earliest levels of proficiency, regardless of age.

These students may not yet be able to string words together in sentences, but they can generate words and phrases. When the teacher helps them to create sentences using their own words, they can read the sentences and more easily retain both the vocabulary and sentence structure.

For example, in a middle school classroom a group of students were talking with their teacher about the high school basketball team and their undefeated status. This small group had read an Internet page on the history of basketball. As the teacher focused their conversation, they agreed on the sentence, "Naismith invented basketball to keep kids out of trouble, not to make a lot of money," which the teacher wrote on a dry erase board. Each of the group members then copied their agreed-upon sentence into their journals and added two sentences on their own. Jamar wrote (corrected for spelling), "His idea was tight and now everybody plays. Hoover could beat the whole state."

Spotlight on Instruction

Language Experience Approach

Listen in as Mr. Velasco uses LEA to develop listening, speaking, reading, and writing with his first-grade class. First he has students talk about what they see in a picture, then they brainstorm relevant vocabulary words. He builds on that vocabulary and subsequently moves the talk into writing by having the students create sentences, extending their use of language through shared writing. Finally the students are able to read what they have written.

T: Before we start talking about the picture, I want you to look at the picture and think about what's going on. Look at everything. Take your time and think about what's happening in the picture.

As the children begin to talk, Mr. Velasco listens closely to their language and writes down what he hears them say.

S1: The girl is taking care of the dog.
S2: The . . . the . . . the boy and the girls, they were, they were, they were washing the dog, and the dog was washing the kids. They got all wet.
S3: The dog shaked.
S4: The girl, the girl and the boy was giving the dog a bath. The dog does . . . doesn't want it. So the dog just wanted to make them wet.
S5: But look at the boy!
T: What's happening with the boy? What's he feeling?
S3: Wet.
T: What's happening in their faces? What are they feeling?
S1: They're wet.
S2: They're laughing.
T: Look at the dog's face. How do you think the dog is feeling?

S2: Sad.

S5: Mad.

T: Leyla, you said, "I think the big girl is washing the dog." Victor, you said, "The girl is showering the dog." Tomás, you used the word *splashing.* What a great word! Do you know what this is called?

Points to the bathtub. Students shake their heads no.

T: Bathtub. Can you say bathtub?

Students repeat "bathtub."

T: What does bathtub start with?

Writes bathtub and sounds it out as she writes. Has students repeat. Repeats this process with "hose" and "towels."

T: What is the dog doing?

S (in unison): Shaking.

S5: Splashing.

As the students come up with vocabulary describing the action in the picture, Mr. Velasco writes each word on a Post-it note and asks the students to place it on the picture.

T: Let's read our words.

Students read the words together.

T: Show me the bathtub.

Students point to the bathtub.

T: Show me what splashing looks like.

Students make splashing movements.

T: Let's make a sentence. What do we want to say about what's happening in our picture? Let's use our new words.

S2: The girl is shaking.

T: The girl is shaking?

S4: No.

T: What is she doing?

S1: She's taking a bath and the dog is shaking.

T: You've got a lot of great ideas. Can I help you with your ideas? What is the girl doing to the dog?

S5: Watering.

T: Watering or washing?

S2: Washing.

Teacher writes sentences as he says them. He makes sure each student is watching.

T: OK. Here's our first sentence. What else is happening?

He points back to the picture with the vocabulary words written on Post-it notes.

S4: Towel.

T: What do you want to say about the towel?

S3: Towel dry.

T: The towels dry everybody.

He writes it on a sentence strip.

S1: The dog is mad.

T: Why?

S5: Because he no want to wash?

T: Because he doesn't want a bath?

S1: Yeah. That's my sentence.

S2: The dog is splashing to the girl and the boy because . . .

S5: The dog is splashing the kids because the dog don't like the bath.

Teacher writes: "The dog is splashing the kids because he doesn't like taking a bath."

Mr. Velasco finishes by praising the sentences, having each student hold one of the strips and read the sentence aloud. Then they switch sentence strips with a classmate and read a second sentence.

2. Interactive writing

Based on the Language Experience Approach (LEA), interactive writing allows the teacher to share the pen with students. Again, students have a discussion about a topic and then agree upon a sentence. The difference between LEA and interactive writing is who controls the pen. As stated before, in LEA the teacher writes while students watch. In interactive writing, students take turns collaboratively creating the message (e.g., McCarrier, Pinnell, & Fountas, 2000). Students complete the writing one word or phrase at a time while the teacher provides additional instruction. This instruction is vital in teaching students how writers make decisions about composition, layout, letter formation, punctuation, grammar, and vocabulary. Although interactive writing was first used with younger students, it is appropriate for older students as well because it provides explicit instruction of the ongoing editing process all writers engage in (Fisher & Frey, 2002).

In a third-grade classroom, the class was discussing a recent visit to the Museum of Art. The topic was focused on artists' use of light to highlight parts of their paintings. The students discussed different artists' work they had seen as well as the textures and styles they liked and didn't like. The teacher guided their conversation and they eventually agreed on the sentence, "Artists use light to focus attention, show perspective, and stress important points." As the first student approached the dry erase board to write the first word, the teacher said to the group, "What do all sentences start with?" to which the class responded "Capital letters!" As the third student approached the board to write the word *light*, the teacher asked her students, "Do you know any other words that use the *-ight* rime?" Several students named words including *fight*, *right*, and *sight*. Each time a word was completed, the class read the sentence as written thus far and then completed the remainder of the sentence from memory. This rehearsal allowed the teacher to initiate instruction about layout and punctuation. When a student spelled a word incorrectly (e.g., *atention*), the teacher asked another student to check and correct. This process continued until the entire sentence was written on the board. At that time, the students read the entire written sentence aloud and began to copy the sentence into their journals. As with LEA, this teacher asked them to use this as a topic sentence of a paragraph they would compose individually.

3. Writing models

Writing models provide students a framework for their writing. Some writing models are created by the teacher; others are based on books or other sources of print. For example, a teacher wrote the following on the board:

> I was walking home one afternoon when . . . I didn't know what to do, so I . . . When I tried to . . . Thankfully, . . . + 3 sentences

Students used this writing frame or model to incorporate their own ideas into a structure provided by the teacher. This level of support provides students an opportunity to incorporate their individual ideas into a structure that provides them a certain degree of success. Anthony responded to this prompt by writing the following (with spelling corrected):

> *I was walking home one afternoon when I was stopped by the cops. I didn't know what to do, so I started to run down the alley. When I tried to jump the fence, I saw a huge dog there. Thankfully, the dog was tied up. But, the cop was on the other side. They caught me. All they really wanted was to tell me was that I dropped a book when I crossed the street.*

We can also use writing models to teach students how to write a particular type of expository text such as cause and effect or compare and contrast. The sentence frames can be composed of particular language structures that are used to express that language function: "*As a result of . . . the gladiators in ancient Rome . . .*" Teachers can differentiate for different levels of language proficiency by using phrases that are more or less complex. (See Table 6.4 for examples of differentiated vocabulary to express a variety of language functions.)

In addition to these teacher-created writing models, books and other printed materials make excellent writing models. The book *Somewhere Today: A Book of Peace* (Thomas, 1998) is one such choice. Each page of the book contains a single sentence that starts with the phrase "Somewhere today." After reading the book aloud to students, a fourth-grade teacher asked each student to complete his or her own sentence starting with "Somewhere today . . ." The teacher then turned down the lights, lit a candle, and asked students to share what they had written so they could hear their work in spoken form. The students' individual sentences were then revised as a class poem. The teacher provided instruction about imagery, rhyme, and alliteration using the students' original writing.

ELLs may need numerous writing models.

4. Generative sentences

Also known as "given word sentences" (Fearn & Farnan, 2001, p. 87), this strategy allows students to focus at the sentence level. As many educators know, if students have difficulty composing a sentence, their writing will appear fragmented, incomplete, and amateurish.

In a generative sentences session, the teacher provides students with a word or phrase as well as a placement requirement for the sentence. For example, in a social studies classroom the teacher asked for the following sentences: one that contained *famine(s)* in the second position; one that contained *rights* in the fourth position; and one that contained *constitution* in the final position. Different students produced the following sentences:

Famine: Worldwide famines threaten peace because hungry people will fight for their lives.
When famine strikes a community, the world must respond.
Rights: The Bill of Rights provides guidance for how people should be treated.
When our human rights are threatened, we sue the oppressor.
Constitution: George W. Bush and his politics could destroy our Constitution.
When we need guidance related to our rights as citizens, we look to the Constitution.

Generative sentence sessions allow the teacher to assess both content knowledge and understanding of grammar and vocabulary. In this way, the teacher can provide instruction that is responsive to the needs of individuals or groups for their writing.

> Try it yourself. Select a key vocabulary word. Write sentences with that word in the second position, then in the third, then in the fourth.

Spotlight on Instruction

Teaching Grammar

Ms. Segal wanted to refocus her students' attention on verbs. She noticed that her fourth graders were making a number of errors in verb usage. She decided to read aloud Ruth Heller's (1988) book *Kites Sail High: A Book about Verbs.* The class listened as their teacher shared the text, which incorporated a number of verbs in a humorous and engaging way. Then she wrote some of the lines on sentence strips and invited students to choral read with her some of the rhyming lines. During her interactive writing lesson, students identified new ideas for the language chart as follows:

VERB	WHAT DOES?	OUR NEW IDEAS
bloom	roses	flowers
run	people	clock, nose
fly	pelicans	airplane, flies, birds

Following her Read Aloud, students participated in learning centers. At one center, students at early levels of proficiency were asked to illustrate the actions of singular and plural nouns such as "the bird flies" and "birds fly." At another center, students at intermediate levels of proficiency sorted word cards into two categories—verbs that show action and verbs that don't. At a third center, students at higher levels of proficiency completed a more complex word sort identifying the types of verbs, as follows:

LINKING VERBS	AUXILIARY VERBS	REGULAR VERBS	IRREGULAR VERBS
is	do	paint, painted	bite, bit
am	does	walk, walked	sink, sank
are	did		shrink, shrank
was	have		
were			
been			

All of these concepts were introduced in Ruth Heller's book. Ms. Segal ended the lesson with generative sentences in which students used regular and irregular verbs in sentences of their own. Her next lesson would focus on constructing sentences using different kinds of verbs. Students at the early levels of proficiency would be given a word bank of linking verbs to use in completing a cloze activity. Students with more proficiency in English would be asked to create sentences using auxiliary and irregular verbs.

Ms. Segal collected several of the grammar books for use with her students, including:

- Heller, R. (1987). *A cache of jewels and other collective nouns.* New York: Putnam Berkley Group.
- Heller, R. (1989). *Many luscious lollipops: A book about adjectives.* New York: Putnam Berkley Group.
- Heller, R. (1990). *Merry-go-round: A book about nouns.* New York: Putnam Berkley Group.
- Heller, R. (1995). *Behind the mask: A book about prepositions.* New York: Putnam Berkley Group.
- Heller, R. (1998). *Fantastic! Wow! And unreal! A book about interjections and conjunctions.* New York: Puffin.

5. Word pyramids

Another useful way to encourage students to explore their word knowledge for writing is through the use of word pyramids (Fearn & Farnan, 2001). This is a simple strategy in which the teacher gives each student a letter and the instructions to "make a word pyramid." Starting with the letter they were given, students write a two-letter word, followed by a three-letter word, a four-letter word, and so on. On some days, teachers provide students access to dictionaries under the condition that they know the meaning of each word they use, while other days students must create their pyramids from memory or students complete this task as partners. Regardless of the approach on a given day, our experience suggests that students "rack their brains," as one fifth grader said, to find good words. This exercise ensures that students think about different words they can use when they write. A sample word pyramid for the letter *N* included:

No

Not

Nail

Naked

Nature

Noticed

Nineteen

Napoleons

Narcissism

Try it yourself. Select a concept word, and create a pyramid first with one word, then two, then three, and so on.

The activity then moves to the sentence level. Students working in pairs or individually select words they have generated from the pyramid for use in sentences. This challenges writers to consider both semantic and syntactic elements to create accurate sentences.

Students can also create pyramids with phrases and sentences using a particular content word. Mr. Gonzalez gave his geometry students the word *area* and asked them to create a pyramid, first using *area* in a two-word phrase, then in a three-word phrase, then four, and so on.

6. Power Writing

Each of the strategies presented thus far is used in the overall writing curriculum and is not necessarily done on a daily basis. Power Writing, however, should be done daily. The goal of this strategy is to improve writing fluency (e.g., Kasper-Ferguson & Moxley, 2002). As Fearn and Farnan suggest, Power Writing is "a structured free-write where the objective is quantity alone" (2001, p. 501).

We recommend that students complete three 1-minute sessions each day. As we observed in a fifth-grade classroom, the teacher can make quite a ceremony out of this. Ms. Allen has students hold their writing instruments high in the air until she gives them the topic and then starts the timer. When the timer rings one minute later, students stop writing and count their words. Each and every time, Ms. Allen begins by saying, "Write as much as you can as well as you can" and then announces the topic. When the timer rings, she says, "Count your words and circle any words you think you have misspelled." They repeat this two times for a total of three 1-minute sessions. Students then graph their highest score on a piece of graph paper at the front of their writing notebooks. Ms. Allen often invites them to use their Power Writing for journal entries, for responses to essay questions later in the day, and for homework completion, during which they revise their writing and present it in complete paragraphs. Ms. Allen consults their Power Writing graphs as she confers with students because it provides students with a way to assess their own progress in writing.

The topics range from social studies content—*slavery, colonies,* or *government*—to the use of grammar such as *they're, their,* and *there.* Regardless of the topic or word provided, the goal is for students to write increasingly longer responses so that they have something to edit later in the day during the writer's workshop (e.g., Dorn & Soffos, 2001).

7. Found poems

Found poems are an excellent strategy for encouraging students to reread what they have written (or read) for a specific purpose. The found poem strategy can be used with just about any text—from the science textbook to students' own Power Writing. The task is to reread the selection and choose specific words and phrases that retell the text in an open verse poem format. For example, Jenny wrote the following poem based on her reading and summary writing of *Phineas Gage: A Gruesome but True Story About Brain Science* (Fleischman, 2002). The opening of her poem read:

> Phineas—the famous patient
>
> A family man—a good man
>
> Survived a rod—a tamping rod
>
> Through his skull—through his brain
>
> Phineas—the famous patient
>
> Became a horrible man—a gambler and cheat

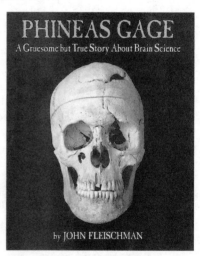

Jenny's found poem demonstrates her understanding of the text as well as her ability to select key ideas and arrange them in order to tell the story. This found poem assignment encouraged her to look for powerful words and phrases to convey the impact of this tragic event on Phineas' life.

8. RAFT

Too often students write for their teacher and do not consider the range of audience members who may be reading their writing. RAFT provides a scaffold for students as they explore their writing based on various roles, audiences, and formats (Santa & Havens, 1995). RAFT is an acronym for:

Cover from PHINEAS GAGE: A Gruesome but True Story About Brain Science. Copyright © 2002 by John Fleischman. Reprinted by permission of Houghton Mifflin Company. All rights reserved.

Role—what is the role of the writer?

Audience—to whom is the writer writing?

Format—what is the format for the writing?

Topic—what is the focus of the writing?

RAFT prompts can be used for a variety of purposes, from teaching perspective in writing to assessing student understanding of a book. For example, in a unit of study on the various Cinderella stories around the world, the teacher read aloud the picture book *Rough Face Girl* (Martin, 1992) and asked students to respond to the following RAFT:

R	Cinderella
A	Rough-Face Girl
F	Letter
T	Our stepsisters

This allowed the teacher to determine whether or not the students understood the similarities and differences between the Cinderella stories they had examined thus far in the unit. In addition, these writers assumed a point of view from the perspective of the protagonists in the tales.

The usefulness of RAFT writing is not limited to narrative texts. Ms. Diaz, a computer technology and business applications teacher, uses the RAFT format to teach students how to apply for jobs. Using an ad for a student clerk position that at least one student will be selected to do, Ms. Diaz asks her students to type their responses to the following:

R	a student at John Adams Middle School
A	Ms. Renee Garcia, Vice Principal
F	Business letter
T	I want the student clerk job!

> Think of a RAFT you could assign to extend learning in a unit you plan to teach.

Through this assignment, these students participate in an authentic writing experience that consolidates their knowledge of the business letter format, the job specifications, and the word processing technology. A number of RAFT prompts, along with their associated language function, can be found in Table 6.11.

9. Writing to learn

In addition to learning to write, students must write to learn. As noted by at least one student, "I didn't know what I thought until I had to write it down." Writing to learn prompts are a powerful way to encourage students to think—to think about the content they are studying. Different from process writing, in which the teacher returns the paper with corrections and the student resubmits the paper, writing to learn papers allow students to clarify their thinking and teachers to assess what students do and do not understand.

Fisher and Frey (2003) provide a number of writing to learn prompts such as:

- Yesterday's news—a review of class from the previous day
- Crystal ball—a prediction of what might come next
- Best thing I learned—a summary or analysis of the best part of class
- Exit slip—a written review of the class completed before leaving the room

Regardless of the prompt, the goal of writing to learn activities is to encourage students to think (Jenkinson, 1988). These writing prompts provide

Table 6.11

RAFT Prompts				
Role	**Audience**	**Format**	**Topic**	**Language Function**
Inventor	Consumers	TV commercial	The wheel	Persuade
Hotel owner	Prospective travelers	Travel brochure	The Gold Rush	Describe
Gardner	Apprentice	Instruction manual	Photosynthesis	Sequence
Prospective employer	Character in a story	Interview	Character traits	Ask questions
Journalist	Newspaper readers	Eyewitness account	Survivor of a volcanic eruption	Sequence using past tense
Writer of the Constitution	Voters	Venn diagram	Forms of government	Compare and contrast
A coordinate	A point	Letter	Slope	Explain
A cell	Children	Game	Mitosis	Describe

Source: Adapted from: Pritchard, R. (2004). Differentiating instruction to develop strategic readers and learners. Presentation for San Diego State University Reading/Language Arts Conference. San Diego, CA. Used with permission.

students with the space and time necessary for them to consider new information, make connections with information, predict new information, and summarize what they have learned.

10. Independent writing assignments

Independent writing is the goal of all of our writing instruction. We want to show students how to respond to prompts in thoughtful ways. Further, we want to ensure that our students can write for a variety of purposes and audiences. The writing instruction we have reviewed thus far ensures that students will be able to do so.

The final instructional strategy involves the creation of independent writing prompts. Prompts are developed for specific writing purposes. For example, expository prompts might require students to explain a procedure or explain a phenomenon. Narrative prompts provide students the opportunity to recount

Students must learn to write and write to learn
Doug Fisher

or tell events from books they have read, their own life, or their imagination. Finally, persuasive prompts require students to convince or persuade someone to do or believe something.

Writing good prompts is key. In creating prompts, we often focus on things that matter to students—things that they care about enough to write about. Similarly, we often attempt to incorporate youth and popular culture into our prompts (e.g., Alvermann, Moon, & Hagood, 1999). Examples of prompts that connect to lives of students include:

- Describe your ideal crib (house, apartment, or other living area).
- In a letter to the principal, persuade him to maintain or eliminate the school uniform policy.
- Relate the school motto to your life.

In response to the school motto prompt, a student at John Adams Middle School in Albuquerque, who is identified as having a behavioral disability, wrote:

"Teach me respect, responsibility, and lifelong learning" is our school motto. In the following essay, I will try to express what it means to me.

First of all, respect means to me to treat others how you want to be treated. Have respect for your elders and people around you. That means not to cuss people out, no talking back to teachers, no fighting, bugging, or picking on people. That's what respect means to me.

Responsibility means to do your chores and remember to feed your dog. Be responsible for doing your homework. Be responsible for your actions and bad actions. Be responsible for getting up in the morning and being on time for school. Be responsible for studying for school and tests, and using good language not bad language. That's what responsibility means to me.

Lifelong learning means to get to know new things forever. It means doing your work in class and accomplishing goals. You need to learn to read so you can read books, newspapers and applications to get a job. You need a good attitude to learn new things. You will have goals all your life.

I think our school motto is a good motto. It will teach you to be a good person and help you accomplish your goals. Respect and responsibility will help you use good manners. Responsibility will keep you on track. Lifelong learning will help you through your whole life.

These 10 writing instructional strategies are useful as teachers provide instruction for their students. However, these strategies do not provide for the curriculum planning and pacing that we need to consider. In addition, there are multiple assessment and feedback systems, including student grading and statewide writing tests. Teaching writing is a complex task—at least as complex as teaching reading. Simply assigning more writing will not ensure that our students become skilled writers and thinkers. Our students need and deserve quality instruction as they hone their craft, express their ideas, dreams, and beliefs, and understand that their words can change the world.

Spotlight on Instruction

Academic Language: From Listening to Speaking to Writing

To help her students become comfortable with writing, Ms. Yarr has created a classroom routine in which students first talk with a partner or small group of peers about their ideas. Talking with a partner or in a small group provides students the time to think through the concepts and rehearse the language. This process of talking in groups also prepares students to share their findings and ideas with others using more explicit language, which then prepares them to write using more academic language.

Once they have talked with their peers, each student or group makes a brief oral presentation or reports information back to the teacher. This allows Ms. Yarr to model increasingly complex academic language, language she would like students to use in their writing. For example, when Yafet said, "The frog, it was green," Ms. Yarr replied, "Yes, as a matter of fact the frog was green."

Once students have had the opportunity to share their thinking aloud with the larger group, they write their responses on paper and commit to their ideas. Ms. Yarr can then use their writing as data for her students' instructional needs. This process is represented visually in Figure 6.9.

Figure 6.9   Classroom Routine Moving from Speech to Print

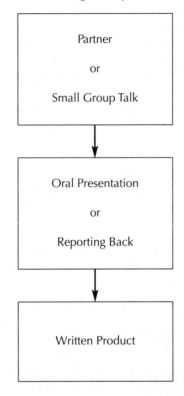

TEACHING GRAMMAR

As with all language instruction, we can best teach grammar in context (see the Spotlight on Instruction box, "Teaching Grammar"). We recommend analyzing student work to identify the types of errors students are making, and determining a focus for grammar instruction based on prioritizing these errors. You can then design mini-lessons using actual student writing and working together to practice the grammatical structure. Student work alone, however, is not sufficient to teach our students everything they need to know about grammar. Their writing may contain many errors that allow us to teach a particular point of grammar, but there are other grammatical structures that they may not be using at all. We can find all these structures within the text we read with our students, and we can use this text to focus on grammar as well as content and organization.

Robin Scarcella (2000) identified 10 major areas of focus for grammar instruction for English language learners. These are the areas where we find errors even with students who are at more advanced proficiency levels. She suggests that we teach these rules to all students in the upper grades every year. Table 6.12 contains a list of these major areas of grammar focus as well as examples and nonexamples for each.

Table 6.12

Grammar Structure		
Rule of Grammar	**Example**	**Nonexample**
1. Sentence Structure All sentences have one subject and one main verb. A main verb is not a part of an infinitive that begins with *to*.	My English *instructor* in high school *was* the key person who taught me.	My English *instructor* in high school *key person* to teach me.
2. Subject-Verb Agreement Subjects agree with verbs in number. Indefinite pronouns such as *everyone* are generally followed by singular verbs.	*Everyone understands* me.	*Everyone understand* me.
3. Verb Tense Use the present tense to refer to events that happen now and to indicate general truth. Use the past tense to refer to events that took place in the past. Generally use the present perfect with words such as *already, yet, since* + a number of years.	My instructor *explained* how important books *are* for students.	My instructor *explain* to me that how important the books *was* for the student.
4. Verb Phrases Certain verbs are followed by *to* + the base form of a verb; others are followed by a verb that ends in *-ing*.	My instructor persuaded me *to read* many books.	My instructor persuaded me *read* many book.
5. Plurals A plural count noun (*table, book, pencil*) ends in an *-s*	My instructor persuaded me to read many *books*.	My instructor persuaded me read many *book*.
6. Auxiliaries Negative sentences are formed by using *do* + *not* + the base form of the verb.	Please *do not make* me lose face.	Please *do not makes* me lose face.

(continued)

Table 6.12 (continued)

Rule of Grammar	Example	Nonexample
7. Articles Definite articles generally precede specific nouns that are easily identifiable because they are modified by adjectives.	I don't speak *the Vietnamese* language.	I don't speak *Vietnam* language.
8. Word Forms The correct parts of speech should be used. Nouns should be used as nouns. Verbs should be used as verbs, etc.	I have *confidence* in English.	I have *confident* in English.
9. Fixed Expressions and Idioms Idioms and fixed expressions, such as *to lose face*, cannot be changed in any way.	Please do not make me *lose face*.	Please do not make me *lose the face*.
10. Word Choice Formal words should be used in formal settings. Informal words should be used in informal settings.	Dear *Professor Scarcella:*	Dear *Robbin:*

Source: Adapted from: Scarcella, R. (2000). Accelerating academic English: A focus on the English learner. Oakland, CA: Regents of the University of California. Used with permission.

ERROR CORRECTION

How do you correct student errors in language?

Correcting students' errors in language use is tricky business. As teachers, we can scaffold students' language by providing them fluent academic language models. We can also rephrase their language into standard form. Before we turn our focus to the use of language in the content areas (chapter 7), let's spend a little time on when and how to correct students' language usage. Let's start with quotes from a couple of students:

Situation 1:

Kelly: But why you will not correct all my mistakes? I will like to know how is the right way to say everything.

Situation 2:

Erica: I go to the house of my aunt yesterday.

Teacher: Oh, you went to your aunt's house yesterday?

The statements above represent two views of error correction from opposite ends of the spectrum. The first statement was made by Kelly Dell Antonio, a university student from Brazil in Carol's Theories of Language Acquisition class, earning a master's degree in TESOL (Teaching English to Speakers of Other Languages). She wanted to get everything right and felt the only way to improve was to receive explicit feedback on all her errors. The exchange between Erica and her teacher, on the other hand, demonstrates the view of error correction to which many teachers of English language learners subscribe—that the best way to correct errors is simply to model.

If Carol had attempted to give Kelly the feedback she wanted, she'd have needed to rewrite most of the paper. In Kelly's two short statements on the previous page we find three errors, each one of which could result in a lesson of its own. At the same time, when Erica hears her teacher restate what she just said, what she knows now that she did not know before is that her teacher heard and understood her description of what she did yesterday. We do not know if she recognized the grammatical difference between her statement and her teacher's.

The truth is, of course, that both giving explicit feedback on errors and modeling correct syntax are appropriate ways to address error correction. Neither, however, is effective for all students at all times. Determining how and when to correct students' errors in English depends on a variety of interdependent factors.

English language learners make a number of common errors. As teachers, we have to predict the types of errors that our students will make and help them understand the errors. Common error types include those found in Figure 6.10.

> Discuss with a partner what you believe about how to correct errors.

Factors to consider in correcting errors

Comprehensibility. When student errors interfere with comprehension, this is a good time to correct. How much you correct depends on the student's level of language proficiency. Given their current level, what is reasonable to expect them to be able to express, and what is reasonable to expect them to retain? Whether you simply restate correctly, briefly explain how it should be stated, or teach a mini-lesson depends on their language proficiency level, the frequency of the error, and how much the error interferes with comprehension. At earlier levels of proficiency, more restating and less explicit correction provides the modeling students need and allows them to focus on communication—*what* they want to say, and not so much *how* it should be said. The principle of the low anxiety environment comes into play here, along with the focus on communication.

Pedagogical Focus. As an ELD teacher, you will want to correct any errors that reflect the current focus of your teaching. If you are working with your students on past tense of irregular verbs and a student has written "He goed to

Figure 6.10   Types of Errors

Listen and look for these types of errors in your students' speaking and writing.

> **Transfer:** When rules from one language are applied to another language. For example, "The house that I used to live in it is big."
>
> **Overgeneralizations:** Application of a general principle to an exception to the rule. For example, "We runned home."
>
> **Avoidance:** Avoiding unknown words or forms in the target language. For example, instead of "I got lost" the student says, "I lost my way" or "I lost my road."
>
> **Idiomatic:** Translation of forms from one language that are not parallel in the target language. For example, the student says "I have hunger" instead of "I am hungry."
>
> **Idiosyncratic:** Errors that are unique to the individual as part of his or her language learning.

the park," you would note the error and likely expect the student to find the resources in the classroom to assist in correcting it.

How can you correct errors when you are not teaching writing?

As a content area teacher, your focus is directed primarily at the subject you are teaching. However, as a teacher of English language learners, you are also a teacher of language, and as such you must share responsibility for teaching the language necessary for students to express their understanding of your content. Correction of grammatical errors in content instruction should relate to the language objectives you have set for your students, as well as to comprehensibility. If you are studying the causes of the Civil War, your students must be able to use specific vocabulary and language structures correctly to express cause and effect.

Frequency. When students repeatedly make the same kind of error, that structure is in danger of becoming fossilized. A student who leaves the *s* off the third person singular of regular verbs, such as "he say," can benefit from a review of present tense conjugations of regular verbs. Again, language proficiency level must be considered. A student who is just beginning to speak in one- or two-word phrases likely is not ready to concentrate on conjugating verbs correctly.

Individual Student Concerns. Some students may be more sensitive to correction than others, some may need more modeling, some are more analytical. How and when you correct students' errors will also depend on their readiness to accept and benefit from the correction as well as their learning style.

Application to Practice

Reflection

Complete the "L" section of the KWL at the beginning of this chapter.

Case Study: *Writing Instruction*

Look back at the writing sample that you collected from your target student. Identify and prioritize three areas of instructional focus to advance your student's language proficiency.

Planning and Instruction: *Planning for Language*

Return to the unit plan and daily lesson plan you developed in chapter 3. Identify the key vocabulary for this unit and revise your plan to include instructional activities that focus on vocabulary and language.

References

Alvermann, D. E., Moon, J. S., & Hagood, M. C. (1999). *Popular culture in the classroom: Teaching and researching critical media literacy.* Newark, DE: International Reading Association.

Anderson, R. C., Wilson, P., & Fielding, L. (1988). Growth in reading and how children spend their time outside of school. *Reading Research Quarterly, 23,* 285–303.

Ashton-Warner, S. (1959). *Spinster.* New York: Simon & Schuster.

Bear, D. R., Invernizzi, M., Templeton, S., & Johnston, F. (1996). *Words their way: Word study for phonics, vocabulary, and spelling instruction.* Upper Saddle River, NJ: Merrill/Prentice Hall.

Beck, I., & McKeown, M. (2001). Text talk: Capturing the benefits of read-aloud experiences for young children. *The Reading Teacher, 55,* 10–20.

Brassell, D., & Flood, J. (2004). *Vocabulary strategies every teacher needs to know.* San Diego, CA: Academic Professional Development.

Brock, C. H., Boyd, F. B., & Moore, J. A. (2003). Variation in language and the use of language across contexts: Implications for literacy learning. In J. Flood, D. Lapp, J. R. Squire, & J. M. Jensen (Eds.), *Handbook of research on teaching the English language arts,* (2nd ed., pp. 446–458). Mahwah, NJ: Lawrence Erlbaum.

Bromley, K. (2002). *Stretching students' vocabulary: Best practices for building the rich vocabulary students need to achieve in reading, writing, and the content areas.* New York: Scholastic.

Carroll, L. (1946). *Through the looking glass.* New York: Grosset and Dunlap.

Cisneros, S. (1991). My Lucy friend who smells like corn. In: *Woman hollering creek and other stories.* New York: Vintage.

Cunningham, A. E., & Stanovich, K. E. (1991). Tracking the unique effects of print exposure in children: Associations with vocabulary, general knowledge, and spelling. *Journal of Educational Psychology, 83,* 264–274.

Cunningham, P. M. (2002). *Prefixes and suffixes: Systematic sequential phonics and spelling.* Greensboro, NC: Carson-Dellosa.

Cunningham, P. M., Hall, D. P., & Sigmon, C. M. (1999). *The teacher's guide to the four blocks: A multimethod, multilevel framework for grades 1–3.* Greensboro, NC: Carson-Dellosa.

Dixon, C., & Nessel, D. (1983). *Language experience approach to reading (and writing): Language-experience reading for second language learners.* Hayward, CA: Alemany.

Dolch, E. W. (1936). A basic sight vocabulary. *The Elementary School Principal, 36,* 456–460.

Dorn, L. J., & Soffos, C. (2001). *Scaffolding young writers: A writers' workshop approach.* York, ME: Stenhouse.

Dutro, S., & Moran, C. (2003). Rethinking English language instruction: An architectural approach. In G. Garcia (ed.), *English Learners: Reaching the Highest Level of English Literacy.* Newark, DE: International Reading Association.

Fagan, M., & Prouty, V. (1997). *Language strategies for children: Keys to classroom success.* New York: Thinking Publications.

Farley, M. J., & Elmore, P. B. (1992). The relationship of reading comprehension to critical thinking skills, cognitive ability, and vocabulary for a sample of underachieving college freshmen. *Educational and Psychological Measurement, 52,* 921–931.

Fearn, L., & Farnan, N. (2001). *Interactions: Teaching writing and the language arts.* Boston: Houghton Mifflin.

Fisher, D., & Frey, N. (2002). Accelerating achievement for adolescent English language learners: Interactive writing grows up. *California English, 7*(4), 24–25.

Fisher, D., & Frey, N. (2003). *Improving adolescent literacy: Strategies at work.* Upper Saddle River, NJ: Merrill/Prentice Hall.

Fleischman, J. (2002). *Phineas Gage: A gruesome but true story about brain science.* New York: Houghton Mifflin.

Frayer, D., Frederic, W. C., & Klausmeier, H. J. (1969). *A schema for testing the level of cognitive mastery.* Madison, WI: Wisconsin Center for Educational Research.

Frey, N., & Fisher, D. (2004). Using graphic novels, anime, and the Internet in an urban high school. *English Journal, 93,* 19–25.

Frey, N., & Fisher, D. (2006). *Language arts workshop: Purposeful reading and writing instructions.* Upper Saddle River, NJ: Merrill/Prentice Hall.

Gibbons, P. (1991). *Learning to learn in a second language*. Portsmouth, NH: Heinemann.

Gibbons, P. (2002). *Scaffolding language, scaffolding learning, teaching second language learners in the mainstream classroom*. Portsmouth, NH: Heinemann.

Graves, M. F., & Slater, W. H. (1996). Vocabulary instruction in the content areas. In D. Lapp, J. Flood, & N. Farnan (Eds.), *Content area reading and learning: Instructional strategies* (2nd ed., pp. 261–276). Boston: Allyn & Bacon.

Greaney, V. (1980). Factors related to amount and type of leisure reading. *Reading Research Quarterly, 15,* 337–57.

Guthrie, J. T., & Greaney, V. (1991). Literacy acts. In R. Barr, M. L. Kamil, P. Mosenthal, & P. D. Pearson (Eds.), *Handbook of reading research* (vol. II, pp. 68–96). New York: Longman.

Halliday, M. A., & Hasan, R. (1976). *Cohesion in English*. New York: Longman.

Heller, R. (1988). *Kites sail high: A book about verbs*. New York: Putnam Berkley Group.

Hoestlandt, J. (1993). *Star of fear, star of hope*. New York: Walker.

Jenkinson, E. B. (1988). Learning to write/writing to learn. *Phi Delta Kappan, 69,* 712–717.

Kasper-Ferguson, S., & Moxley, R. A., (2002). Developing a writing package with student graphing of fluency. *Education and Treatment of Children, 25,* 249–267.

Krashen, S. D. (1993). *The power of reading: Insights from the research*. Englewood, CO: Libraries Unlimited.

Krull, K. (2003). *Harvesting hope: The story of Cesar Chavez*. San Diego: Harcourt.

Martin, R. (1992). *Rough face girl*. New York: Scholastic.

McCarrier, A., Pinnell, G. S., & Fountas, I. C. (2000). *Interactive writing: How language and literacy come together, K–2*. Portsmouth, NH: Heinemann.

McDougal-Littell. (2006). *Language of Literature*. Evanston, IL: Author.

National Center for Educational Statistics. (2003). *The nation's report card: Writing highlights 2002*. Retrieved February 28, 2004 from http://nces.ed.gov/nationsreportcard/writing/results2002/.

Payne, R. K. (1995). *A framework for understanding and working with students and adults from poverty*. Baytown, TX: RFT.

Pittleman, S., Heimlich, J., Berglund, R., & French, M. (1991). *Semantic feature analysis*. Newark, DE: International Reading Association.

Romaine, S. (1994). *Language in society: An introduction to sociolinguistics*. New York: Oxford University Press.

Santa, C., & Havens, L. (1995). *Creating independence through student-owned strategies: Project CRISS*. Dubuque, IA: Kendall-Hunt.

Scarcella, R. (2000). *Accelerating academic English: A focus on the English learner*. Oakland, CA: Regents of the University of California.

Scarcella, R., & Rumberger, R. (2000). *Academic English key to long term success in school*. University of California Linguistic Minority Research Institute Newsletter, 9:4. Santa Barbara, CA.

Scott, J. A., & Nagy, W. E. (1994). Vocabulary development. In A. C. Purves, L. Papa, & S. Jordan (Eds.), *Encyclopedia of English studies and language arts, Vol. 2* (pp. 1242–1244). New York: Scholastic.

Stanovich, K. E., & Cunningham, A. E. (1993). Where does knowledge come from? Specific associations between print exposure and information acquisition. *Journal of Educational Psychology, 85,* 211–229.

Taba, H. (1967). *Teacher's handbook for elementary social studies.* Reading, MA: Addison-Wesley.

Thomas, S. M. (1998). *Somewhere today: A book of peace.* Morton Grove, IL: Albert Whitman.

Tompkins, G. E., & Blanchfield, C. (2004). *Teaching vocabulary: 50 creative strategies, grades K–12.* Upper Saddle River, NJ: Merrill/Prentice Hall.

Trueman, T. (2003). *Inside out.* New York: HarperCollins.

Ulanoff, S. H., & Pucci, S. L. (1999). Learning words from books: The effects of read-aloud on second language vocabulary acquisition. *Bilingual Research Journal, 23,* 409–422.

Williams, V. (1982). *A chair for my mother.* New York: Scholastic.

7

Grade-Level Content: Integrating Language and Learning

Anne Vega/Merrill

THE PROPS assist the house
Until the house is built,
And then the props withdraw—
And adequate, erect,
The house supports itself;
Ceasing to recollect
The auger and the carpenter.

Just such a retrospect
Hath the perfected life,
A past of plank and nail,
And slowness,—then the scaffolds drop—
Affirming it a soul.

—Emily Dickinson

Focus Questions

1. What does it mean to "scaffold" learning?
2. How can you use graphic organizers to support your ELLs' access to grade-level text? How can you differentiate these graphic organizers for students at different levels of proficiency in English?
3. How can you "frontload" language to prepare your students to talk and write about a new concept?
4. How can you teach learning strategies that will help build independence?
5. What are some of the unique challenges for ELLs in learning math, science, social studies, and reading literature?
6. What strategies can you use to differentiate instruction for your ELLs as they meet these challenges?
7. What are the most essential standards for your students to achieve?

ACCESSING PRIOR KNOWLEDGE: MAKING MEANING FROM TEXT

The findings of our study also reveal that there is nothing especially difficult about setting up a mental representation for a new lexical item as presumably children would have to do for unknown words. For example, for localist versions of connectionist viewpoints, it seems probable that one would first have to create a new lexical node before orthographic, phonological, and semantic information could become connected with it. Presumably, if substantiating a mental representation for a new lexical item was particularly difficult, we would expect to see that the development of unknown words was slower than for partial knowledge words because partial knowledge words already have an existing lexical node with corresponding orthographic and phonological features but few semantic features. (Stahl, 1999, p. 3)

As you read this text excerpt, observe what strategies you use to make meaning.

What strategies did you use?
What else would help your comprehension?

MAKING CONTENT COMPREHENSIBLE: SCAFFOLDING

> *Scaffold—"a temporary or movable platform for workers (as bricklayers, painters, or miners) to stand or sit on when working at a height above the floor or ground"(Merriam-Webster, 2005).*

> *Scaffold—". . . support mechanisms to allow learners to handle tasks involving complex language. Without such support students might not succeed. Scaffolds are by definition temporary, that is, as the teacher observes that students are capable of handling more on their own, she gradually hands over responsibility to them" (Walqui, 1992).*

We have used the term *scaffolding* for a long time, an idea defined by Jerome Bruner as a process of helping a child learn something new, beginning with easy, successful experiences, and then gradually handing over more responsibility as the child's skill increases (Bruner & Sherwood, 1975). Similar to the scaffolding that construction workers use, scaffolding for students allows them to complete tasks that they could not otherwise do on their own. As with construction scaffolding for buildings, educational scaffolding is temporary—as the students become more capable, they can provide the support they need on their own. It is important to recognize the dynamic interaction between the scaffold itself, or the structure of the support, and the actual content of a task. As you observe and evaluate your students as they engage with the content, you can determine when and how to modify the scaffold. Aida Walqui (1992, 2003) describes six scaffolds that assist English language learners in accessing grade-level content: modeling, bridging, contextualization, schema-building, metacognition, and text re-presentation.

As you read, think of a lesson you are planning and jot down ideas for each scaffold that would support what you want your students to learn.

Research in Focus: Classroom Conditions That Support English Language Learners

Based on her experience and review of research, Aida Walqui identified general approaches for creating classroom conditions that are particularly supportive for English language learners:

- Instead of presenting the curriculum as a linear progression of concepts, teachers *reintroduce* key information and ideas at increasingly higher levels of complexity and interrelatedness.
- Teachers help students understand their own learning, in particular, the feelings of vagueness and frustration that are a natural part of the learning process. For students

with the extra task of learning English, such feelings can have an especially strong, undermining effect if not understood.

- Teachers become expert at observing students in order to know when to gradually hand over more responsibility as students become capable of handling it.
- Teachers learn to amplify and enrich—rather than simplify—the language of the classroom, giving students more opportunities to learn the concepts involved. For example, rather than avoid a complex term, a teacher might use it in context and then paraphrase it.

Source: WestEd, *A framework for teaching English learners,* 2004 (http://www.wested.org/cs/we/view/feat/36). Used with permission.

Language patterns + functions usage

Modeling

It would be difficult to find a teacher today who does not recognize the importance of modeling for students. In elementary school, the children's day often begins with a Read Aloud in which the teacher also "Thinks Aloud," modeling his or her thought processes in making meaning of the story. Science lessons often begin with a demonstration, and every math teacher we have met ends the day with ink-stained hands from demonstrating math problems on the overhead projector. For English language learners, who may not be able to rely primarily on language for understanding, modeling becomes even more critical. They may need more models than fluent English-proficient students, and they may need more explicit modeling of processes and directions. When we consider Pearson and Gallagher's model of gradual release of responsibility (1983) or the "to, with, and by" model (e.g., Cappellini, 2005), the balance of time spent in the "to" and "with" portions can shift for English language learners who may require additional support. It can be helpful to do small group instruction in order to differentiate and provide additional modeling for those students who need it while other students work on another task or on the same task independently of the teacher.

What are different ways you can model for your students?

Bridging

The process of learning consists of making connections, linking new information to that which we already know. By activating students' prior knowledge, we activate their thinking about something they already understand and show them how new ideas or skills are connected. These links are made both to prior learning and to personal experience. As teachers, we automatically see the link between what we are about to teach and what we taught yesterday, last week, or in a previous unit. Our students, without the depth of knowledge about the content that we have, don't always make those connections. We can help them make connections through bridging activities. Bridging can be as simple as asking for a quick recap of related, previously learned material and then explaining how it

What can you say, or have your ELLs do, to make connections to their personal experience? (Think about the different cultures they come from and the background experiences they bring.) What about connections with their prior learning?

Research in Focus: Modeling through Read Alouds

Fisher, Flood, Lapp, and Frey (2004) studied 25 expert teachers and 120 randomly selected teachers as they conducted Read Alouds. The goal of the study was to identify the essential features of an interactive Read Aloud. While "many researchers have demonstrated that Read Alouds are an effective way to introduce students to the joy of reading and the art of listening (Morrow, 2003) while developing their vocabularies, experiential backgrounds, and concepts of print and story" (pp. 8–9), Fisher, Flood, Lapp, and Frey (2004) wanted to determine if there were common features that could be used as an instructional model. Their data suggest that there are at least seven common factors, including:

1. *Text selection*—Selection was based on the interests and needs of the students.
2. *Preview and practice*—The text was not read for the first time, which allowed teachers to pause and use questions.
3. *Clear purpose*—The reason for the Read Aloud was clear to students.
4. *Fluent reading model*—The teacher modeled fluent oral reading.
5. *Animation and expression*—The teacher made the Read Aloud interesting with his or her voice and expressions.
6. *Discussing the text*—Read Alouds were not a passive experience; students were encouraged to talk with one another and the teacher about the reading.
7. *Connected to other reading and writing tasks*—The Read Alouds were not "commercials" but were connected with the overall content or focus of the class.

---

is related. Or it can be more involved, using an Anticipation Guide (such as the one we did at the beginning of chapter 2 in this book), doing a Think-Pair-Share (chapter 3), or a brainstorming activity.

Contextualization

How can you create a context to help make the new learning more concrete?

As we discussed in detail in chapter 2, providing a context for new information facilitates comprehension and learning. Grade-level texts are often full of dense language and lack visuals or other contextual clues to meaning. Manipulatives, realia (real objects), video clips, metaphors, and analogies related to students' lives can help to create a context that supports comprehension.

Schema-building

What can you do to help students see where or how the new ideas fit into "the scheme of things"?

The brain as a natural pattern seeker functions most efficiently when it can make connections between ideas and see how the parts relate to the whole. Much like the frame of a new house, a schema is a framework into which we can place or catalogue new experiences and build new understanding upon the existing structure. Graphic organizers (discussed later in this chapter), particularly advance organizers, are one of the most effective ways to build schema.

Metacognition

"Thinking about your thinking" plays an important role in preparing to learn, monitoring learning, and assessing learning. As learners grow older, we rely more on explicit systems of meaning than on implicit learning (Zadina, 2005). It follows, then, that metalinguistic (discussion of how language works) and metacognitive (discussion of thinking and learning processes) information will foster academic development. It is the awareness of which strategies can assist in learning that leads students to become independent learners. We will discuss an approach to teaching these strategies, CALLA (Cognitive Academic Language Learning Approach) in more depth later in this chapter.

What can you have students do that requires them to plan, monitor, and think about their learning?

Text re-presentation

You may know text re-presentation by another name. This is the "after" part of the before, during, and after reading model of instruction. It is the "beyond" part of the into, through, and beyond model of instruction. In other words, this is where students apply their learning and demonstrate their understanding by taking the text and doing something new with it. They may write a new ending to a story, describe life on a wagon train in a letter to a friend, or create a brochure for a recycling campaign.

What can you have students do to extend and apply their learning?

Spotlight on Instruction

Scaffolding in Action

Understanding sequence of events is an important goal for young readers. Ms. Alvarez knew this and collected a number of books that use a cause-and-effect sequence to tell their story. She knew that focusing on sequence stories for several weeks would allow her students, all English language learners from around the world, an opportunity to make connections—bridges—between the books and the bigger idea of sequence. The books she used included:

- Charlip, R. (1964). *Fortunately* New York: Aladdin.
- Peters, L. W. (1994). *When the fly flew in.* New York: Scholastic.
- Rice, D. (1999). *Because Brian hugged his mother.* Nevada City, CA: Dawn Publications.
- Taback, S. (1997). *There was an old lady who swallowed a fly.* New York: Viking.
- Taback, S. (1999). *Joseph had a little overcoat.* New York: Viking.
- Wood, A. (1984). *The napping house.* San Diego: Harcourt.

By David L. Rice   Illustrated by K. Dyble Thompson

Used by permission of Dawn Publications.

Ms. Alvarez also selected these books because the topics they covered were humorous yet familiar—both of which assist students with bridging and schema-building. Ms. Alvarez knew that she needed to provide context for these books. As such, she ensured that each book was paired with a number of photos, manipulatives, and realia. For example, while the class was focused on *The Napping House* (Wood, 1984), she used several photographs of different beds, a recording of a person snoring, and stuffed animals that matched the animals in the illustrations.

As she read *The Napping House* (Wood, 1984) aloud, she regularly paused, asked her students what they were thinking about the text, and checked their understanding of the text. Given that her students had had a number of experiences with sequence stories before reading this particular book, Ms. Alvarez wanted them to make predictions and notice their predictions—metacognition—as she read.

As she finished each book, Ms. Alvarez provided her students with an opportunity for text re-presentation. Of course, she provided her students with several choices in their individual text re-presentations, ranging from retellings, to illustrations, to sequencing pictures related to the story, to writing letters to the author about favorite parts.

DEVELOPING INDEPENDENCE IN USING EFFECTIVE LEARNING STRATEGIES: GRAPHIC ORGANIZERS

We know graphic organizers assist in learning. Thinking about what you know about language acquisition and learning in a new language, why would they be particularly useful for ELLs?

In her teacher education class, "Instruction for English Language Learners," Carol used to give the teachers a handout with a couple of questions related to the ideas discussed in class that evening. She would ask them to reflect on those ideas in relation to their own practice. She would watch these teachers, successful adults, sit, sometimes for several minutes, before they would begin to write. Some of them would write in very large handwriting, filling up the page with very little said; others would write for a few moments and stop. One evening she decided to give them a T-chart with the ideas they had discussed in class listed in one column and space for their reflections in the other column. Most began to write immediately, and their responses were far more detailed and comprehensive. This simple graphic with a few words and a few boxes provided a support for the teachers to express their learning.

How do graphic organizers support ELLs?

Even teachers, who are generally successful learners, found the graphic organizer helpful. For students who are not yet proficient in English, graphic representations of ideas are even more beneficial (Dye, 2000; Ritchie & Gimenez, 1995–1996). More specifically, graphic organizers assist English language learners because they:

- Require critical thinking
- Organize information visually
- Build schema
- Categorize information
- Lower the affective filter

Let's consider each of these concepts in greater detail.

Require Critical Thinking. Too often, classroom activities for English language learners require very little critical thinking. When students have limited proficiency in expressing their thoughts, it can be difficult to discuss complex ideas. It can be difficult for teachers to think of higher-order questions or tasks that don't rely on use of complex language. We may use low-level texts and limit our questions to those with yes or no answers. Many times we will even discard the text altogether, providing all the information ourselves so that students will not have to read difficult text. The danger here is that instruction becomes "watered-down" and students not only do not learn grade-level concepts, but neither do they learn to read academic text, nor do they gain the critical thinking skills necessary for academic success.

Graphic organizers require a high level of thinking without requiring a high level of English language proficiency. It takes a deep understanding of ideas in order to organize them graphically, yet because we generally only write single words and phrases, grammar demands are reduced, and students can devote their energy to thinking about the concepts rather than worrying about how to express them. Using a graphic organizer limits the pressure on the student's linguistic resources even as it raises the cognitive demand.

Organize Information Visually. Graphic organizers assist students in seeing the relationships between the ideas, without relying on complex language to express those relationships (Carlson, 2000). The language that describes the relationship between two ideas is often precisely the language that is not explicitly taught. It is taken for granted that students know and understand words and expressions such as *cause, one of the characteristics of,* or *if . . . then.* In a statement such as *One of the characteristics that lipids have in common is that they all consist of fatty acids,* which words do you think would be the focus vocabulary for this lesson? Most science teachers would likely spend time teaching *lipid* and *fatty acid,* assuming that students understand the surrounding words that actually carry a good deal of the meaning. The words *characteristics, have in common, consist of,* are just as important to understanding the sentence as the content-specific words, yet we generally wouldn't take the time to teach them in a science lesson. An English language learner reading this sentence might see the words that have been taught, recognize that there is some link between *lipid* and *fatty acid,* but without understanding *characteristics, have in common, consist of,* will not be clear as to what that connection is. A graphic organizer can support the language by demonstrating the relationship.

How can you ensure that a graphic organizer does not become a "worksheet"?

What kind of graphic organizer would be useful to express this statement about lipids?

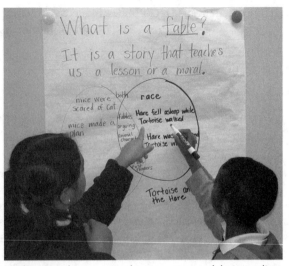

Students working on graphic organizers of their reading
Doug Fisher

Build Schema. Graphic organizers help build schema for students, one of the key scaffolds we discussed earlier for making content comprehensible for English language learners (e.g., Rock, 2004). Brain research has shown us that the brain learns best by making its own sense out of new information, finding patterns, and constricting meaning on its own (Caine & Caine, 1991). Graphic organizers can help students construct their understanding of new concepts by providing them with a structure that allows them to place the new information into a known context. When Ms. Lesher begins a new unit in her high school physics class, she posts and briefly discusses a chart with a graphic organizer of all the key concepts in the unit. This allows her students to see how the concepts are interconnected.

Categorize Information. When students place information into a graphic organizer, they are "chunking" that information, a strategy that facilitates retention. When information is "chunked," we are better at retaining and understanding it. If you are learning a new language and you are reading a story about a family that takes a vacation, it is a good time to focus on other words used when talking about families, rather than to try to learn all the new words in the story.

To perceive is to categorize, to conceptualize is to categorize, to learn is to form categories, to make decisions is to categorize.—Jerome Bruner

When studying the desert habitat, Ms. Shirley used a Matrix/Process Grid to help her third graders describe adaptations that plants and animals have made to survive in the desert (see Table 7.1). Similarly, in an ELD lesson focused on describing feelings, students can use a graphic organizer such as a Word Web to organize words that describe feelings into categories of *happy* and *sad*.

Lower the Affective Filter. Have you ever sat down to write a paper or a report and found yourself staring at a blank page of paper, unable to come up with the first sentence? Imagine that you were given an assignment asking you to demonstrate your understanding of the life cycle of a frog. Figure 7.1 contains

Table 7.1

Graphic Organizer		
Desert Life	**Adaptation**	**How It Helps Survival**
Plants	Retain water	Need less water
	Thorns	Keep predators away
Animals	Nocturnal	Cooler at night

Figure 7.1   Life Cycle of the Frog

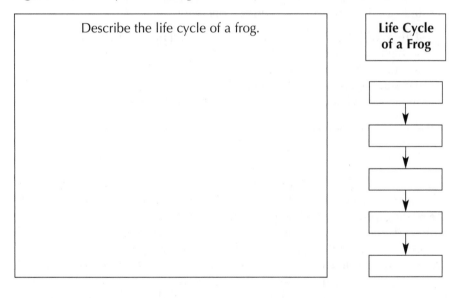

two options for the assignment: writing the report on a blank piece of paper or developing a graphic representation of the information. Which of the two papers in Figure 7.1 would you prefer to be asked to complete? Why?

TEXT STRUCTURE: FROM TEXT TO GRAPHICS AND BACK AGAIN

The tendency in many classes designed for English language learners is to simplify the content, using below-grade-level texts with short sentences, basic vocabulary, and simple language structures, often resulting in a "watered-down" curriculum. When we do this with literature, we eliminate the richness of the language. When we do this with expository text, we deprive our students of the opportunity to

Research in Focus: Graphic Organizers

As Merkley and Jefferies (2000/2001) noted, graphic organizers (GO) help students understand complex texts and ideas. They are especially useful as a during-reading or after-reading activity (Alvermann & Boothby, 1986). When combined with metacognitive instruction and tasks such as summarizing and retelling, the impact of graphic organizers is enhanced (Bean, Singer, Sorter, & Frasee, 1986). Teachers who are not experienced with the use of graphic organizers sometimes use them as worksheets—something for students to fill out. Based on their review of research from schema theory, classroom discussions, and concept development, Merkley and Jefferies (2000/2001) identified five attributes for the effective implementation and use of graphic organizers. As they note, "When presenting the GO to students, the teacher should do the following:

- verbalize relationships (links) among concepts expressed by the visual,
- provide opportunity for student input,
- connect new information to past learning,
- make references to the upcoming text, and
- seize opportunities to reinforce decoding and structural analysis." (p. 352)

---

acquire an essential skill—learning how to make meaning from grade-level text. If we want students to learn to access difficult text we must find ways to scaffold the reading, provide support for constructing meaning, and teach them the skills that will enable them to become autonomous, independent readers.

Gloria Tang (1993) proposed a model of instruction using graphic organizers as a way to help students first read and comprehend difficult text and then write their own expository prose based on the reading. This model, "From Text to Graphics and Back Again," involves a sequence where students use a graphic organizer to identify the major concepts from the text, and then use the graphic form to organize writing. This sequence of planning, instruction, and practice is as follows:

Planning

1. Determine the organization of the text.
2. Select a graphic organizer.

   You begin by examining the text with three questions:
   - What is the "big idea" that you want students to walk away with?
   - What is the organization of the text?
   - What is the language and vocabulary (linguistic and cohesion devices—see chapter 6) needed to talk or write about the big idea?

You then focus on the challenges in the text:
- What is the structure of the text?
- What linguistic and cohesion devices will students need to understand in order to fully comprehend the text and to talk and write about the ideas in the text?

The following is a selection from a seventh-grade social studies text.

> But during the 1600s and 1700s, large landowners began buying up the holdings of small landowners and then fencing in, or enclosing, the land. Once the land was enclosed, the owner could farm it any way he liked. Landowners introduced new agricultural techniques, which boosted the amount of food produced on the same amount of land. But many peasants were left without land of their own. They bitterly resented enclosure but could not stop it. Deprived of land, many headed to cities to find work. (Cordova, et al., 1999, p. 492)

In this reading selection, what is the big idea?

As you read, you may have identified the key concept as how changes in farming methods affected life at that time. The text is organized, or structured, to describe cause and effect. Some cohesion devices students will need to express their understanding might be: *because, the effect of . . . was . . ., resulted in, so, as a result of . . . ,* or others, depending on the proficiency of your students in English. Beginners might use the words *because* and *so,* where you might focus on expressions such as *as a result of . . .* with more advanced students. Other language that students will need to use includes past tense verbs. Content-specific words might include *landowner* and *peasant.* Vocabulary for general academic use might include *produced* (and *production*) and *techniques.*

What type of graphic organizer could you use to teach students to recognize cause and effect? How might you teach the linguistic and cohesion devices students will need to use?

Instruction

3. Use the graphic organizer to teach the major concepts.
4. Direct students' attention to key language—vocabulary and cohesion devices.

You might have chosen a graphic organizer like one of those in Figure 7.2—a Two-Column Chart or a Cause and Effect Chain.

The sequence of instruction follows the same sequence as any instruction—modeling, guided practice, and independent practice. You can begin the lesson by showing a graphic organizer you have already constructed and completing it as you teach (modeling). After presenting the key concepts, highlighting the focus language, and discussing the structure of the graphic organizer, you can proceed to the next section of text and co-construct a graphic organizer with the students as you read (guided practice).

Practice

5. Set student tasks that require construction of graphic representations of ideas.
6. Set student tasks that require them to write expository text from graphic representations of ideas.

Figure 7.2 Two-Column Chart

Cause	Effect
Landowners bought up and enclosed land.	Peasants left without land.
Landowners introduced new techniques.	Food production boosted.
Peasants left without land.	Peasants moved to the cities.

Cause and Effect Chain

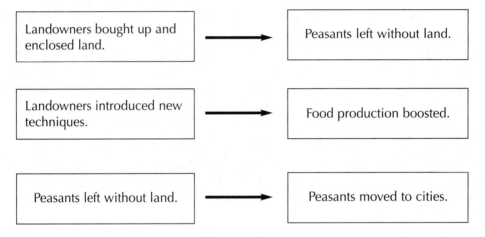

After seeing how the graphic organizer is organized to represent the ideas of the text, students can begin to work in small groups or with partners to construct their own graphic representations of the next section. This step, for many ELLs, will likely come only after you have modeled the process and guided their practice many times. Depending on their level of English proficiency, the reading level of the text, and the difficulty of the concepts, you may find that students are unable to do this independently until well into the school year. Having students work in small groups will allow you to differentiate your level of support. You can spend more time modeling with a group that needs more assistance, or you can provide more information on the graphic organizer for those who need it. It is helpful to begin the gradual release of responsibility with text structures that are easier for students to identify—sequence, for example, where the graphic organizer might be a timeline or a sequence of events flowchart.

The co-constructed graphic organizers provide an effective source of support for writing. The arrows and spatial arrangement serve as a graphic representation of the cohesion devices. Students can then translate these graphics into text using the language they have been taught. And because the ideas in the graphic organizer are not written in complete sentences, the pervasive problem of students copying directly from the text is minimized or eliminated.

Create a graphic organizer that will help students compare and contrast two ideas in a lesson you will teach. Fill in the key ideas. What mortar words will they need to construct sentences from the graphic organizer?

Integrating Language and Content: Teaching the Academic Language That Allows Students to Express Their Learning

When we think about what it takes to become proficient in another language, to be able to understand and use language in an academic context, it is apparent that 20 minutes a day of ESL/ESOL, even an hour or two, is not nearly enough for most students to attain proficiency before they have completed high school. Language must, therefore, be a consideration all day long—during math or social studies, PE or art. (In bilingual programs, as students learn concepts and skills in their primary language, teachers can introduce key vocabulary in English. A strong foundation in their primary language will facilitate transfer to English. As students progress through each year and through each grade, teachers can incorporate progressively more English into content-area instruction.) All teachers must take responsibility for teaching the language and vocabulary used in whatever subject area they are teaching. In order to be able to talk about and write about academic content, students not only need to understand the concepts, but they also need to be able to use the language that expresses those ideas. As we discussed in chapter 6, the *mortar* is as necessary as the *bricks*.

Clearly, a secondary school math teacher cannot be expected to teach language as explicitly as an English teacher. An elementary school teacher would not spend as much time teaching language during social studies time as during the reading/language arts block. However, there are specific language structures and general utility vocabulary that it makes sense to teach during math, social

Students also learn language during art
David Mager/Pearson Learning Photo Studio

studies, or other content areas, language that is directly related to the ability to discuss, read, and write about the concepts being learned.

Integrating language and content: Frontloading

We can scaffold learning of our ELLs by frontloading language they will need in order to understand, talk, and write about the content. When we ask students to summarize the plot of a novel, participate in a classroom discussion, present an oral report, write a science lab report, or frame an argument about the causes of a historical event, we can provide support for learning and promote development of academic language proficiency by teaching the language they need to complete the task.

As we looked at planning in chapter 3, we began to think about planning for language learning, creating language objectives alongside the content objectives in each lesson. Let's examine this process in more detail.

Dutro (2005) suggests that integrating language and content teaching requires three steps:

1. Analyze the linguistic demands of a content task.
2. Pre-teach the vocabulary and language structures needed to comprehend and participate.
3. Move from talking about content to talking about language and back again during the lesson.

Think of a language function you might ask your students to perform (comparing, hypothesizing, describing, etc). What language structures will they need to be able to complete the task? What vocabulary will they need?

If we begin by determining what the task is that we are asking students to complete and the language function they must use to accomplish that task, we can then determine the language structures and the mortar vocabulary they will need. (See chapter 6 for a list, differentiated by proficiency level, of signal words used to perform various academic tasks.) Prior to the actual content lesson, we can teach some of the key vocabulary—both content-specific (brick) and general utility (mortar).

We can also provide sentence frames to assist students in constructing sentences. During the content lesson, students can use the language they have practiced. Then, as we teach, we can focus on the content, highlighting how the language is used to express the ideas. This process of frontloading not only helps students develop academic language, but it also minimizes the challenges that language can present, allowing students to concentrate on the content.

Spotlight on Instruction

Using Sentence Frames

In Ms. Shirley's desert unit, she wanted her third graders to understand the differences between how people have used the resources in the desert and how they have used them along the coast. They needed, first, to be able to describe those resources. Then they would need to compare and contrast how they have been used. She also wanted them to use evidence to draw conclusions regarding the influence of geography on how people adapt to and change their environment. Through scaffolding instructional activities with visuals, Read Alouds, and bridging to prior learning, she helped her ELLs understand the concepts. As she observed them in partner and small group work, listening to their discussions and asking questions, she judged that they appeared to understand the key concepts. However, what she came to realize was that they could not always express that understanding clearly. So she pulled them aside in a small group and taught a mini-lesson on some of the vocabulary that would facilitate their participation in the group and, later, help them write their reports. Teaching words such as *both, neither,* and *unlike,* and a few sentence frames like the ones that follow, she gave them practice with the language structures they would need to talk and write about what they had learned. Here are some sample writing frames:

Unlike the _____, the _____ used/ate _____.
Both _____ used/ate _____ because _____.

The students practiced the structures briefly by talking about similarities and differences between themselves and their siblings, using familiar content to teach new language. Then they returned to their small groups and prepared to write their conclusions.

DEVELOPING INDEPENDENCE: TEACHING LEARNING STRATEGIES

CALLA: Cognitive Academic Language Learning Approach

Think of yourself as the learner for a moment. Describe what you do in each situation to help you understand, remember, and complete the task.

Listen to a lecture on the westward expansion in the United States.	Write an essay comparing two characters in a story.
Learn new vocabulary words in a foreign-language class.	Solve a word problem in math.

You probably listed a variety of strategies that help you accomplish different kinds of academic learning tasks. In the 1980s, Ana Chamot and Michael O'Malley conducted a research study investigating the learning strategies used by English language learners who had been identified by their teachers as successful learners. What they found was, first, that these students used a variety of strategies to learn English, and second, that they were keenly aware of the processes they used. From their research, Chamot and O'Malley developed a model to teach students to use specific strategies to learn language and academic content. The CALLA (Cognitive Academic Language Learning Approach) model integrates language, content, and strategy instruction. The strategies fall into three categories.

Metacognitive strategies

Metacognitive strategies are those that help us plan for a task and monitor and evaluate our learning. Using advance organizers, scanning for information, and self-assessment are tools that require learners to think about what is important to learn, what will be the best approach to learning it, and how well they have learned it.

How do you prepare to accomplish a large or unfamiliar task? What strategies do you use to monitor your progress?

Cognitive strategies

These are strategies we use during learning to help make sense of new information. Activating prior knowledge, using graphic organizers, and taking notes are strategies that help learners understand and remember the key points.

Social/affective strategies

These strategies utilize both interpersonal and intrapersonal skills. Working with others, asking questions for clarification, and self-talk to lower anxiety level are as important to facilitate learning as the metacognitive and cognitive strategies.

Think of a time when working with others helped you learn something new or complete a task. What skills did you use to work with others?

Types of learning: What, how, and why

Cognitive theory describes three types of learning (e.g., Paris, Cross, & Lipson, 1984; Sternberg & Williams, 2002):

- Declarative
  What we know, for example, math multiplication facts or how to conjugate a verb in the past tense.
- Procedural
  What we know *how* to do, for example, solve a math problem or ask a question.
- Conditional
  Knowing *when* and *why* to use a procedure, skill, or strategy, for example, determining what operation is necessary to solve a word problem or knowing how to ask for assistance.

We address these three types of knowledge as we teach *content* and as we teach *language*. In the CALLA model, which is grounded in cognitive theory, we also want our students to know the *what, how, when,* and *why* of using specific strategies for learning. Instruction on using a learning strategy such as a graphic organizer might look like this:

- Declarative
  What is a graphic organizer?
- Procedural
  How do I find the key information in the text and complete the graphic?
- Conditional
  When is it helpful to use a graphic organizer?
  Why are some types better for a given task than others?

How do we teach learning strategies?

Most teachers model and use a variety of learning strategies frequently, if not daily. The step that may be left out, however, is the explicit instruction of the learning strategy itself for the purpose of teaching students to use the strategy on their own. Current best practice in literacy instruction centers around the teaching of strategies to make meaning—predicting, making connections, summarizing, visualizing, inferring, and questioning. We teach students to monitor their comprehension and give them a bag of tools to use when comprehension breaks down ("fix-up" strategies). These are cognitive learning strategies that are usually taught in elementary school and in classes for struggling readers at secondary school. Although the strategies are commonly used in other subjects, time is rarely spent on overt instruction of their application subjects other than literacy. And while we often ask students to use metacognitive and social/affective learning strategies, we seldom teach these strategies as explicitly as the cognitive learning strategies.

> With a partner, compare and contrast: having students *use* a learning strategy, and *teaching* them to use it.

The sequence of instruction on learning strategies follows the gradual release of responsibility model we have discussed previously.

> See the section in chapter 5: "How Do We Teach Students to Ask Questions?"

Sequence of instruction

Step 1: Explicit Teaching. You can begin your lesson by making connections to students' personal experiences. Have them think and talk about what learning strategies they already use, what they do that helps them learn. You might ask students to complete a questionnaire of the types of strategies they use in various situations, and then follow with a discussion of how those strategies help them.

Step 2: Modeling. Select a learning strategy that is appropriate to the task at hand and model its use, thinking aloud as you go. Name the strategy, chart the steps in using it, and describe how it will help them.

Step 3: Guided Practice. Guided practice can be conducted with the whole class or in small groups. The amount of guidance needed will vary with individual students. As students read you might ask them to *summarize* each chunk of text and stop and share with the group. Or if you are teaching them the strategy of *organizational planning*, after you assign the task, ask them to break that task into logical steps and again share with the group. Discuss the steps they listed and how they will use this list to approach the task. They might construct a checklist or a graphic organizer to guide them as they work.

Step 4: Independent Practice. As students work individually, monitor their use of the strategy. Confer with students. Check to see how they are using the strategy. Offer suggestions and support as needed. Continue to ask students to use the strategy with other assignments.

Step 5: Reflection. After using a strategy, students are ready to reflect on how they used it, how it helped them, how they might use it more effectively, and in what other situations it would be helpful.

Assessing use of learning strategies

What questions might you ask your students to find out what strategies they use to facilitate their learning?

To assess your students' prior knowledge and use of learning strategies, you might ask them questions similar to those at the beginning of this section of the chapter. In Chamot and O'Malley's *CALLA Handbook*, you can find a questionnaire that asks students to reflect on how they approach a variety of learning tasks across the curriculum (Chamot & O'Malley, 1994, p. 77).

MATH, SCIENCE, SOCIAL STUDIES, AND LITERATURE

Some considerations when teaching English language learners . . .

Mathematics

Language. English language learners are often placed in mainstream math classes while still in the early stages of English proficiency. The thinking behind this practice is that they will be able to participate more easily in the math class because math is not as heavily language dependent as subjects such as science or social studies. We generally think of the language of mathematics as being universal. When we examine the language requirements in math classes today, however, we find that many difficulties can arise for students who are not yet proficient in English. Students are expected to listen to explanations, read technical text, write word problems, and often explain and justify their work—all language-dependent activities that require a highly sophisticated and specialized use of language.

What language and vocabulary can you think of that might cause problems for an ELL in math?

Collaborative tasks provide the opportunity for students to develop a conceptual framework, practice mathematical skills, and use mathematical language. The more time students spend actively engaged in working in groups or with a partner, the more proficient they become in using academic language. The same collaborative structures we use in language arts, social studies, or science work just as well in math. We can introduce a concept using a Think-Write-Pair-Share to activate prior knowledge and get students talking about math—perhaps brainstorming what they know about factors in preparation for a lesson on factoring polynomials. Students can work together to solve problems, create a poster showing the process they used, and explain their work to other students, building a deeper understanding of the concept and practicing the mathematical skills as they talk through and justify their approach. Just as in any other content area, we must remember that math lessons are also opportunities to develop language, and so the same principles of instruction apply—providing comprehensible input, contextualizing concepts, creating a low-anxiety environment, and engaging students in meaningful activities.

> See chapter 2 for additional information on comprehensible input and a low-anxiety environment.

Vocabulary. The vocabulary of mathematics can also present a challenge for ELL students. Many words may be familiar to the student, but have specialized meanings in the context of math, such as *round, square, table,* and *function. At least* takes on a completely different meaning in math than students may have encountered in literature—*He had at least as many marbles as she did* expresses a different idea than *At least he had a coat to keep him warm.* Other familiar words can cause challenges for English language learners as well—*he* and *she,* words commonly found in word problems, might confuse a student who does not yet control the use of pronouns. Prepositions, one of the most troublesome grammatical features even for highly proficient non-native speakers, are small, everyday words that can completely change the meaning of the statement. *Divided into* requires a different response than *divided by.* Phrases such as *how many more* and *less than* can require the same operation, even though the student has learned in the ESOL class that *more* and *less* are opposites. When first introduced to word problems, students are often taught to look for key words that signal the mathematical operation to be used. This can be misleading if students do not carefully read the entire problem. Consider the following two problems.

> Marta has three dollars. Carmen has five. How much *less* money does Marta have than Carmen?

> Marta has three dollars. She has two dollars *less* than Carmen. How much money does Carmen have?

If students have been taught that when they see the word *less,* they should subtract, they may be led astray in the second problem. A vocabulary chart such as the one in chapter 6 (Figure 6.10) helps students to learn the specialized mathematical meanings of familiar words. When the words all relate to a particular unit, they can use this same chart to tally the number of times their partner uses these mathematical terms during an assigned task, thus encouraging them to interact multiple times with the new vocabulary. To build conceptual understanding while developing language, students can use a Venn diagram to compare and contrast two graphs, two equations, or two geometric shapes. Here students will need to use the mathematical vocabulary as well as the language needed to make comparisons.

Lack of Redundancy. In chapters 2 and 5, we discussed the importance of redundancy for students who are learning a new language, particularly important when they are learning the new language at the same time as they are learning new content. Restating ideas in different ways gives students the opportunity to process the language and think about the concept. The language used in mathematics texts generally lacks redundancy. It tends to be sequential, with little paraphrasing, providing few clues to the meaning (Chamot & O'Malley, 1994). Collaborative tasks provide a scaffold for ELLs through the natural redundancy that occurs as students talk with each other about the concepts.

Background Knowledge. Lack of familiarity with the mainstream culture can also hinder understanding. Mr. Martinez, a high school math teacher, wrote the following word problem for a quiz in his ninth-grade sheltered algebra class:

> You are buying decorations for your math class party: 4 rolls of crepe paper and 20 balloons cost $5.40. Later you buy 2 more rolls of crepe paper and 8 balloons for $2.60. Find the cost of a roll of crepe paper and a balloon.

What could you do to support your ELLs in solving this problem?

Many of his students didn't even attempt the problem. When he investigated, he discovered that they had read the problem, come to the words *crepe paper*, and skipped the problem entirely because they had no idea what *crepe paper* was. Mr. Martinez had assumed, quite logically, that the average high school student would be familiar with an item so commonly used to decorate school events in this country. Unfortunately, few of his ELLs had participated in those events, and many of those who had taken part had been so inundated with new things to learn about, they had not paid attention to the crepe paper.

We can eliminate some of these kinds of challenges by paying careful attention to test design, and by teaching students how to approach problems when they don't know some of the words. In chapter 2 we explored the importance of background knowledge in helping to provide a schema for students when they are learning a new concept. There are some concepts in mathematics that are quite abstract and don't have concrete, real-world applications that are within the everyday world of our students. But most concepts do have a real-world connection, and if we activate students' background knowledge by helping them make those connections, we have helped them to build the schema that provides the framework for their conceptual understanding.

Assessment. When older students are newly arrived in this country, speak little or no English, and bring no school records with them, they are often placed in the most basic math class offered at the school. The reasoning behind this placement is that, if the content load, or level of difficulty, is lighter, then the students will be more able to understand the English. This seems reasonable until we consider that some students enter with high levels of skill in math, and the class would serve only as unnecessary review for them. Ms. Wilson, a high school calculus teacher, has found that many English language learners do much better than the native English speakers in her advanced-level math classes. They enter

How are students placed in math classes at your school? What do you know about the math skills of your target student?

with strong math backgrounds and, because of their lack of proficiency in English, often take more care in reading the problems than other students.

Just as we assess students' English language skills when they first enter the school system, we need to assess their math skills to assure that they are placed in the appropriate level of math. It is difficult, however, to get an accurate picture of a student's skills when the assessment relies heavily on language.

The same issue arises in evaluating student progress in math. In order to determine whether students have gained the competency they need to score "proficient" on the standardized tests used for accountability purposes, many schools are beginning to design unit tests that use language that is similar to those standardized tests. The thinking behind this approach is that students will become familiar with "test language." The result, however, for students who are not yet proficient in English, is that they score poorly, and we are left without accurate information regarding their math proficiency. When tests rely on language, we are unable to determine whether the student scored poorly because he or she did not know the math, or because he or she did not know the English. As we discussed earlier in chapter 3, the purpose of the assessment drives the design. If we want to evaluate progress in a content area, we must differentiate assessments according to the language proficiency level of the student. It is critical, then, that we are keenly aware of the language demands of our assessments, and that we modify and scaffold language in order to gain a true picture of our students' skill and understanding of the mathematical concepts. It is also helpful to use a variety of assessments that ask students to demonstrate their knowledge

What are some ways to assess student understanding of a mathematical concept without heavy reliance on language?

Students work in partners to solve math problems
Doug Fisher

in a variety of ways. We can also gain a truer picture of our students' progress by providing multiple assessment opportunities so that we do not rely on their performance at a single point in time.

Science

Language and Vocabulary.   Science teachers often tell us that teaching science is akin to teaching another language—for all their students, even native English speakers. The vocabulary load is immense as students learn technical ways to talk about ideas and processes that explain the why's and how's of the world around us. Everyday words, as in mathematics, take on new meanings—*table, mass, energy.* And new, complex words describe new, complex ideas with which students have little or no familiarity. Learning the word *cell* entails more than just learning the word. Students must learn a host of additional words such as *nucleus, cytoplasm, membrane, permeable,* among others. They also must learn the concepts that are the reason for learning about cells—photosynthesis, for example.

Reading a science text is significantly different from the type of reading to which most ELLs are accustomed in their ESL/ESOL classes. As in mathematics texts, the text tends to be dense, each paragraph containing many important facts with little redundancy. Many ELLs, taught the key vocabulary, become adept at getting the gist of what they have read, but may miss the precise meaning as they gloss over the mortar words.

The following is a selection from a high school chemistry text:

> Organisms are composed of as few as one cell or as many as billions of cells. Two major cell designs occur in nature. Prokaryotic cells are the cells of bacteria. The cells of all other organisms, including green plants and humans, are called eukaryotic cells. The prokaryotic cell is the more ancient of the two. Microscopic examination of fossilized remains shows that prokaryotic cells were present on Earth at least 3 billion years ago. Eukaryotic cells did not appear until about 1 billion years ago. (Wilbraham, Staley, Matta, & Waterman, 2002, p. 809)

Although we might look at this text and think that it would be difficult for anyone without background knowledge about the structure of cells, the language used presents additional challenges for those not familiar with English. Constructions such as *as few as, as many as, the more ancient of, did not appear until* do not use unfamiliar or difficult words, and they do not express difficult ideas. They are constructions that would not trouble a native speaker, even a struggling reader, leaving him or her free to focus on the scientific terms and ideas. An English language learner, however, might struggle with the scientific terms as well as the everyday vocabulary found in the passage.

One advantage that Spanish-speaking ELLs have is the frequency of words with Latin roots. Words such as *velocidad, aceleración, penúltimo, impermeable, examinar,* considered to be high-level academic vocabulary for native English speakers, are not only commonly used in Spanish, but are also cognates or near-cognates (words that are similar and have the same meaning in two

What must students look for in this reading selection besides the main idea? Aside from the science-specific terms, what are some of the language structures that might cause an ELL to miss the meaning?

What words can you think of that are similar in English and another language?

languages, e.g., *teléfono* and *telephone*) that Spanish-speaking ELLs will easily understand. Cognates assist students in transferring between two languages. (See the Teacher Tools for a list of some common English-Spanish cognates.)

Background Knowledge. While key strategies for ELLs such as demonstrations and hands-on activities are used perhaps more in science than in any other subject area, many science courses are now based on "discovery learning," an approach that requires students to "discover" the scientific theory being taught, an approach that, if not carefully structured, can preempt the strategy of activating prior knowledge. We know that possessing background knowledge about a concept, along with a schema into which the new information fits, can help students fill in some of the gaps in understanding that may have been left by a lack of proficiency in English. When we expect students to make these connections on their own, after conducting the experiment, we take away a valuable scaffold to learning new concepts in a new language. It is important to find ways to activate students' background knowledge and build schema while still organizing the lesson in such a way that they can construct their own meaning. One way to build background knowledge is through teacher Read Alouds of science texts such as *Gregor Mendel: The Friar Who Grew Peas* (Bardoe, 2006). The inquiry method may also pose problems for students who come from a culture where they are taught that the teacher is the source of knowledge and that questioning authority is a sign of disrespect.

How can you balance activating or building background knowledge with discovery learning?

At the same time, science lends itself handily to concrete, hands-on experiences that build background knowledge, providing a foundation for abstract thinking and for reading and writing about academic topics. In chapter 6 we examined a continuum of language, from the informal language of a discussion during a shared experience, to the more explicit language needed to report on that experience to those who were not present, to the academic language required to write about the experience. Science provides an ideal forum to build language along this continuum. The lab experiment first gets students talking about an academic topic. From that concrete experience and the ensuing discussion, they build background knowledge and understanding, practice language around the concepts, and then use that new understanding and language to write.

Used by permission of Abrams Books for Young People; Amulet Books.

Assessment. As we saw in our discussion of mathematics and ELLs, the language of the test can prevent us from gaining an accurate assessment of student progress in science. The following sample science question is designed to assess the student's understanding of plants and plant cells.

What language in
this question might
prevent an ELL from
demonstrating his or
her understanding of
the scientific
concept?

Which causes tomatoes to ripen much more slowly in a refrigerator than they do if left on a table at room temperature?

A. Tomatoes need sunlight to ripen.
B. Humidity accelerates the ripening process.
C. Low temperatures reduce the action of ripening enzymes.
D. Enzymes produced by bacteria inhibit ripening.

Here is a revised version of the stem for the same question.

Tomatoes get ripe more slowly in the refrigerator than at room temperature. Why?

What differences do
you see between the
two versions? How
are the changes
helpful to an ELL?

If we truly want to assess our students' progress towards the science standards, we must be sure that we provide assessments in which the language used does not prevent them from demonstrating their understanding. (See chapter 3 for another example of modifying test questions in science.)

Social studies

Language and Vocabulary. Instruction and materials in social studies are heavily language-dependent—requiring comprehension and use of both oral and written language. Unlike for math and science, it can be difficult to find hands-on materials to use in teaching the abstract concepts that underlie the events of history. The texts used are almost exclusively expository, with information organized in ways that are very different from the literary texts with which students may be most familiar. The following passage from a high school history text is typical.

What kinds of hands-
on materials can you
use to teach social
studies?

> If Higgins found oil, it could serve as a fuel source around which a vibrant industrial city would develop. (Danzer, Klor de Alva, Krieger, Wilson, & Woloch, 2003, p. 230)

What language
and/or vocabulary
might cause difficulty
for an ELL? How can
you support
understanding?

Note the verb tenses, the cause/effect sentence structure, and the pronouns. Sentences in secondary-level social studies texts tend to be long, contain multiple clauses, and use pronouns frequently. In conversation we primarily use the present and past tenses. Social studies texts commonly use the conditional—*could build*—and the past perfect—*had been built* or *would have been built*. While texts written for the elementary level generally use more simple sentence structures. Challenges can arise here if the text is simplified in a way that removes the language that provides cohesion. Students still may need support to understand how the ideas are connected.

ELD instruction typically focuses on writing sentences using a common structure—subject + action + object. We ask students to include descriptive words and vary their word choice and sentence length. We teach complex structures to express cause and effect, hypothesis, and comparison, but many of the structures found in a social studies text are beyond what we teach in ESL/ESOL. In the following statement, the subject is embedded in the middle of the sentence with the predicate (the verb phrase related to the subject) at the beginning.

> Spawned in the process were vast new constituencies of government bureaucrats and beneficiaries whose political clout made it difficult to kill programs off. (Danzer, et al., 2003, p. 693)

Here, a verb becomes the subject of the sentence.

> But funding the Great Society contributed to a growing budget deficit. (Danzer, et al., 2003. p. 692)

Even in a third-grade text, in a selection about making money choices, where the content is relevant to students' lives and the vocabulary itself may pose no obstacle, the structure of the sentence with a negative gerund (the *ing* form of a verb) phrase as the subject—*not getting the pink camera*—may obscure the meaning for some ELLs.

> In a way, not getting the pink camera or the cord is part of the cost of being able to buy film. (Banks et al, 2007, p. 269)

Although we may be able to give students the meaning of the text without using these complex structures, it is critical that they learn to read them independently. This is the language of school. Students may not be exposed to this type of language during their ELD time, so the social studies texts provide authentic, meaningful situations to use to teach this language.

Here again, Spanish-speaking ELLs can make use of cognates to facilitate understanding. Many of the key words in social studies are similar in both Spanish and English. *Democracy* and *representation* are easily recognizable in Spanish as *democracia* and *representación*. Words such as *libertad* and *responsibilidad* provide an opportunity to teach students about suffixes—the *-tad/-dad* ending in Spanish equates to the *ty* ending in English. The meaning of these words, however, may be somewhat obscure for students coming from countries where there is a different type of government. Finding ways to contextualize these abstract concepts and make them more concrete then becomes particularly important.

Background Knowledge. Students who have attended school in the United States since kindergarten have been exposed to U.S. history numerous times throughout their schooling. By the time they enroll in their high school U.S. history class, they may have studied various topics related to American history in easily five of their 10 or 11 years in school. So it is not surprising that teachers often assume that their students have studied U.S. history in previous years. ELL students may not have this background knowledge of our nation's past and they may need additional instruction.

How can you assess your students' background knowledge in social studies?

Even studies of world history typically have an emphasis on the past from the point of view of the United States. In one middle school standards-based textbook we looked at, the first four units focus on life in the Roman Empire, the roots of Islam, West Africa from 5000 B.C. until the 1600s, and ancient Asian civilizations. As the chapters move from medieval times into the 18th century, the focus is on Europe and America, with two chapters on the native civilizations of the Americas. While the text does include references to events that occurred in the 18th and 19th centuries in Asia, Africa, and the Middle East, it might be

Interacting with history increases comprehension
Doug Fisher

interpreted that the cultures outside of the Euro-American world stagnated or even disappeared when Western cultures began to flourish.

When students have little proficiency in English, how can you assess what they have learned in the content?

Assessment. Luz had arrived in the United States from Mexico just four weeks earlier. When Ms. Voeltner asked the Beginning ELLs in her eighth-grade U.S. history class to write three sentences about the Civil War, Luz wrote the words "The United States . . ." and then sat quietly waiting for the bell to ring. Carol, who was visiting the class that day, asked Luz a few questions in Spanish about what she had learned during the lecture and discovered that she did indeed understand a good deal of what had been discussed. Ms. Voeltner's use of graphic organizers during her lecture had facilitated Luz's understanding, but she still did not have enough English to be able to express what she knew.

Assessment of progress in social studies, like instruction, is often heavily dependent upon language. If Ms. Voeltner had relied solely on Luz's written product, she would have assumed that Luz needed reteaching. Clearly, an assessment that relies on language will not always give accurate information regarding content knowledge. For Beginning ELLs, it may be helpful to allow them to write first in their native language. Then, using a graphic organizer, they may be able to fill in some of the key words or complete a sentence frame. Yes/no questions, selecting from a list of words, matching pictures to labels, or even drawing a picture are ways that students may be able to demonstrate their learning. This is not to say that they should not be writing sentences or paragraphs about the content, merely that a writing task may not be an appropriate assessment tool for students at the earliest levels of language proficiency.

Even for students at higher levels of proficiency in English, some scaffolding may help teachers gain an accurate view of the student's understanding. Students can use graphic organizers completed during the lesson to assist them in structuring their writing (text to graphics and back again). Sentence frames also allow students to focus on the concepts and events rather than on how to formulate the sentence. By differentiating our assessments for language proficiency level, we can assess the same content knowledge and clearly identify what each student has learned about that content.

Literature

Language and Vocabulary

"This for store bill," she would mutter, making a little pile. "This for c'llection. This for piece o'gingham" . . . (Collier, 2006 p. 252).

The language of literature is rich with nuances and descriptions woven together to transport the reader to a different time and place. For an ELL, the very richness we want our students to experience can be an obstacle to comprehension. In the short passage from Eugenia Collier's *Sweet Potato Pie*, found in a high school literature anthology, the language Mama uses as she counts the money transports us to the sharecropper's cabin, and we know before the sentence ends that, while there might be enough money to go around, the family is just barely surviving. If we understand this from the beginning of the sentence, we quickly grasp the meaning and visualize the image projected in the conclusion of the sentence:

> . . . and so on, stretching the money as tight over our collective needs as Jamie's outgrown pants were stretched over my bottom.

An English language learner, however, may wonder what *this* refers to, what *c'llection* is (partly because of the colloquial spelling and partly because of a lack of background knowledge), and become confused by the sentence structure. They may miss the powerful analogy of the tight money and the tight pants. We find them reading for the gist, missing the richness of the author's craft.

These issues are not limited to the secondary school English classroom. Consider the following lines from a very popular children's book, *Olivia* (Falconer, 2000):

> She is very good at wearing people out. She even wears herself out.

For readers without background in the various uses of *out*, these two sentences can be very confusing. Similarly, you have to know that the pig is the character and that *wearing* is used in different ways in the story.

It can be difficult to find quality fiction at students' independent reading levels that also has a high enough interest level for a middle or high school student who is just beginning to learn English. Alternative format texts such as *ttyl* (Myracle, 2005) are one good source of reading material. Older ELLs who are reading well below grade level may be more motivated to read nonfiction text at that level than fiction. Even

How do you select literature for your ELLs? How do you determine what vocabulary to teach, and what vocabulary to simply tell the meaning and move on?

Used by permission of Abrams Books for Young People; Amulet Books.

Select a piece of literature that you might read with your students. What background knowledge will help them understand the story? Do all your students have that background knowledge? If not, what might you do?

upper-grade elementary students often find that easy-to-read nonfiction captures their interest more than the fiction at their level.

Background Knowledge. As we discussed earlier, the way we organize and express our thoughts is culture-bound. The organization of a short story, the sequencing, the emphasis on plot or character may vary from culture to culture. Some cultures emphasize character over action. Some develop themes by talking around the central idea and never address it directly. In the literature of some cultures, there is almost always a lesson to be learned. In English, stories tend to be driven by the action—the nouns and verbs draw us in. This is not so for all languages. In Korean, for example, adjectives and adverbs are often more important to the descriptive nature of the language. For ELLs who come from a culture where stories are told with a different emphasis, it may be more difficult to recognize foreshadowing, predict events or outcomes, even to determine the plot, and thus to comprehend the story fully. Inclusion of literature from many cultures, along with comparing and contrasting the ways they are organized, may help make story structures more transparent and enable students to use reading comprehension strategies such as prediction and visualization more independently.

How can you assess ELLs' understanding of literature without relying on writing?

Assessment. Typically, the way in which we assess students' understanding of a piece of literature is by asking them to write a response of some kind. Just as we saw with Luz in social studies, it is entirely possible that an ELL has understood the story, but does not yet have enough proficiency in English to be able to express understanding. And when they do write, there may be so many grammatical errors that it is difficult to know how to score their work. One approach to this dilemma is to give two grades—one for content and one for grammar.

This encourages teachers to analyze student understanding of the literature apart from their skill in using English. It also provides feedback to the students regarding what they know and what they need to work on. As we discussed in chapter 6, we still must circumscribe our correction of errors, taking into consideration the student's developmental stage of language proficiency, the focus of our instruction, the frequency of the type of error, and its effect on the reader's comprehension.

Another solution to the dilemma of assessing the understanding of students who are still learning English is to provide alternatives to the written response to literature. Students can demonstrate their understanding through posters, skits, dioramas, or other projects. Students at early levels of proficiency can complete matching or cloze activities, or use a word bank to help them with their writing. Clearly, it would not be appropriate to provide sentence frames, word banks, or matching activities for all students. Native English speakers have the language background to be able to express their ideas without these kinds of support. In order to be able to use assessments to inform our instruction for English language learners, however, it is important to assess in such a manner that we obtain an accurate and complete picture of student understanding. Assessment, like instruction, can be differentiated to facilitate the learning process.

Spotlight on Instruction

Less Is More

The first year that Carol taught Spanish was a year of academic reform at the inner city high school where she worked. One of the new graduation requirements for the incoming freshman class included three years of high school foreign language. Many students who would have previously completed their world language, visual, performing, or practical arts graduation requirement by taking music or art now would need to study a foreign language for three years. Until that time, world language classes had been filled primarily with self-motivated, college-bound students with good study skills and an interest in learning another language. Suddenly, the classes were larger, the students were not always motivated, and the teachers in the department struggled to make a new language comprehensible to monolingual English speakers. As the teachers built background knowledge, provided lots of comprehensible input, and offered multiple opportunities for students to practice language in authentic contexts, they found that they could not move as quickly through the textbook. As a result, at the end of the year, in the first-year language classes, the students had completed only six of the 12 chapters in the book. The following year, as the school began to gain a new reputation for academic rigor, many neighborhood students who had chosen to attend schools in other parts of the city returned, lured back by the opportunities available as the staff implemented many new ideas. Consequently, the second-year language classes now had a mix of continuing students who had completed only the first half of the textbook and new students from other schools where they had completed all 12 chapters. The first day of school, many of the students in Carol's second-year Spanish class groaned when they saw they would be using the first-year book again, complaining that they had already "been there, done that." By the end of the first week of school, however, as Carol listened to her students, read their writing, and informally assessed their proficiency in Spanish, it became clear to her that the students she had taught the previous year were actually able to communicate more clearly and more easily than the students who were new to the school. While the new students might have "covered" more of the material, they had not retained as much as the students who had more opportunities to practice and apply their skills. It appeared that the depth of instruction counted for more than the breadth of instruction: a classic case of "less is more."

FOCUS ON KEY IDEAS

In this age of accountability, teachers feel the pressure of making sure that they have *addressed* all the standards for their grade level and subject. This commendable goal can conflict with the goal of making sure that students can actually *meet* the standards. Especially for students who are learning a new language at the same time as they are learning new content, it simply takes more time. Lessons that build background, engage students in conversations about the content, provide

How can you balance the need to address all the standards with the need to make sure students gain mastery?

opportunities for students to practice and apply new concepts require more time than more traditional "sit and get" lessons. It is not always possible to "cover" the same amount of material. "Covering" less, however, need not mean that students learn less or leave the class less prepared for the next level. Figure 7.3 provides a number of tips for teaching content to English language learners.

Identify essential standards

Look at your content standards. Which are essential? Why? How do we reconcile this dichotomy and ensure that our English language learners are gaining access to the grade-level standards?

We do believe that all students must be held to grade-level standards. We also recognize that meaningful instruction for ELLs may require spending a significant amount of time, perhaps more than typically allotted, on each concept.

In each state, a cadre of teachers and experts in their field have written content standards that detail the important concepts and skills for students to learn in each subject area. Obviously, it would be ideal to thoroughly address each of these standards. Given that the Differentiated Approach we have described in this book requires more time, the resulting reality in many classrooms is that there simply is not enough time to provide this type of instruction for all the standards. By identifying those standards that are most essential to a grade-level understanding of the content, we can, in effect, buy ourselves more time. It is true that students will not have been exposed to all the standards. However, if we look closely at the standards, we can see that many are intertwined and can conceivably be addressed together. Others, while certainly important, may be considered to take a back seat, addressed once students have gained sufficient understanding of those we have identified as most important.

Carol's friend Shelley, an elementary math specialist, argues that, if we do not expose students to a standard, they have absolutely no chance of understanding it. She contends that a well-designed curriculum revisits the concepts in succeeding years at increasingly more complex levels, and that when we introduce students to a concept or skill, even if they do not master it, it will facilitate their learning the next time they encounter it. When we introduce them to

Figure 7.3 Tips for Teaching Content

- Be aware of language use in your speech and in the text, both vocabulary and structure, in written text, oral discussions, and assessments.
- Be aware of cognates when possible and help students to recognize and look for them themselves.
- Be aware of language demands, including vocabulary and structures that are not content specific, such as prepositions or words that give directions, and so on.
- Use graphic organizers to help students understand the structure of the text.
- Teach students how to recognize the necessary parts of word problems in math and work around words they don't know.
- Use manipulatives—shapes and colors to help students understand such concepts as fractions. Model using colored shapes made for overhead projectors.

a new concept that builds upon a skill they have not yet mastered, they will still be more successful than if we had not exposed them at all to the prerequisite skill. We acknowledge that the sequence and pacing of instruction cannot rely solely upon mastery. We also believe that when students have a deep understanding of a few key concepts, this understanding provides a solid foundation on which to build future understanding. And while we are not proponents of "teaching to the test," we believe that students with this solid foundation will perform better on the tests than those who have "covered" or been exposed to all the standards, without having actually met them. This again, it seems, is part of the art of teaching—maintaining a calculated balance between giving students a strong foundation in the subject area (*depth* of knowledge), and exposing them to everything we would like them to learn (*breadth* of knowledge). This is the art of knowing our students, knowing our content, determining the essential content, and choreographing the dance: when to move into more depth and when to move on.

Spiral the curriculum

Some of this dilemma can be resolved through the scaffolding process of cyclical teaching that Aida Walqui describes—reintroducing key ideas at increasingly higher levels of complexity, building understanding by first introducing an idea and laying a foundation. When we move to the next idea, we demonstrate a clear connection to prior learning and engage students in using that learning to bring their understanding to a more complex level. The instructional sequence begins to look more like a spiral than a linear progression as students continually deepen their understanding of key concepts. This process entails more than merely a periodic review of ideas. It requires students to think about and use their knowledge as they explore new ideas.

Suppose that you are a novice with the latest handheld technology and you want to buy a new PDA (personal digital assistant). The assistants in the store will likely give you an overview of the multitude of its capabilities and show you how to use it. Most of you will go home and immediately begin to enter your contact list, referring to the instruction manual to see once again how to use your new device. You will probably begin by using the simplest functions and the ones that are most familiar to you from whatever previous experience you have. As you continue to use it, you may begin to explore its other functions and eventually become proficient. If, on the other hand, you are a bit of a technophobe, you may find that you do not venture beyond the basic functions. Without revisiting the more complicated functions, without repeated practice and application of those functions, you are not likely to become a proficient user, even though you have been "taught" everything your PDA can do.

Similarly, the students in Carol's Spanish class first learned how to form past tense verbs and then to use them in simple sentences. As the year progressed, and they moved on to learn other verb tenses, they continued to describe events that took place in the past, expanding their sentences and conversations as their vocabulary grew. They still used the simple past tense, but now were beginning

Does your school have a curriculum map? How are concepts revisited throughout the year?

See the Research in Focus box on page 188, "Classroom Conditions that Support English Language Learners," for more information on spiraling the curriculum.

to incorporate the imperfect past tense. They didn't simply see a unit on the past tense, speak only of events in the past, and then move on to the future tense and speak only of events that had not yet taken place. They continually expanded their skill as they learned new language, talking and writing about increasingly complex ideas.

Redundancy

In chapter 2 we discussed the importance of redundancy in second language acquisition and learning. The value of redundancy applies to learning content as much as to learning a new language. Restating ideas in a variety of ways, presenting new information through multiple modes, amplifies important ideas rather than simplifying them. If students didn't quite understand a statement, when they hear it reworded in another way, they have an opportunity to catch what they didn't get the first time. When Carol was studying Spanish literature at a university in Mexico she was not yet proficient in Spanish. She could follow the lectures and class discussions, but when she tried to take notes or formulate her thoughts in order to ask a question or voice an opinion, she had to concentrate on thinking how to write or say what she wanted, and thus missed much of the discussion. Had the professor stopped to expand on key statements, she would have had the extra time she needed to process the language she heard, the ideas being discussed, and the language she needed to express her thoughts. When we give students an opportunity to hear the same concepts in a variety of ways, we give them more time to comprehend both the language and the ideas, in turn leading them to develop both academic language and understanding of content.

As we can see, it takes more time to amplify ideas. It takes more time to provide ample opportunities for students to practice and apply their new learning. The result may well be that we are not always able to "cover" the entire curriculum with students who are learning English at the same time as the content. However, if we identify essential standards, revisit the key concepts at a continually more sophisticated level, and provide multiple opportunities for students to practice and apply their learning, we can provide a rigorous curriculum and lay a strong foundation of understanding of key grade-level skills and ideas.

Application to Practice

Reflection

1. What are the five most important ideas discussed in this chapter? Why are they important?
2. What is one key idea you want to implement in your classroom? How will you do this?
3. What is something you have a question about?

Case Study: *Teaching Content*

1. What do you know about your target student in relation to these five ideas?
2. What do you want to investigate about your target student in relation to these five ideas?

Planning and Instruction: *Revise Your Unit of Study*

Use the outline in Figure 7.4 to continue to revise your unit of instruction. As you think about how to improve the outcomes your students will experience, incorporate your important ideas from this chapter.

Figure 7.4   Unit of Study

Class: _____   Unit (Topic) of Study: _____

Date: _____   Teacher: _____

Key Concept(s)
What is the big idea (essential question) you want students to walk away with?

Standards, Objectives, and Expectations
Use your content standards, ELD Standards, and what you know about your students to write content, language, and social objectives.

Assessments
What task(s) will students complete that demonstrates their learning?
How will you differentiate the task for students at different levels of English proficiency?

Materials
What core text(s) will you use?
What supplemental texts will you use?
What text will you use to differentiate for students at different levels of English proficiency?
What is the structure of the text(s)?
What types of graphic organizers will you use to help ELLs at different proficiency levels comprehend, talk, and write about the text?

Language and Vocabulary
Content-specific and general academic use (bricks)

Language structures (mortar)

What signal words are necessary in order to comprehend, talk, and write about the key concepts? (mortar)
How will you teach them?

What sentence (question) frames might support your ELLs at different proficiency levels?

Background Knowledge
What do students need to know before you begin the unit?
How will you introduce the unit and connect to understanding they already have?

Instructional Arrangements
How will you scaffold your students' learning?
What learning strategies will help students learn this content? How/when will you teach them?
How will you build on ideas at increasingly more complex levels?
What opportunities will there be to develop listening, speaking, reading, and writing?

Projects, Homework, and Assignments
What instructional tasks will provide opportunities to practice and apply new learning?

References

Alvermann, D. E., & Boothby, P. R. (1986). Children's transfer of graphic organizer instruction. *Reading Psychology: An International Quarterly, 7,* 87–100.

Banks, J., Colleary, K., Cunha, S., Echevarria, J., Parker, W., Rawls, J., et al. (2007). *California communities.* New York: Macmillan McGraw-Hill.

Bardoe, C. (2006). *Gregor Mendel: The friar who grew peas.* New York: Abrams.

Bean, T. W., Singer, H., Sorter, J., & Frasee, C. (1986). The effect of metacognitive instruction in outline and graphic organization construction on students' comprehension in a tenth-grade world history class. *Journal of Reading Behavior, 18,* 153–169.

Bruner, J., & Sherwood, V. (1975). Peekaboo and the learning of rule structures. In J. S. Bruner, A. Jolly, & K. Sylva (Eds.), *Play: Its role in development and evaluation* (pp. 277–85). Harmondsworth, England: Penguin Books.

Caine, R., & Caine, G. (1991). *Making connections: Teaching and the human brain.* Alexandria. VA: Association for Supervision and Curriculum Development.

Cappellini, M. (2005). *Balancing reading and language learning: A resource for teaching English language learners, K–5.* York, ME: Stenhouse.

Carlson, C. (2000). Scientific literacy for all. *The Science Teacher, 67*(3), 48–52.

Chamot, A., & O'Malley, M. (1994). *The CALLA handbook, implementing the cognitive academic language learning approach (CALLA).* New York: Addison-Wesley.

Collier, E. (2006). Sweet potato pie. In McDougal-Littell, *The Language of Literature* (grade 10, p. 252). Evanston, IL: McDougal-Littell.

Cordova, J., Klor de Alva, J., Nash, G., Ng, F., Salter, C., Wilson, L., et al. (1999). *Across the centuries,* p. 492. Boston, MA: Houghton Mifflin.

Danzer, G., Klor de Alva, J., Krieger, L., Wilson, L., & Woloch, N. (2003). *The Americans* (California ed.). Evanston, IL: McDougal-Littell.

Dickinson, E. (1924). *Complete poems. Part Five: The Single Hound XXVI.* Boston: Little, Brown. Retrieved June 14, 2005 from *http://www.bartleby.com/113/5026.html.*

Dutro, S. (2005). Questions teachers are asking about courses of study for secondary English language learners. *The California Reader, 39*(1), 45–58.

Dye, G. A. (2000). Graphic organizers to the rescue! Help students link—and remember—information. *Teaching Exceptional Children, 32*(3), 72–76.

Falconer, I. (2000). *Olivia.* New York: Atheneum Books for Young Readers.

Fisher, D., Flood, J., Lapp, D., & Frey, N. (2004). Interactive read alouds: Is there a common set of implementation practices? *The Reading Teacher, 58,* 8–17.

Merkley, D. M., & Jefferies, D. (2000/2001). Guidelines for implementing a graphic organizer. *The Reading Teacher, 54,* 350–357.

Merriam-Webster Online Dictionary. (2005). Retrieved December 16, 2005 from: *http://www.m-w.com/dictionary/scaffold.*

Morrow, L. M. (2003). Motivating lifelong voluntary readers. In J. Flood, D. Lapp, J. Squire, & J. Jensen (Eds.), *Handbook of research on teaching the English language arts* (2nd ed., pp. 857–867). Mahwah, NJ: Erlbaum.

Myracle, L. (2005). *ttyl (talk to you later)*. New York: Abrams.

Paris, S. G., Cross, D. R., & Lipson, M. Y. (1984). Informed strategies for learning: A program to improve children's reading awareness and comprehension. *Journal of Educational Psychology, 76*, 1239–1252.

Pearson, P. D., & Gallagher, M. C. (1983). The instruction of reading comprehension. *Contemporary Educational Psychology, 8*, 317–344.

Ritchie, D. C., & Gimenez, F. (1995–1996). Effectiveness of graphic organizers in computer-based instruction with dominant Spanish-speaking and dominant English-speaking students. *Journal of Research on Computing in Education, 28*, 221-233.

Rock, M. L. (2004). Graphic organizers: Tools to build behavioral literacy and foster emotional competency. *Intervention in School and Clinic, 40*(1), 10–37.

Stahl, S. (1999). *Vocabulary development: Reading research to practice, a series for teachers*. Brookline, MA: Brookline Books.

Sternberg, R. J., & Williams, W. M. (2002). *Educational psychology*. Boston: Allyn & Bacon.

Tang, G. (1993). Teaching content knowledge and ESOL in multicultural classrooms. *TESOL Journal, 2*, 8–12.

Walqui, A. (1992). *Sheltered instruction: Doing it right*. San Diego, CA: San Diego County Office of Education.

Walqui, A. (2003). *Conceptual framework: Scaffolding instruction for English learners*. San Francisco: WestEd.

Wilbraham, A., Staley, D., Matta, M., & Waterman, E. (2002). *Chemistry*, p. 809. Boston, MA: Addison-Wesley.

Zadina, J. (2005). *Brain research and instruction*. Presentation for the Office of English Language Acquisition. Washington, DC: U.S. Department of Education.

8

Differentiated Instruction: High Expectations for All

Bob Daemmrich/The Image Works

Do not train children to learning by force and harshness, but direct them to it by what amuses their minds, so that you may be better able to discover with accuracy the peculiar bent of the genius of each.

—Plato

Focus Questions

1. What teacher expectations make a difference for student learning?
2. What is differentiation?
3. How do you group your students for differentiated instruction?
4. How can you use the idea of multiple intelligences to differentiate your instruction?
5. What are strategies you can use to differentiate your instruction?

ACCESSING PRIOR KNOWLEDGE: LEARNING STYLES

You are sitting down with some friends to play a board game you have never played before. Do you . . .

1. Ask one of your friends to read the directions to you while you set up the board?
2. Reach for the directions and read them before you begin?
3. Say to your friends: "Let's just play and figure it out as we go"?

If you selected number:

1. You are an auditory learner.
2. You are a visual learner.
3. You are a kinesthetic learner.

We have spent a great deal of time in this book focused on student learning needs. We have discussed planning, assessment, and instruction. We have focused on students' need to learn the English language (both oral and written) and how to develop language within content areas. Taken together, these ideas and strategies will result in significant learning for students. However, there are a few things that teachers can do to ensure that English language learners reach the highest levels of achievement. First, teachers must hold high expectations for all of their students. The specific behaviors that teachers engage in clearly communicate their expectations for students. We will focus on the ways in which teachers can ensure that their students understand that they have high expectations as well as ways for helping students meet those expectations.

Second, teachers must differentiate instruction to address the diverse learning styles, needs, and skills found in the classroom. Through differentiated instruction, students are challenged but not frustrated and teachers are able to facilitate learning.

Research in Focus:
Teacher Expectations

Nearly all schools claim to hold high expectations for all students. In reality, however, what is professed is not always practiced. Although some schools and teachers maintain uniformly high expectations for all students, others have "great expectations" for particular segments of the student population but minimal expectations for others. And in many urban and inner city schools, low expectations predominate.

Asa Hilliard III (1991) contends, "Our current ceiling for students is really much closer to where the FLOOR ought to be." Many believe there is great disparity between what youngsters are capable of learning and what they are learning (Bishop, 1989). Evidence suggests that schools can improve student learning by encouraging teachers and students to set their sights high.

Do Teachers' Expectations Affect Student Performance?

The expectations teachers have for their students and the assumptions they make about students' potential have a tangible effect on student achievement. According to Bamburg (1994), research "clearly establishes that teacher expectations do play a significant role in determining how well and how much students learn."

Students tend to internalize the beliefs teachers have about their ability. Generally, they "rise or fall to the level of expectation of their teachers. . . . When teachers believe in students, students believe in themselves. When those you respect think you can, YOU think you can" (Raffini, 1993).

Conversely, when students are viewed as lacking in ability or motivation and are not expected to make significant progress, they tend to adopt this perception of themselves. Regrettably, some students, particularly those from certain social, economic, or ethnic groups, discover that their teachers consider them "incapable of handling demanding work" (Gonder, 1991). Teachers' expectations for students—whether high or low—can become a self-fulfilling prophecy. That is, students tend to give to teachers as much or as little as teachers expect of them.

A characteristic shared by most highly effective teachers is their adherence to uniformly high expectations. They "refuse to alter their attitudes or expectations for their students—regardless of the students' race or ethnicity, life experiences and interests, and family wealth or stability" (Omotani & Omotani, 1996).

In What Ways May Teachers' Beliefs Translate into Differential Behavior toward Students?

Either consciously or unconsciously, teachers often behave differently toward students based on the beliefs and assumptions they have about them. For example, studies have found that teachers engage in affirming nonverbal behaviors such as smiling, leaning toward, and making eye contact with students more frequently when they believe they are dealing with high-ability students than when they believe they are interacting with "slow" students (Bamburg, 1994).

When teachers perceive students to be low in ability, they may also give them fewer opportunities to learn new material, ask them less stimulating questions, give them briefer and less informative feedback, praise them less frequently for success, call on them less frequently, and give them less time to respond than they do for students they consider to be high in ability (Cotton, 1989).

In addition, we sometimes "dumb-down" instructional content for students we consider to be low in ability. Teachers in low groups and tracks usually offer students "less exciting instruction, less emphasis on meaning and conceptualization, and more rote drill and practice activities" than they do in high or heterogeneous groups and classes (Cotton, 1989).

When teachers summarily categorize or label students, typically some students end up receiving "a watered-down curriculum and less intense—and less motivating—instruction" (Gonder, 1991).

Source: Lumsden, L. (1997). *Expectations for students.* ERIC Digest, Number 116. (http://www.ericdigests.org). Used with permission.

TEACHER EXPECTATIONS AND STUDENT ACHIEVEMENT

Good (1987) defines teacher expectations as "inferences that teachers make about the future behavior or academic achievement of their students based on what they know about these students now" (p. 32). He notes that there are two kinds of expectation effects: *self-fulfilling prophecy* and *sustaining expectations.* Self-fulfilling prophecy effects are based on erroneous expectations that lead teachers to behave toward a student in ways that may be damaging to that student's learning. Some of the behaviors that distinguish teachers' treatment of higher from lower achieving students are found in Figure 8.1.

Nearly 30 years ago, staff from the Los Angeles County Office of Education decided to address the issue of differentiated teacher expectations. They reviewed the available research and identified 15 factors, or interactions, that can facilitate student achievement. These interactions connect student achievement with teacher expectation and are known as Teacher Expectations and Student Achievement or TESA. The research for their model has been updated regularly, but the 15 interactions have remained constant. The 15 interactions can be found in Figure 8.2. A summary of each interaction can be found in Figure 8.3.

While the TESA staff focuses on students who are not performing at grade level for any reason, our work has focused on using the TESA interactions with English language learners. We'll discuss each of the 15 interactions and why they are important for English language learners.

As you can see, TESA consists of three main strands: response opportunities, feedback, and personal regard. Each of these strands goes deeper and deeper

Figure 8.1   Behaviors That Can Indicate Differential Teacher Treatments of High and Low Achievers *(Source: Adapted from: Good, T. L. (1987). Two decades of research on teacher expectations: Findings and future directions. Journal of Teacher Education, 38(4), 32–47. Reprinted by permission of Sage Publications.)*

- Waiting less time for low achievers to answer.
- Giving low achievers answers or calling on someone else rather than trying to improve their responses by giving clues or rephrasing questions.
- Rewarding inappropriate behavior or incorrect answers by low achievers.
- Criticizing low achievers more than high achievers for failure.
- Praising low achievers less frequently than high achievers for success.
- Failing to give feedback to the public responses of low achievers.
- Paying less attention to low achievers or interacting with them less frequently.
- Calling on low achievers less often to respond to questions.
- Seating low achievers farther away from the teacher.
- Demanding less from low achievers.
- Interacting with low achievers more privately than publicly and monitoring and structuring their activities more closely.
- Giving high achievers more than low achievers the benefit of the doubt when grading tests or assignments.
- Having fewer friendly interactions with low achievers.
- Providing briefer and less informative feedback to the questions of low achievers.
- Making less eye contact and other forms of nonverbal communication with low achievers.
- Providing less time on instructional methods with low achievers when time is limited.
- Not accepting or using low achievers' ideas.

as you progress down the units. Our goal in presenting this information to you is for you to think about your classroom and how your behaviors, actions, and interactions can facilitate student learning.

Interactions that facilitate student achievement

Reflect on your own teaching in relation to each of these interactions.

Equitable Distribution of Response Opportunity.   The first interaction focuses on the students who are encouraged to participate in class. Research evidence suggests that teachers call on lower-performing students less often than higher achievers. In addition, we know that we call on boys more often than girls. In terms of English language learners, teachers often allow them to sit quietly in the class.

Figure 8.2   Teacher Expectations and Student Achievement Interaction Model
(Source: Los Angeles County Office of Education (http://streamer.lacoe.edu/teas). Used with permission.)

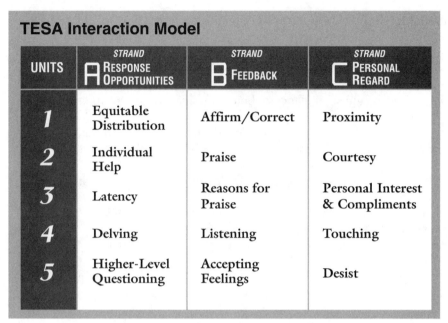

UNITS	STRAND A RESPONSE OPPORTUNITIES	STRAND B FEEDBACK	STRAND C PERSONAL REGARD
1	Equitable Distribution	Affirm/Correct	Proximity
2	Individual Help	Praise	Courtesy
3	Latency	Reasons for Praise	Personal Interest & Compliments
4	Delving	Listening	Touching
5	Higher-Level Questioning	Accepting Feelings	Desist

TESA Interaction Model

Some teachers report that this is so that students won't be embarrassed. Others say that this is because English language learners don't understand the content and can't answer the questions. Of course we don't advocate requiring a Beginner to answer in fully formed complete English sentences. However, we do know that students need practice in speaking English and that teachers can structure their classrooms such that all students have many opportunities to participate orally.

Affirmation or Correction. When students do participate in the class, they want to know what their teachers think about their responses. At minimum, teachers should acknowledge the response—whether it be orally, in writing, on a test, or on a project. We know that students gauge their teachers' reactions to their participation and make decisions about future participation based on this information. If incorrect information is presented, students expect that teachers will correct them, but correct them in ways that honor them as individuals. Unfortunately, lower achieving students are often ignored or do not receive feedback. Our English language learners need affirmation and corrections. These corrections must be responsive to their language development level and current skills, while clearly communicating increased performance expectations. Importantly, we know that constant correction can lead to low self-esteem and poor performance. The effective teacher balances affirmation and correction to facilitate student learning. (See chapter 6 for further discussion of error correction.)

Figure 8.3   Fifteen Interactions for Teacher Expectations and Student Achievement (TESA) (*Source: Los Angeles County Office of Education (http://streamer.lacoe.edu/teas). Used with permission.)*

- **Equitable Distribution of Response Opportunity**: The teacher learns how to provide an opportunity for all students to respond or perform in classroom learning situations.
- **Affirmation or Correction**: The teacher learns how to give feedback to students about their classroom performance.
- **Proximity**: The teacher learns the significance of being physically close to students as they work.
- **Individual Helping**: The teacher learns how to provide individual help to each student.
- **Praise for the Learning Performance**: The teacher learns how to praise the students' learning performance.
- **Courtesy**: The teacher learns how to use expressions of courtesy in interactions with students.
- **Latency**: The teacher learns how to allow the student enough time to think over a question before assisting the student or ending the opportunity to respond.
- **Reasons for Praise**: The teacher learns how to give useful feedback for the students' learning performance.
- **Personal Interest Statements and Compliments**: The teacher learns how to ask questions, give compliments, or make statements related to a student's personal interest or experiences.
- **Delving, Rephrasing, Giving Clues**: The teacher learns how to provide additional information to help the student respond to a question.
- **Listening**: The teacher learns how to apply active listening techniques with students.
- **Touching**: The teacher learns how to touch students in a respectful, appropriate, and friendly manner.
- **Higher-Level Questioning**: The teacher learns how to ask challenging questions that require students to do more than simply recall information.
- **Accepting Feelings**: The teacher learns how to recognize and accept students' feelings in a nonevaluative manner.
- **Desisting**: The teacher learns how to stop a student's misbehavior in a calm and courteous manner.

Where in the classroom do you spend most of your time when you are teaching?

Proximity. The physical presence of the teacher in the classroom is a powerful motivator. We know that teachers use proximity as a classroom management tool. Proximity also communicates value. Teachers often stand near students who are performing well or who are in trouble behaviorally. In terms of seating patterns, lower achieving students are often placed in the back of the room or clustered in corners. The goal of this interaction is to ensure that the teacher gets physically near each of his or her students. This communicates value and provides the teacher an opportunity to develop a bond with each individual.

Proximity aids learning and can correct problem behaviors
Doug Fisher

Individual Helping. Most teachers know that students who struggle in school need individual help to succeed. However, students who are performing at grade level and students above grade level typically are more assertive in seeking the teacher's assistance. This TESA factor reminds us to focus our instructional interventions equitably. Consistent with Vygotsky's theory of the Zone of Proximal Development, every student, including our English language learners, needs access to an adult model who can facilitate learning.

Praise for the Learning Performance. Everyone likes to hear praise. As humans, we like to know that we do some things well. For students who find school difficult, praise is especially important. While they are statistically less likely to receive praise, our English language learners need praise to develop their sense of self as they explore the English language. Importantly, the verbal praise must match the nonverbal clues and cues that the student is receiving. These nonverbal clues include looking at the student, tone of voice, using a student's name, facial expressions, and honesty. It is also important to note that praise builds the bond between the teacher and his or her students. Figure 8.4 includes a number of ways for teachers to say "good job."

Courtesy. While it may seem obvious that we should interact with students in a courteous way, research indicates that we do not always do so with students from traditionally underrepresented ethic groups. There is evidence that English language learners are treated and spoken to harshly. For example, Cesar Chavez reported having to wear a sign that said "I am stupid. I speak Spanish." Although this incident took place many years ago, it is not so very different from an attitude

Figure 8.4   Ways to Say "Good Job"

Aren't you proud of yourself?	Much better!	Well, look at you go.
Bravo!	Nice going.	Wonderful!
Congratulations!	Nothing can stop you now.	Wow!
Congratulations. You got it right!	Now that's what I call a fine job.	You are learning fast.
Couldn't have done it better myself.	Now you have it!	You are really learning a lot.
Exactly right.	Now you have the hang of it.	You are very good at that.
Excellent!	Now you've figured it out.	You certainly did well today.
Fantastic!	One more time and you'll have it.	You did a lot of work today.
Fine!	Outstanding!	You did it that time!
How impressive!	Perfect!	You did that very well.
Good for you!	Right on!	You figured that out fast.
Good going.	Sensational!	You have great potential.
Good job, (person's name).	Super!	You haven't missed a thing!
Good remembering.	Superb!	You must have been practicing.
Good thinking.	Terrific!	You outdid yourself today!
I knew you could do it.	That kind of work makes me happy.	You really make my job fun.
I like that.	That was first-class work.	You remembered!
I think you're doing the right thing.	That's better than ever.	You're doing a good job.
I think you've got it now.	That's coming along nicely.	You're doing beautifully!
I'm happy to see you working.	That's how to handle that.	You're doing fine!
I'm proud of the way you worked today.	That's it!	You're doing that much better today.
I'm very proud of you.	That's much, much better!	You're getting better every day.
I've never seen anyone do it better.	That's quite an improvement.	You're improving.
It's such a pleasure to teach when you . . .	That's right!	You're on the right track now!
Keep it up!	That's the best ever.	You're really going to town.
Keep on trying.	That's the best you've ever done.	You're really improving.
Keep up the good work.	That's the right way to do it.	You're really working hard today.
Keep working on it.	That's the way!	You've got it made.
Kudos!	That's the way to do it.	You've got that down pat.
Marvelous!	Tremendous!	You've just about got it.
	Way to go!	You've just about mastered it.

still prevalent today. There are many who, when listening to a non-native speaker of English, find a French accent charming and believe a Spanish one to indicate an uneducated or even ignorant person. As teachers we must remember that our interactions with students leave lasting impressions in their minds about who they are and what they can do. At the very minimum, every student deserves to be treated with respect and courtesy. Ideally, every student knows that he or she is loved and valued.

Latency. Wait time, or latency, refers to the amount of time between a teacher asking a question and then either moving on or answering the question him or herself. There are a number of benefits of ensuring that students are provided at least a five-second wait time before the teacher moves on, calls on someone else, or answers the question him or herself. By ensuring that students are provided sufficient time, the variety of students who volunteer to answer will increase as will the length of their responses. In addition, there is evidence that providing wait time results in responses that demonstrate critical thinking and that are supported by evidence or logic. For English language learners, latency is critical. As students become increasingly proficient in English, they begin to think in English and do less translation into and back from their heritage language. However, regardless of their level of proficiency, English language learners need time to compose their response. A few seconds' delay does not mean that they do not have profound things to offer the class.

See also chapter 5.

In addition to the latency period between asking the question and expecting a response, teachers should wait for the student to finish and let the response linger in the air for one or two seconds. This gives everyone in the room an opportunity to consider what was just said. We're sure you've been part of a conversation in which the person you're talking with has clearly already formulated his or her response. What happens to you? It makes you want to curtail your conversation in frustration. We don't want to do that to our students.

Reasons for Praise. As we delve deeper into the TESA interactions, we note that students also need reasons for the praise they receive. When possible, the praise students receive should be based on a specific action or response. The recommendation from TESA is that we strive for a ratio of four praises for each correction. For English language learners attempting to master the language, reasons for praise are critical. We can shape or influence students' language when we provide specific praise for their usages. TESA (2002) recommends that praise should:

Observe yourself in your next lesson. How often do you praise students? Who are you praising? Who aren't you praising? What types of things do you say?

- Immediately follow the accomplishment.
- Be specific to the accomplishment.
- Be informative or appreciative.
- Be varied and credible.
- Be natural rather than theatrical.
- Be private most of the time.
- Be individualized.
- Be attributed to effort and ability. (p. D-31)

Personal Interest Statements and Compliments. Another way we make connections with our students and show them that we care is to make statements that indicate that we have a personal interest in their life. It may be as simple as noting that "Arian, you're from the same country that we're reading about. How interesting." Teachers may also ask students to share their experiences and backgrounds when they are connected with the focus of the class. In addition, teachers can make compliments about students, including comments about their clothes, performance at a sports event, or anything else the student engages in. In doing so, the student knows that the teacher has taken personal interest and cares enough to remember. For our English language learners, many of whom have world experiences that their teachers do not share, this interaction is a prime opportunity to draw on the student's "funds of knowledge" and allow him or her to demonstrate skills, knowledge, and interests.

Delving, Rephrasing, Giving Clues. As we have already discussed, we tend to ask fewer questions of low-achieving students than higher achieving students. In addition, when we ask low-achieving students a question, we typically ask easier questions or excuse them from answering if they pause, look confused, or avert their eyes. If this were not enough, teachers tend to rephrase the question less often for lower achieving students and rarely give this group of students clues to be able to answer. This cycle is problematic for English language learners. They need to develop oral language proficiency, but aren't provided as many opportunities to do so. When they are provided opportunities, they are asked "easy" questions, which reinforces for the teacher that the student doesn't know much. Although we aren't suggesting that English language learners be asked questions beyond their language skills, we hope that teachers scaffold their questions and provide the supports necessary for students to successfully respond in the classroom. We know that leveling questions is a good practice, provided that we give students opportunities to stretch their thinking, rephrase questions as necessary to aid their understanding, and give them clues rather than pass over them to another student.

Listening. We know that listening is a critical literacy skill. Unfortunately, students spend a great deal of their class time listening and not engaging in other literacy skills and practices. Several decades ago, Flanders (1970) noted that teachers of high-achieving students talked about 55% of the class time. He compared that with teachers of low-achieving students who monopolized class, talking at least 80% of the time. Clearly, as teachers, we need to listen more. By listening, we mean that students talk with their teacher and with one another. As listeners, we give our attention to the person speaking, make eye contact with that person, engage in nonverbal clues that we understand, and can ask questions or comment about what the person said. Listening to our English language learners is critical—they must develop a sense that someone is listening and that someone understands what they are saying. In addition, listening facilitates the bond between teacher and student and lets students know that we value them.

Respectful human contact develops positive relationships
Doug Fisher

Touching. In this era of lawsuits, touching has become taboo. We are warned of cultural and gender customs around touching, and teachers across the country have taken a "hands-off" approach to education. TESA challenges that assumption and suggests that students respond to touch and that teachers can and should touch students in respectful ways. While this may be uncomfortable to some teachers (and some students at first), the relationships that develop when you can shake the hand of a student entering the room, place a hand on a shoulder to communicate that they are doing a great job, or "high-five" a student who has completed a major project are amazing. In addition, it should be noted that teachers can "touch" with their eyes and words—a wink for a job well done, a smile at the end of a presentation, the use of pronouns such as "we" and "our"—all communicate value and respect.

Higher-Level Questioning. As we have noted before in this discussion of the TESA interactions, we generally ask fewer and easier questions of students who struggle with schooling. Importantly, this does not result in their becoming critical and creative thinkers who can solve problems. Every student needs the opportunity to engage in complex thinking and to receive the support to do so. Benjamin Bloom (1956) created a taxonomy or classification system for educational objectives. This system has been applied to questions as well. To ensure that students develop cognitive flexibility and thinking skills, they need to consider a wide range of question types. They need teachers who ask these kinds of questions and who provide the language support for them to answer them. Our work with English language learners suggests that we need to prepare these questions in advance. It is very difficult, even for veteran teachers, to create good questions on the spot that expand student thinking.

See chapter 5 for an in-depth discussion of questioning.

Table 8.1 contains Bloom's taxonomy as well as an example from two class-rooms, one reading "Goldilocks and the Three Bears" and the other studying the formation of oceans. In addition, Table 8.1 provides a list of the range of words found in each type of question.

Table 8.1

Bloom's Taxonomy with Examples		
Category	**Example**	**Key Words**
Knowledge: Recall data or information.	1. Recall the items used by Goldilocks in the three bears' house. 2. List the major oceans of the world; name the largest ocean in the world.	define, describe, identify, know, label, list, match, memorize, name, outline, recall, recognize, repeat, reproduce, select, state
Comprehension: Understand the meaning, translation, interpolation, and interpretation of instructions and problems. State a problem in one's own words.	1. Explain why Goldilocks liked Baby Bear's chair best. 2. Locate and identify all the oceans on a map; describe four kinds of sea life found in the ocean.	comprehend, convert, defend, discuss, distinguish, estimate, explain, extend, generalize, give examples, infer, interpret, paraphrase, predict, rewrite, summarize, translate
Application: Use a concept in a new situation or unprompted use of an abstraction. Apply what was learned in the classroom into novel situations in the workplace.	1. Demonstrate what Goldilocks would use if she came into your house. 2. Illustrate the different levels of the ocean; dramatize what might happen on an underwater expedition.	apply, change, compute, construct, demonstrate, discover, manipulate, modify, operate, predict, prepare, produce, relate, show, solve, use
Analysis: Separate material or concept into component parts so that its organizational structure may be understood. Distinguish between facts and inferences.	1. Compare the story to reality. What incidents could not have happened? 2. Compare the differences between fresh and salt water (oceans and rivers); diagram the food chain in the ocean.	analyze, break down, compare, contrast, diagram, deconstruct, differentiate, discriminate, distinguish, identify, illustrate, infer, outline, relate, select, separate

Category	Example	Key Words
Synthesis: Build a structure or pattern from diverse elements. Put parts together to form a whole, with emphasis on creating a new meaning or structure.	1. Propose how the story would be different if it were "Goldilocks and the Three Fishes." 2. Design a model of the ocean floor; construct a three-dimensional diorama of ocean life.	categorize, combine, compile, compose, create, devise, design, explain, generate, modify, organize, plan, rearrange, reconstruct, relate, reorganize, revise, rewrite, summarize, tell, write
Evaluation: Make judgments about the value of ideas or materials.	1. Judge whether Goldilocks was bad or good and be prepared to defend your opinion. 2. Evaluate the programs that are in place to protect the ocean. Rate the effectiveness of these programs.	appraise, compare, conclude, contrast, criticize, critique, defend, describe, discriminate, evaluate, explain, interpret, justify, relate, summarize, support

Accepting Feelings. Humans have feelings. We react to the world around us. As teachers, we have to accept the feelings of our students. We must acknowledge their joys and sorrows. And we can help them think about their feelings and what they want to do with them. This is a critical component in the teaching of English language learners. As we discussed in chapter 2, we have to create an environment that is safe for learning. That safety includes accepting feelings. Our English language learners will experience a range of emotions such as loss of loved ones, excitement of finding a new living arrangement, embarrassment with language mistakes, joy when acknowledged for work well done. As teachers, we must be on the lookout for these feelings, help our students name them, and help students decide what they want to do with these feelings.

Desisting. The final interaction outlined by TESA focuses on the actions that teachers take to stop misbehavior. Most teachers use a wide range of strategies to manage their classrooms. In too many classrooms, lower achieving students are punished more frequently. Desisting should be impartial and equitable. The teacher must clearly demonstrate that he or she expects the same behavior and interest in learning from all students. Regardless of the systems in place, the effective teacher knows that the results of desisting are an end to the problem behavior *and* a continued respect for the learner.

See *The Effective Teacher's Guide* by Nancy Frey (2005) for a list of 50 effective classroom management strategies.

Addressing each of these 15 interaction factors that comprise the TESA model is an important component of the Differentiated Approach to teaching English language learners. When combined with the focus on oral and printed language, which we have discussed previously, and differentiated instruction, which will we will discuss presently, teacher expectations will result in proficiency for our students.

From this discussion of teacher expectations, we hope that it is clear that what teachers must hold alike for all students is high expectations. Some students may take longer to reach those expectations, some may need to reach them in a different manner, some may need more support to reach them. The expectations still remain the same—high.

So if the expectations, or the end goal, remain the same for all our students, and we know that each student has unique needs, how do we support them so that they can all achieve to the highest levels? As we have seen in each of the preceding chapters, we can differentiate both instruction and the assessment to guide that instruction. But how do we organize in order to accomplish that? Let's look first at how we organize overall classroom placement, and then we will look at ways to organize within the classroom.

Heterogeneous or Homogeneous Classrooms?

Across the nation, perhaps the only characteristic of our students that remains constant are the unique differences our children bring. Each classroom consists of students from different backgrounds, who speak different languages and arrive with different strengths and different needs. We have students with special needs, students who excel at math but struggle with reading, students who are visual learners, and others who need to be physically active as they learn. And, of course, we have the students who are the focus of this book, those who are at different stages of learning English, many of whom cannot rely on language alone to drive their learning.

While some schools have special, temporary programs for students who are brand-new to the country and brand-new to English (newcomer programs), most schools place students in classrooms according to grade level and space, perhaps with consideration to maintaining a balance of gender, ethnicity, and special needs. This results in a marvelous diversity that we believe strengthens our classrooms, our schools, our communities, and our nation. It also results in a wide spectrum of learning styles, skills, interests, and readiness to meet the established standards.

How does your school place ELL students?

In secondary schools, English language learners at the earlier levels of proficiency—Beginning, Early Intermediate, and Intermediate—typically are placed in one class of ESL/ESOL (English as a Second Language/English for Speakers of Other Languages) comprised of students at like proficiency levels. The remainder of their day, however, is generally spent in "regular" classrooms with a mix of native and fluent speakers, along with students at varying levels of English proficiency. In elementary schools, even when ELL students are initially placed in classrooms according to proficiency in English, as the year goes on, students progress at varying rates; some leave the school and others come in, placed in the class because there is room for them at that point in the year. And the result is a classroom with a wide range of learning styles, skills, interests, and readiness to meet the established standards.

These heterogeneous classrooms reflect the world outside our classrooms and provide a richness of experiences for our students. But the mix of students will lead to improved achievement only if we are prepared to meet each student's point of readiness. Carol Ann Tomlinson (1999) suggests that there are two common practices in heterogeneous classrooms that prohibit progress of both the native speaker and the English language learner. First, students who are still learning English are often placed in classrooms with native speakers in order to provide them with fluent models. Mere inclusion, without scaffolds to support full participation with proficient students, does not result in academic progress. We may see some growth in social language (BICS) as a result of increased opportunities to interact with native speakers of English, but this will not transfer to growth in academic language simply by virtue of the placement.

The second practice relates to the progress of the proficient speakers. They are often asked to act as tutors for students who are new to English. Clearly, there are benefits to students teaching other students, both academic and social, and we encourage teachers to use peer and cross-age tutors and buddies to facilitate language development (Jacobson, et al., 2001). When the tutoring replaces time they could be spending engaged in challenging activities within their own Zone of Proximal Development, however, it limits opportunities for their own academic growth. Pacing can also take time away from learning for proficient speakers as they wait for ELLs who often need extra time to grasp new ideas presented through unfamiliar language. Let's explore how a differentiated classroom maximizes the learning opportunities for *all* students.

> Tomlinson addresses the issue of struggling students and those who are gifted; we will look at her ideas from the point of view of English language learners.

> What are the pros and cons of asking a proficient student in your class to assist a student who is new to English?

> See chapter 5 for guidelines on students helping students.

Diverse students working together mirrors the real world in which students will live, work, and play
Scott Cunningham/Merrill

WHAT IS DIFFERENTIATION?

So what is differentiation? Paula Rutherford (2005) says it's a way of thinking—a way of thinking about instruction that is based on the recognition of the diversity of our students. If we begin with Vygotsky's belief that learning takes place in the Zone of Proximal Development, if we understand that our students come to us with differing levels of *readiness,* and if we believe that we must hold high expectations for all of our students, we know that we must design learning activities that address the same standards *and* take into consideration the differing levels of our students. If we also believe that students will be most engaged when we ask them to participate in activities that capture their *interest,* we then must think about our content from a variety of perspectives. And if we recognize that all our students have different *styles of learning,* we can design learning activities that utilize their preferred style, as well as ones that develop other styles. For English language learners, this may mean that learning activities relying solely on language, whether verbal or written, are relying on a learning style that, at this point in their development, is not their strongest means of learning.

In short, differentiating instruction means that we think about our content from different perspectives. Figure 8.5 depicts what we can differentiate and what we need to consider in planning.

Differentiating sources, processes, products

When we know our students' level of readiness and we are aware of their interests and specific learning styles, we can select varied sources, use different processes, and provide a choice of products to match.

Sources. When you hear people talk about differentiating instruction, you may hear them talk about differentiating content. We prefer to think about differentiating the *sources* used to teach/learn the content. Our standards remain the same for all our students, regardless of readiness or language proficiency level. So, in order to help all our students reach the standards, the differentiation lies in making the same content more accessible through a variety of resources and scaffolds. If your sixth graders are learning about plate tectonics in their science class, some might be asked to conduct their own Internet search about volcanoes or earthquakes, others might use only sites that you have selected for their level of readability, still others might read a children's book that contains basic information along with pictures and charts to support their reading. In a unit on legends, fourth-grade students might read legends or fairy tales from their own culture to compare with a similar story from another culture.

Process. You can choose to differentiate the *processes* in which students will engage as they learn. The processes are the strategies and structures you use to teach the content; they are the "how" of teaching. You may use small group activities, a variety of cooperative learning structures; you may assign tasks that vary in the level of complexity or abstractness, or that rely on a particular learning style.

What do you think it means to differentiate instruction? Close your eyes for a moment and visualize a differentiated classroom. What do you see?

As you read, think of a lesson you have taught.

What additional resources could you use to support learning for students? Think about readiness, interest, and learning style.

What are three ways for students to engage with the content of your lesson?

Figure 8.5   Differentiating Instruction *(Source: Adapted from Tomlinson, C. (1999). The differentiated classroom: Responding to the needs of all learners. Alexandria, VA: Association for Supervision and Curriculum Development. Reprinted by permission. The Association for Supervision and Curriculum Development is a worldwide community of educators advocating sound policies and sharing best practices to achieve the success of each learner. To learn more, visit ASCD at www.ascd.org.)*

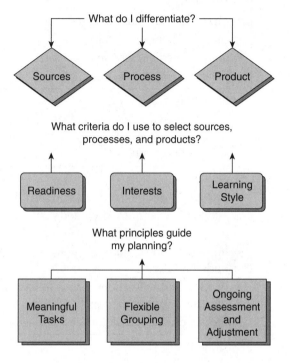

Moving between large and small group, partner, and individual activities allows you to address readiness, interest, and learning style at the same time as providing multiple opportunities for students to practice and apply their learning.

Products. *Products* are the ways in which students demonstrate their learning. Students at early levels of language proficiency may have understood the content and yet be unable to express their understanding in a written report. (Remember Luz in Ms. Voeltner's U.S. history class?) These students might complete a graphic organizer that compares or classifies, or you might ask them to construct a chart, diagram, or timeline. Others who still make numerous errors in speaking may be uncomfortable giving an oral presentation but can create a poster report that can be shared with the class. Understanding that, it is also important to remember that English language learners are also required to participate in standards-based, or standardized, tests. Figure 8.6 includes a list of ways to provide testing accommodations for English language learners.

What are three ways for students to demonstrate their understanding of your lesson?

Figure 8.6   Common Testing Accommodations: Assessment Accommodations for English Language Learners *(Source: Fisher, D., Lapp, D., Flood, J., & Suarez, L. (2001). Assessing bilingual students: When policies and practices meet in the classroom. In S. R. Hurley & J.V. Tinajero (Eds.), Literacy assessment of second language learners (pp. 104–114). Boston: Allyn & Bacon. Copyright © 2000 by Pearson Education. Reprinted by permission of the publisher.)*

Flexible Scheduling Time extension Duration Successive administrations Multiple days	Student is . . . • provided with extended time • provided periodic breaks • administered the assessment in sections over time • given several days to complete the assessment
Setting Individual administration Small group administration	Student is . . . • administered the assessment in a separate location • given the assessment in a separate location with a • small group of peers
Test Directions Rewriting directions Emphasizing key words in directions Reading directions aloud Native language	Student is . . . • provided simplified language in directions; provided additional examples; provided cues (e.g., arrows or stop signs) on the answer form • given directions with highlighted instructions or underlined verbs • provided oral directions for the assessment; reread directions for each page of questions • provided with instructions in language of choice.
Use of Aids Special equipment Proctor/reader Equipment to record responses Scribes Computational aids	Student is . . . • provided auditory tape of test items; provided with markers to maintain place • reread oral comprehension items; read passages, questions, items, and multiple-choice responses; provided cues to maintain on-task behavior • provided tape recorder for taping responses; • provided typewriter or word processor grammar check • provided adults to record answers on paper • provided use of calculator, abacus, or arithmetic tables

Uniqueness in learning

Each of us learns in different ways. We use different senses to help us learn, and we connect with new material from unique perspectives (Armstrong, 2000). Yet our classrooms most often ask students to participate using their auditory skills.

And, while this may be the case more as students move up through the grade levels, we find that students at all grade levels, kindergarten through high school, must rely on their listening skills as they encounter new information and concepts. For English language learners, even those with strong auditory skills, listening in an unfamiliar language can be a challenging way to learn. In this chapter we will discuss ways to design instruction that utilizes the diversity of student strengths to facilitate access to grade-level content. We know that students all have unique learning profiles and strengths. We also know that no one learns through just one style or type of intelligence. While some people may prefer kinesthetic activities, they can also interact with others, use visual representations, reason logically, and classify plants and animals. And indeed, virtually all these styles are necessary in varying degrees.

For information on a multiple intelligences assessment, see Christison, M.A. (1999). *A guidebook for applying multiple intelligences theory in the ESL/EFL classroom.* Burlingame, CA: Alta Book Center.

Research in Focus: Multiple Intelligences

Intelligence has traditionally been defined in terms of intelligence quotient (IQ), which measures a narrow range of verbal/linguistic and logical/mathematical abilities. Howard Gardner (1983) argues that humans possess a number of distinct intelligences that manifest themselves in different skills and abilities. All human beings apply these intelligences to solve problems, invent processes, and create things. Intelligence, according to Multiple Intelligences (MI) theory, is being able to apply one or more of the intelligences in ways that are valued by a community or culture. The current MI model outlines eight intelligences, although Gardner (1999) continues to explore additional possibilities.

- *Linguistic Intelligence:* The ability to use language effectively both orally and in writing.
- *Logical/Mathematical Intelligence:* The ability to use numbers effectively and reason well.
- *Visual/Spatial Intelligence:* The ability to recognize form, space, color, line, and shape and to graphically represent visual and spatial ideas.
- *Bodily/Kinesthetic Intelligence:* The ability to use the body to express ideas and feelings and to solve problems.
- *Musical Intelligence:* The ability to recognize rhythm, pitch, and melody.
- *Naturalist Intelligence:* The ability to recognize and classify plants, minerals, and animals.
- *Interpersonal Intelligence:* The ability to understand another person's feelings, motivations, and intentions and to respond effectively.
- *Intrapersonal Intelligence:* The ability to know about and understand oneself and recognize one's similarities to and differences from others.

Source: Christison, M. A., & Kennedy, D. Multiple intelligences: Theory and practice in adult ESL. ERIC Digest. (http://www.ericdigests.org/2001-1/multiple.html). Used with permission.

Using varied grouping configurations
to differentiate instruction

It is possible to differentiate instruction for readiness, interest, and learning style while teaching in whole class configurations. You can simply vary the products that you assign. It is difficult, however to differentiate the sources and processes that match the diversity of your students without incorporating some small group activities. Differentiating instruction is not the same as individualized instruction. We don't assign every student different work, rather we assign them to work in different groups. Flexible grouping is one of the key principles of a Differentiated Approach.

There are times when the whole class will come together to participate in a focus lesson or a class discussion, observe a demonstration, or share their learning. At other times, you will pair students to brainstorm ideas, clarify their understanding, or accomplish a task. And at times, you will ask students to work in groups, whether for small group instruction or to complete an assignment. While individual conferences and assistance are vital supports for students who do not yet have the language proficiency to participate fully without help, it is within the small group configuration that you will find the most effective opportunities to differentiate sources, processes, and products. In small groups students practice language, process understanding, and learn from each other. So what is the best way to group students for maximum learning?

Teachers often ask us, "What is the best way to group my students? Heterogeneously, or homogeneously?" If we had to answer this in two words or less, our answer would be "It depends." It depends on your purpose. In chapter 4, we discussed other important elements of effective grouping. Varying grouping configurations allows you to provide both the supports that your ELL students require, and to offer the challenges that stimulate your more proficient students.

Grouping for Purposeful Instruction. Sometimes you will want to pull aside a small group of ELLs for a quick preview of the content you are about to introduce to the class. In this group you can build background knowledge or introduce vocabulary that your native English speakers already possess. You might highlight particular language structures that are needed to understand the lesson and express the ideas—language structures such as *if . . . then* to express cause and effect in a science experiment, or *first . . . then . . . finally* to retell the sequence of events in a story. You might also want to work with a small group after a lesson to review the concepts, assess their understanding, and reteach anything they may have missed. For these mini-lessons, you may want to group your students by language proficiency level.

Grouping to Practice Language. When your purpose is to have students practice academic language and build understanding, you want to form groups that

Think about the students in your classroom. Divide them into three groups based on similar needs for an upcoming lesson.

bring together students of varying language and academic proficiency. One way to determine these groups is to create a list of all your students in one class, putting them in rank order by language proficiency or by academic skill. You can then form your groups by taking the first student, the last one, and two from the middle to form the first group. In the next group, you place the second student, the second to last, and the two who are now left closest to the middle. You continue drawing students from the top, bottom, and middle of the list until you have formed all your groups. Once the groups are formed, you can adjust them based on other concerns such as students who do not work well together. Remember not to assume that students who are at an early level of proficiency in English have weak academic skills or little understanding of the content.

Grouping for Learning Styles. When your planning incorporates consideration of individual learning styles or interests, you might group students according to their learning style to complete a project that matches that particular style. Literature circles and book clubs will be composed of students with like interest in a particular book.

Grouping to Build Community. Sometimes you may want to allow students to select their own teammates, other times your focus might include building a collaborative environment and have students grouped randomly. In this case you could distribute matching cards as students enter the classroom, perhaps a picture with a statement that describes it, or the steps of a process, each written on a separate card, and students form a group by finding the students whose cards match theirs.

Grouping to differentiate language instruction

For the purposes of focused language instruction, which is only a portion of the students' day, we advocate placing students in groups according to language proficiency level.

Beginners may need to learn how to form regular plurals and write simple sentences in the present tense. They would be virtually unable to participate in a lesson on using figurative language or writing a persuasive essay. And obviously, students at more advanced levels of proficiency would have little to gain from practice with regular plurals. Students who are in the process of developing proficiency in English should have a time in their day when the teacher's instruction is aimed precisely at their level. For elementary school students, this may be a portion of the literacy block, or it may occur during another part of the day. In schools where each classroom is composed of students at varying levels of proficiency, you can redeploy students to other classrooms for their ELD time. For secondary students, this time should be a class period that focuses specifically on language instruction for English language learners.

So again, the short answer to the question, "What is the best way to group my students?" is, "Vary them according to your purpose."

Follow the steps listed here to create heterogeneous groups in your classroom.

See chapter 3 for a discussion of the instructional framework for teaching English language learners.

Spotlight on Instruction

Differentiating Sources and Processes

Ms. Johnson wanted her seventh-grade students to develop their skills in writing an essay, taking notes, outlining, summarizing, and using effective transitions to unify ideas. She decided to use the topic of the sinking of the *Titanic*, having discovered previously that her students tended to be very interested in this event. To build background knowledge and capture their interest, she showed a few short clips from the film with Leonardo diCaprio—a clip of the passengers boarding the ship, one of the life in first class versus the life in steerage, and one of the ship as it began to sink. Following each clip she asked the students to talk in pairs about what they noticed and what they could infer about society at the time, how they thought the characters were feeling and why, and so on.

After a whole class discussion of the event, Ms. Johnson divided her students into groups based on language proficiency and reading level. She gave each group a selection of reading material and assigned them a role for their RAFT. Chris gave two of the groups different excerpts from books that describe the lives of individual passengers in steerage and in first class. The students were directed to compose a journal entry that their RAFT character might have written, describing their experience. Two other groups were given a variety of books that describe the ship, its unique construction, the size of the iceberg, and the sequence of events taking place among the crew. They were to write their RAFT from the point of view of the ship's architect, and their task was to explain to the investigating committee how the sinking happened. Ms. Johnson assigned two different groups to write an editorial commentary on the division between the upper and lower class society of the time, using selections from books that include primary source documents, illustrations, quotations, and descriptions of the differences in the living conditions aboard the ship. Each RAFT asked students to look for information, take notes, interpret what they were reading, and organize their writing to include anecdotes, descriptions, and examples, all strategies directly from the grade-level standards for English language arts. Ms. Johnson differentiated the sources she provided and the processes she used to vary the level of structure and abstractness so that students could focus on the writing skills, rather than struggling with the text. These groups are flexible and students in Ms. Johnson's class are grouped and regrouped regularly based on the various tasks at hand.

RAFT prompts are explained in chapter 6.

She varied the level of structure for each group by using different graphic organizers. The journal writers used a partially completed graphic organizer to help guide their search for information in the text. Those writing the editorial were given a Venn diagram to compare and contrast living conditions. And she asked the ship's architects to create their own graphic organizer that would support their presentation to the investigating committee.

Some of the books she selected included:

- Ballard, R. (2002). *Exploring the Titanic.* New York: Scholastic.
- Hoh, D. (1998). *Titanic: The long night.* New York: Scholastic.
- Marschall, K. (1997). *Inside the Titanic.* Toronto, Ontario: Madison Press.
- White, E. (1998). *Voyage on the great Titanic.* New York: Scholastic.

As we discussed in chapters 6 and 7, language development occurs not only during ELD time, but throughout the day, across the content. Differentiating language instruction during math, science, social studies, or other content may be as simple as highlighting and explaining language structures during the lesson itself, or it may entail pulling aside a small group of students for a front-loading lesson before the whole group lesson. For example, before showing a film on the Great Wall of China, Ms. Mathews met with a group of English language learners to provide specific instruction in vocabulary, explained the main ideas from the film, and modeled the note-taking she would expect of the students in her class.

PLANNING FOR DIFFERENTIATED INSTRUCTION

Figure 8.5 depicts what you can differentiate, the criteria to use to determine what sources, processes, and products you will select, as well as the three basic principles to keep in mind while planning. These three principles are important for any type of instruction, whether you are differentiating the lesson or not. Without attention to them when planning for differentiation, you won't end up with a differentiated lesson. Considering student interests helps to ensure that tasks are *meaningful*. Knowing your students' proficiency levels in English, background knowledge related to the lesson, and reading levels (in other words, their *readiness*), as well as their *interests* and *learning styles,* helps you determine appropriate grouping configurations. And, of course, the *ongoing assessment* is what provides this information for planning and helps you know how to *adjust* your lessons accordingly.

Differentiation and scaffolding

In the preceding chapter we saw a variety of ways to scaffold learning. Differentiating instruction allows you to build in different scaffolds for different groups of students, using what you know about your students and what it is you want your students to learn. Rutherford (2002) suggests some guiding questions to ask as you plan. We have added some of the considerations that relate specifically to English language learners.

As you read this section, think of a lesson you are going to teach and answer the questions listed here.

How Abstract Are the Ideas? Do I need to make the ideas more concrete for some of my students? What is the best way to do that? Are there pictures, charts, graphs, realia, demonstrations that will help to contextualize the content and provide comprehensible input for my ELLs? What connection to background knowledge will help to build a bridge from old knowledge to new?

How Accessible Are the Resources? What materials and resources can I provide at a level that will challenge all my students without frustrating them? How can I make the materials more accessible? Are there *graphic organizers* that help to *build schema*? Can I *model* reading the text through a Think Aloud? Is there *background knowledge* that I need to provide for my ELLs to help them understand the material? Is there *language* or *vocabulary* that my proficient students know that my ELLs may not?

How Complex Is the Task? Are there specific *metacognitive learning strategies* such as organizational planning (providing benchmark deadlines) or *cognitive learning strategies* such as summarizing chunks of text that will help my students by breaking the task into simpler parts? How can I make sure that my ELLs understand the directions for the task?

What Is the Level of Independence? How can I adjust the level of independence? Do some of my students require more "to" and "with" than others? Do I need to provide more frequent feedback to help some of my students adjust their learning? Are there *language structures* that I can introduce to my ELLs that will facilitate their participation? Can I provide some of the information on a *graphic organizer* that will guide my ELLs and provide a scaffold? What type of *grouping configuration* should I use for my ELLs—same language so they can discuss the ideas in their native language? Same proficiency level so I can provide specific language support or background knowledge? Partnered with proficient students to help facilitate the discussion and provide opportunity to practice language?

What Is the Pacing? How can I allow adequate time for those who need it and still provide well-paced, challenging learning experiences for those who demonstrate understanding in a short time? My ELLs may require more time to read as they encounter unfamiliar vocabulary. They may require more time to discuss the assignment as they search for the language to express their ideas.

Application to Practice

Reflection

1. What is the first step you will take toward differentiating instruction in your classroom? Why did you select this step? How will you go about implementing it?
2. What is something you have a question about?

Case Study: *Learning Styles and Interests*

1. Assess your target student's learning style and decide how to change your instruction as a result.
2. Conduct an interest inventory with your student and develop a plan to address the findings. How might you incorporate this student's interests in planning and teaching?

Planning and Instruction: *Design a Differentiated Lesson*

1. Using the plan for the unit of study that you developed previously, consider the instructional needs of your entire class. Which strategies from this chapter could be added to ensure that all of your students reach high standards?
2. Evaluate yourself on each of the 15 TESA interaction factors. What are you good at? Are there areas in which you can improve?

References

Armstrong, T. (2000). *Multiple intelligences in the classroom.* Alexandria, VA: Association for Supervision and Curriculum Development.

Bamburg, J. (1994). *Raising expectations to improve student learning.* Oak Brook, IL: North Central Regional Educational Laboratory.

Bishop, J. (1989). Motivating students to study: Expectations, rewards, achievement. *NASSP Bulletin, 73*(520), 27–38.

Bloom, B. S. (1956). *Taxonomy of educational objectives, Handbook I: The cognitive domain.* New York: David McKay.

Cotton, K. (1989). *Expectations and student outcomes.* Portland, OR: Northwest Regional Educational Laboratory.

Flanders, N. (1970). *Analyzing teaching behavior.* Reading, MA: Addison-Wesley.

Frey, N. (2005). *The effective teacher's guide: 50 ways for engaging students in learning.* San Diego, CA: Academic Professional Development.

Gardner, H. (1983). *Frames of mind: The theory of multiple intelligences.* New York: Basic Books.

Gardner, H. (1999). Are there additional intelligences? The case for naturalist, spiritual, and existential intelligences. In J. Kane (Ed.), *Education, information and transformation* (pp. 111–131). Englewood Cliffs, NJ: Prentice Hall.

Gonder, P. O. (1991). *Caught in the middle: How to unleash the potential of average students.* Arlington, VA: American Association of School Administrators.

Good, T. L. (1987). Two decades of research on teacher expectations: Findings and future directions. *Journal of Teacher Education, 38*(4), 32–47.

Hilliard III, A. (1991). Do we have the will to educate all children? *Educational Leadership, 49*(1), 31–36.

Jacobson, J., Thrope, L., Fisher, D., Lapp, D., Frey, N., & Flood, J. (2001). Cross age tutoring: A literacy improvement approach for struggling adolescent readers. *Journal of Adolescent and Adult Literacy, 44,* 528–536.

Omotani, B. J., & Omotani, L. (1996). Expect the best: How your teachers can help all children learn. *The Executive Educator, 18,* 8–27, 31.

Raffini, J. (1993). *Winners without losers: Structures and strategies for increasing student motivation to learn.* Needham Heights, MA: Allyn and Bacon.

Rutherford, P. (2002). *Instruction for all students.* Alexandria, VA: Just ASK Publications.

Rutherford, P. (2005). *Presentation for PEAK.* Denver, CO.

Teacher Expectations and Student Achievement (TESA). (2002). *TESA coach's manual.* Los Angeles: Los Angeles County Office of Education.

Tomlinson, C. (1999). *The differentiated classroom: Responding to the needs of all learners.* Alexandria, VA: Association for Supervision and Curriculum Development.

Epilogue

MARY'S TOP TEN: A GUIDE FOR TEACHING ENGLISH LANGUAGE LEARNERS

Mary Waldron is principal of a small elementary school in San Diego, California. Her school of 384 students includes 136 English language learners spread across all grade levels, K–5. In such a small school, each classroom includes significant numbers of students who are in varied stages of English language development.

With her background first as a bilingual teacher and then as a staff developer, Mary is working with her teachers to reflect on their practice and extend their knowledge of instruction for all students, particularly for that 35% of their student population who are learning English at the same time as they are learning to read, write, do arithmetic, and build a foundation in science and social studies.

We sat down with Mary to talk about her work with her teachers and with her students. What does she look for when she walks into a classroom? What advice does she give to her new teachers? These are Mary's Top Ten:

1. *Believe in your students.*

   This is my number one piece of advice. One that's difficult to observe, difficult to quantify, but essential to everything we do with our students, from assessing and planning, to teaching and interacting. I believe that all our students, including our English language learners, have an endless capacity, an infinite potential for learning. I believe that it's my responsibility as a teacher to help my students uncover the boundless possibilities within themselves. If you operate on that belief, you operate with high expectations for all your students, and your students will rise to your expectations.

2. *Know your students.*

   Assessment is at the heart of everything we do as teachers. Assessment is about getting to know your students, knowing their strengths and their areas of need, knowing what they already know. And for English language learners, part of knowing your students is knowing about language acquisition—knowing the characteristics of the developmental stages students progress through as they acquire a new language, knowing what to expect them to be able to do, knowing where they are in their development, and knowing how to help them move through those stages.

   Knowing your English language learners requires close study of the language they use. Listen to how they use language orally. Listening to students is like tuning into a channel we don't access regularly when we don't have English language learners. We generally listen for the content of what students say and pay little attention to the form. What language do they use to express themselves? Are they using the precise, academic language of school, or is their language more like what we hear at lunchtime? Knowing how students use language also requires looking at their writing. What language structures do they have control of? What language structures are they beginning to use? What can you teach them next?

3. *Know your text.*

   This is planning. There is so much in a text that can be supportive, or that can be challenging. Knowing your text well lets you identify the supports and the challenges. Careful planning helps you anticipate the areas where they might have difficulty, determine how to scaffold their understanding, and identify strategies they can use to become progressively more independent. Look at the language. Are there words they need to know ahead of time? Words you can teach as you read together? Structures that help students comprehend and express the ideas? Think about what background knowledge they will need going into the text. Do they all have that knowledge? How can you introduce the text to help them focus on the key understanding? Identify the structure of the text. How can you help them recognize that structure and determine the purpose of the text?

4. *Maintain a clear purpose for the lesson.*

   When you are clear about your purpose for the lesson, and you are clear with your students about that purpose, you can help them focus on the intended learning, and you can stay focused on that purpose. There is an art to maintaining a clear purpose. It's the art of balancing your well-prepared lesson with what you hear your students saying and see them doing during the course of a lesson. Being able to be flexible as your students grasp, or don't, the ideas, yet always staying on target.

   Having a clear purpose for a lesson also means having a literacy or a content objective along with a language objective. Understanding character development is a literacy objective. The language objective might be describing a character.

   So telling students what you expect them to learn, to be able to do, telling them what they should be listening for will help them focus their attention and make those connections that build their understanding.

5. *Connect learning across the day.*

   Something I've begun to think about is how a coherent focus across the day can build students' learning and help to develop language. I've noticed a disconnect between the students' independent work and the work they are doing with their teacher. I see generic learning centers that don't reinforce the purpose of the day, lost opportunities for students to go deeper in their learning. If you look at the day from the perspective of an English language learner, you see how a day where the learning is connected—Read Alouds and shared readings that focus on the current science unit, or learning centers where students practice what they just learned—gives students a chance to hear and practice a focused set of language and vocabulary, gives them time to develop their understanding of the content. It's that notion that "less is more," that learning is recursive—we learn more when we have multiple opportunities to see the same ideas from different perspectives.

6. *Use, teach, reinforce academic language.*

It's easy to fall into the trap of thinking ELLs need only vocabulary development. Because they do need vocabulary development. But that is only one piece of proficiency in a language. Academic language is multidimensional. It requires accuracy in vocabulary and in grammar, varied register for varying audiences, use of cohesive devices to link ideas. It requires use of complex language structures to express complex ideas, not the simplified language we often use with students who are learning English.

Be aware of your own language. Are you using the vocabulary you want students to learn? Are you focusing your students' attention on the specific linguistic features that are used to express specific language functions? Are you asking and expecting them to use those features themselves?

7. *Structure lessons to include multiple opportunities for student-to-student interaction.*

If you look at the day through the lens of language development, it becomes easy to see how to structure learning through opportunities for students to interact with each other, to practice oral language, building academic language that they can use in their reading and their writing. Most of us don't learn a language by listening and reading alone—we need opportunities to produce language, to practice speaking and writing. As you plan your lessons, think about where you can build in meaningful opportunities for students to talk about what they are learning.

We've always talked a lot about comprehensible input. Students need opportunities to develop comprehensible output. Time for students to engage in using language helps them develop language, develop their capacity to make themselves understood about complex academic ideas.

8. *Provide strong environmental supports.*

The first thing I look at when I walk into a classroom is the room environment. I look at the room arrangement. Does it support partner and small group work? Does it facilitate that student-to-student interaction that is so important to developing language proficiency? Is it flexible enough to provide for different kinds of interaction?

I look at the charts that students and teachers have co-constructed as they work. Do they support learning for students' proficiency in English? Is there a title, a sentence that explains the purpose behind the information captured on the chart? Is it just a list of words, or does it use language in sentences that will trigger deeper understanding?

I look at the classroom library. Is it organized in a way that makes sense to students? Is it organized in a way that supports developing independence as a reader? Are there leveled books? Is there a good variety that captures students' interests?

9. *Build background knowledge.*

The more background knowledge students have about a topic, the better they will be able to comprehend what they're reading. It's important to spend time building background—going into a Read Aloud, for instance, spend time talking about what they already know in relation to the key ideas of the text, what they need to know. Build their knowledge of the content. One way to do this goes back to the idea of coherence across the day. Find a thread that links the learning throughout the day. Begin your planning with your content—whether it's science or social studies or an essential question. As you go through the day, you are constantly building background knowledge, helping students develop understanding, language, and skill.

10. *Expect students to take responsibility for their learning.*

It's too easy to let students become passive learners when they don't have enough English to express themselves clearly. The gradual release of responsibility model of learning entails more than "I do it. We do it. You do it." It also means releasing responsibility to students to become actively engaged in their own learning. We need to help our students establish learning goals for themselves. Daily, weekly, monthly—it depends on the age and maturity of the students. What's important is for them to think about what they are going to learn, how they are going to learn it, what they learned, and how well they learned it. This is part of the process of developing independent learners, which is, after all, our goal.

Ms. Waldron ends her Top Ten list by saying:

I've learned that much of what applies to our students as learners, applies to teachers as learners as well. Both teaching and learning are dynamic processes. Just as our students are constantly developing their understanding and their skill, we as teachers are constantly developing our understanding of how our students learn and our skill in planning and teaching. In my own growth as an educator, I let this quote by Roland Barth guide my way:

Let us constantly juxtapose the way things are with fresh visions of what they might become.

Teacher Tools

The following pages may be copied for your classroom or personal use.

1. *Self-Assessment Tool.* Use this tool to assess your knowledge about teaching English language learners and for planning your future professional development.

2. *Instruction for English Language Learners Observation and Reflection Guide.* This tool allows you to observe yourself or other teachers and reflect on the instruction, assessment, materials, and environment.

3. *Instruction for English Language Learners Observation and Reflection Guide 2.* This tool provides you an alternative way to observe and reflect on quality instruction for English language learners.

4. *Unit of Study.* This tool is used to plan instruction. It builds on earlier lesson planning tools presented in this book and incorporates all of the information presented in the chapters.

5. *Anticipation Guide.* This tool can be used to create anticipation guides for your students.

In addition, we have provided you with reference lists on common English and Spanish cognates as well as an academic word list.

Teaching English Language Learners
Self-Assessment

Rate yourself:

Key Elements	How often do I. . .?				
	Always		Sometimes		Never
1. Make sure students know and understand the purpose of the lesson?	4	3	2	1	0
2. Access prior knowledge?	4	3	2	1	0
3. Build background knowledge when necessary?	4	3	2	1	0
4. Examine text for language and vocabulary that may present challenges?	4	3	2	1	0
5. Consider my own language and vocabulary to ensure that my students can understand?	4	3	2	1	0
6. Use a variety of scaffolds for the variety of learners in my class?	4	3	2	1	0
7. Provide opportunities for student-student interaction?	4	3	2	1	0

Which of these is/are easiest for you? Why?

Which of these is/are most difficult for you? Why?

Instruction for English Language Learners
Observation and Reflection Guide

Instruction, assessment, materials, and environment demonstrate evidence of:

❏ **Principles of language acquisition**
- Comprehensible input
- Contextualized instruction
- Safe environment
- Meaningful engagement

❏ **Principles of academic language development**
- Opportunities to practice and develop listening, speaking, reading and writing
- Explicit instruction on vocabulary and language structures

❏ **Principles of content instruction for ELLs**
- Access to grade-level content standards is scaffolded according to language proficiency level.
- Assessments are differentiated for language proficiency level.

Teacher
- *Knows ELLs' prior knowledge and current proficiency in listening, speaking, reading, writing.*
- *Language is comprehensible and academic, reflects purpose.*
- *Questioning promotes critical thinking for all students.*

Students
- *Students are actively engaged and talk frequently about key content using academic language.*
- *Students ask questions to support learning.*
- *Students know the purpose of the lesson.*

Environment
- *Visuals reflect current instruction and key concepts, support understanding for all proficiency levels.*
- *Room arrangement facilitates student interaction.*

Materials
- *Materials at variety of levels support access to grade-level standards for students at all proficiency levels.*

Strengths:

Focus for Professional Development:

Instruction for English Language Learners
Observation and Reflection Guide 2

High Expectations
- *Questioning promotes critical thinking for all students*
- *Instruction, resources, assessment are differentiated to support and challenge all students*
- *Clear, and clearly articulated purpose*
- *Student responsibility for learning: student choice, self-monitoring, self-reflection*

Meaningful Context	**Demonstration**	**Interaction and Engagement**	**Language Focus**
• *Authentic purpose* • *Links to prior knowledge, prior learning* • *Builds schema*	• *Comprehensible input* • *Models of language, content, process*	• *Opportunities to practice oral language and apply academic concepts*	• *Explicit teaching of key vocabulary and language structures* • *Opportunities to listen, speak, read, write, practice language*

Room Environment
- *Models of exemplary products*
- *Visual support for learning, reflects purpose: visuals, charts, etc.*
- *Easily accessible variety of resources*
- *Organization facilitates varied grouping*

Adapted from Kelli McMillan, 2006. Used with permission.

Unit of Study

Class: _____ Unit (Topic) of Study: _____

Date: _____ Teacher: _____

Key Concept(s)
What is the big idea (essential question) you want students to walk away with?

Standards, Objectives, and Expectations
Use your content standards, ELD standards, and what you know about your students to write content, language, and social objectives.

Assessments
What task(s) will students complete that demonstrates their learning?

How will you differentiate the task for students at different levels of English proficiency?

Early	Middle	High

Materials
What core text(s) will you use? What supplemental texts will you use? What is the structure of the text(s)?

What texts will you use for students at different levels of English proficiency?

(continued)

What types of graphic organizers will you use to help ELLs at different proficiency levels comprehend, talk, and write about the text?		
Early	Middle	High

Language and Vocabulary
Content-specific and general academic use (bricks)

Language structures (mortar)

What signal words are necessary in order to comprehend, talk, and write about the key concepts? (mortar) How will you teach them?

What sentence or question frames might support your ELLs at different proficiency levels?		
Early	Middle	High

Background Knowledge
What do students need to know before the lesson begins? How will you introduce the unit and connect to understanding they already have?

Instructional Arrangements
What opportunities will there be to develop listening, speaking, reading, and writing? What learning strategies will help students learn this content? How/when will you teach them?

(continued)

How will you scaffold learning for ELLs at different proficiency levels?		
Early	Middle	High

Projects, Homework, and Assignments
What instructional tasks will provide opportunities for ELLs at different proficiency levels to practice and apply new learning?

Early	Middle	High

Anticipation Guide

Read each statement. Mark "A" if you agree or "D" if you disagree. Tell why.

A	D	Statement	Justification

Common Cognates: English and Spanish

accident	accidente	energy	energía	ordinary	ordinario
accompany	acompañar	examine	examinar	oxygen	oxígeno
action	acción	exclaim	exclamar	pair	par
activities	actividades	family	familia	paper	papel
adaptar	adapt	famous	famoso	part	parte
algebra	algebra	favorite	favorito	perception	percepción
alphabet	alfabeto	finally	finalmente	pioneer	pionero
analysis	análisis	flexible	flexible	planet	planeta
atmosphere	atmósfera	fruit	fruta	plans	planes
attention	atención	galaxy	galaxia	plants	plantas
bacteria	bacteria	group	grupo	practice	practicar
bicycle	bicicleta	history	historia	prepare	preparar
biography	biografía	human	humano	present	presentar
brillant	brillante	idea	idea	problem	problema
bulletin	boletín	identify	identificar	reference	referencia
calendar	calendario	independence	independencia	repetition	repetición
capture	capturar	information	información	rich	rica
catastrophe	catástrofe	introduction	introducción	route	ruta
cause	causa	investigate	investigar	series	serie
center	centro	justice	justicia	special	especial
centigrade	centígrado	language	lenguaje	statistics	estadística
character	carácter	leader	líder	stomach	estómago
circle	círculo	legend	leyenda	study	estudiar
colony	colonia	lesson	lección	subject	sujeto
color	color	line	línea	synonym	sínonimo
common	común	locate	localizar	telescope	telescopio
comparison	comparación	machine	máquina	temperature	temperatura
complete	completo	map	mapa	terrible	terible
continent	continente	memory	memoria	totally	totalmente
contribution	contribución	metal	metal	triple	triple
decide	decidir	microscope	microscopio	tube	tubo
depend	depender	million	millón	uniform	uniforme
describe	describir	minute	minuto	unique	único
desert	desierto	much	mucho	unity	unidad
destroy	destruir	music	música	urgent	urgente
determine	determinar	natural	natural	vacant	vacante
diagram	diagrama	necessity	necesidad	version	versión
dictator	dictador	nectar	nectar	vision	visión
different	diferente	object	objeto	visit	visite
distance	distancia	ocean	océano	vocabulary	vocabulario
distribute	distribuir	office	oficina	volleyball	voleibol
double	doble	order	orden	vote	votar
electric	eléctrico	operation	operación	zone	zona

Source: ColorinColorado. (2005). *Helping English language learners read . . . and succeed!*
Retrieved January 12, 2006 from www.colorincolorado.org. Used with permission.

Academic Word List

Group 1	Group 2	Group 3
analyze	achieve	alternative
approach	acquire	circumstance
area	administrate	comment
assess	affect	compensate
assume	appropriate	component
authority	aspect	consent
available	assist	considerable
benefit	category	constant
concept	chapter	constrain
consist	commission	contribute
constitute	community	convene
context	complex	coordinate
contract	compute	core
create	conclude	corporate
data	conduct	correspond
define	consequent	criteria
derive	construct	deduce
distribute	consume	demonstrate
economy	credit	document
environment	culture	dominate
establish	design	emphasis
estimate	distinct	ensure
evident	element	exclude
export	equate	framework
factor	evaluate	fund
finance	feature	illustrate
formula	final	immigrate
function	focus	imply
identify	impact	initial
income	injure	instance
indicate	institute	interact
individual	invest	justify
interpret	item	layer
involve	journal	link
issue	maintain	locate
labor	normal	maximize
legal	obtain	minor
legislate	participate	negate
major	perceive	outcome
method	positive	partner
occur	potential	philosophy

(continued)

Group 1	Group 2	Group 3
percent	previous	physical
period	primary	proportion
policy	purchase	publish
principle	range	react
proceed	region	register
process	regulate	rely
require	relevant	remove
research	reside	scheme
respond	resource	sequence
role	restrict	sex
section	secure	shift
sector	seek	specify
significant	select	sufficient
similar	site	task
source	strategy	technical
specific	survey	technique
structure	text	technology
theory	tradition	valid
vary	transfer	volume

Source: Adapted from Scarcella, R. (2000). *Accelerating academic English: A Focus on the English learner.* Oakland, CA: Regents of the University of California. Used with permission.

Index